GOD'S
GREATER
GLORY

The Exalted God of Scripture and the Christian Faith

BRUCE A. WARE

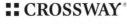

WHEATON, ILLINOIS

God's Greater Glory: The Exalted God of Scripture and the Christian Faith

Copyright © 2004 by Bruce A. Ware

Published by Crossway
        1300 Crescent Street
        Wheaton, Illinois 60187

First printing 2004

Printed in the United States of America

Unless otherwise indicated, Scripture quotations are from the ESV® Bible (*The Holy Bible, English Standard Version®*), copyright © 2001 by Crossway. Used by permission. All rights reserved.

Scripture references marked NASB are from the *New American Standard Bible®*. Copyright © The Lockman Foundation 1960, 1962, 1963, 1968, 1971, 1972, 1973, 1975, 1977, 1995. Used by permission.

ISBN-13: 978-1-58134-443-1
ISBN-10: 1-58134-443-0
ePub ISBN: 978-1-4335-1710-5
PDF ISBN: 978-1-4335-1422-7
Mobipocket ISBN: 978-1-4335-0814-1

Library of Congress Cataloging-in-Publication Data
Ware, Bruce A., 1953-
  God's greater glory : the exalted God of Scripture and the
Christian faith / Bruce A. Ware.
     p. cm.
  Includes bibliographical references and index.
  ISBN 13: 978-1-58134-443-1 (alk. paper)
  ISBN 10: 1-58134-443-0
  1. Providence and government of God—Christianity. 2. Providence
and government of God—Biblical teaching. 3. Open theism. I. Title.
BT135.W37   2004
231'.5—dc22   2004018926

Crossway is a publishing ministry of Good News Publishers.

I know of no living person I would rather hear unfold the majesty of God in providence than Bruce Ware. One reason is that I have come to trust his heart as well as his head. He is utterly unlike those whom Jesus chastised in Luke 11:46 with the words, "Woe to you lawyers also! For you load people with burdens hard to bear, and you yourselves do not touch the burdens with one of your fingers." Bruce Ware has heavy things to say (that is the meaning of "glory"!); but his heart moves him to lift these weighty things with biblical and pastoral wisdom—not so that they become weightless (the curse of our breezy age), but so that they become wings. We find ourselves carried not burdened by the majesty of God in providence.

— JOHN PIPER
Founder, desiringGod.org; Chancellor, Bethlehem College & Seminary

One thing that the recent discussion about "open theism" has exposed is the need for evangelicals to have a better understanding of the Bible's teaching about God's providence. So Bruce Ware's presentation of God's holy, wise, and powerful preserving and governing of all his creatures and all their actions is just what the doctor ordered. In *God's Lesser Glory*, Dr. Ware exposed the deficiencies and dismantled the foundations of so-called "open theism" (a better name for which is "diminished theism"). Now, in *God's Greater Glory*, he sets forth a positive biblical proposal for a robust doctrine of God's sovereignty and providence in relation to human freedom and responsibility. Pastors, seminarians, and intelligent church members will all benefit from Ware's clear and accessible articulation of a mind-bending but pastorally important subject. Rather than attempting to tame and limit the doctrine of God, as so many have done in our time, Ware is determined to let the Scriptures set the table for our understanding of God.

— J. LIGON DUNCAN III
Chancellor and CEO, Reformed Theological Seminary, Jackson, Mississippi

This is a marvelous, spiritually refreshing, soul-enriching, peace-giving, joy-awakening book. It is a thoughtful analysis of a complex problem by a first-rate thinker who has understood the complex debates over God's sovereignty and responsibility and has reached wise and reverent conclusions richly supported by Scripture. The author is aware of many other books but he is clearly subject to only one Book. I strongly recommend this volume.

— WAYNE GRUDEM
*Research Professor of Bible and Theology
Phoenix Seminary*

Bruce Ware has done it again. In *God's Lesser Glory*, Professor Ware set the record straight, confronting the claims of limited theism with the reality of the biblical doctrine of God. Now, in *God's Greater Glory*, he points to the grandeur, majesty, and perfection of the God who revealed himself in the Bible. This brilliant defense of the doctrine of God, rich in historical and biblical documentation, belongs on the bookshelf of every pastor and Christian believer. This book is not only an exercise in faithful theology, reading it is also a devotional experience, as the reader encounters the glory of God as revealed in the Scriptures. Dr. Bruce Ware is one of the finest and most faithful theologians serving the church in this generation. With this book, he places us once again in his gracious debt.

—R. Albert Mohler, Jr.
President, The Southern Baptist Theological Seminary

Dedicated to my beloved and precious wife, Jodi,
whose love, tenderness, kindness, encouragement,
faithfulness, intimate friendship, and zest for life
are constant reminders of the very good and gracious gifts
of God's providence.

Contents

Preface

Readers of my earlier book, *God's Lesser Glory* (Crossway, 2000), cannot help but notice the striking similarity and difference between the titles of this earlier work and the present volume. And of course, the similarity in the two titles—God's glory—only accentuates the fundamental difference between them; in open theism, the theological understanding critiqued by that earlier work, God's glory is cheapened and diminished, while in the view I present in this work, I believe that his glory is honored and exalted. This is my deep conviction, and I can only hope and pray that readers of both books will be compelled to the same conclusion.

Why does it matter? Certainly, the answer is not because I want people to agree with me and not with "them." This isn't a popularity contest. This has nothing to do with personal ego or theological one-upmanship. What is at stake is neither political nor personal nor partisan, strictly speaking. Rather, my deep and abiding conviction is that what is at stake, most centrally, is what is announced in the titles of these two books themselves. Whether we behold, and believe, and adore, and trust, and honor, and love the true and living God, or whether we belittle, and distort, and minimize, and diminish God as we conceive him in order to magnify and enlarge and overextend the significance of "us"—this, at bottom, is what is at stake. In a culture saturated with the esteem of the "self" and marred by the decline of Deity, we stand in need of beholding God for who he is. We need desperately to be humbled and amazed at the infinite splendor of his unrivaled Greatness and the unspeakable wealth of his lavish Goodness. We must marvel at his blinding Glory and fall astonished at his benevolent Grace. If we are to escape the cult of self and find, instead, the true meaning of life and the path of true satisfaction, if we are to give God the glory rightly and exclusively owed to him—that is, if we are to know what truly promotes both our good and his glory—we must behold God for who he is. To this end both of these books are aimed. I present both, then, in full recognition that the only opinion of my work that matters ultimately is the one that will be given before a heavenly throne, and in light of that day, I offer both my previous critique and now, my constructive proposal. To understand and portray God more fully as he is—this is my heart's longing and deepest desire.

Dear family members and friends have once again encouraged me greatly in the writing of this book. Nearly every phone call to my parents, Bill and Ruth Ware, included a question about how the book was coming and their never-failing pledge and promise, "We're praying for you every day in your writing." And in similar fashion, my wife's mother, Esther McClain, and my sister and her husband, Bonnie and Wayne Pickens, also told me of their regular prayers that God would accomplish his will in this writing. In that coming day before the heavenly throne of which I just spoke, no doubt much of any of the value that resides in this book will be shown to trace to these and other prayers. While our parents' physical strength declines with age, their strength of soul and fervency of prayer grow ever larger. How blessed I am, and how gracious God is.

My wife and my daughters also constantly supported me in my writing. No wife has ever been a greater encouragement for her husband than is my precious wife, Jodi. And no children have ever loved their heavenly and earthly fathers with such longing as do my precious daughters, Bethany and Rachel. I yearn for these three women in my life to know ever more fully the God whose character they display to me daily. I can only pray that to the extent that this book assists in knowing him better, they, above all others, will be enabled more fully to see him, and know him, and love him, and worship him.

Todd Miles and Rob Lister assisted both in research and critical evaluation of this work. Both are excellent doctoral students in theology who give me great hope that the vision of God presented here will live on to another generation. Members of my small group also prayed and supported me throughout the writing. My gratitude and love, then, are extended to Ken and Beth Aebersold, Bill and Mae Croft, Mark and Brenda Janke, John and Marilyn McAloon, and Chip and Doris Stam. Marvin Padgett and Bill Deckard of Crossway Books have worked hard to see this project to completion. The keen editorial eye that Mr. Deckard brings to his work has made this book better in a thousand places. And I owe a special debt of thanks to President R. Albert Mohler, Jr., and to the Board of Trustees of The Southern Baptist Theological

Seminary, where it is my great privilege to teach, for the generous sab-
batical leave that granted time needed to complete this work.

Finally, I have sensed both the presence and the pleasure of God
as I have written this book. For God's sustaining and strengthening
grace, I am eternally grateful. I've been regularly humbled by the task
of writing about God, but I've also been stirred at the joyous prospect
of commending to others the One I love and adore. From the bottom
of my heart and from the depths of my soul I express this, my prayer:
May the God whose name is holy, who lives in a high and holy place,
make himself known as the God he is. May his majesty and mercy, his
greatness and goodness, his supremacy and sufficiency, be to those who
see him aright their source of unending joy—for his eternal glory and
our everlasting good. Amen.

Introduction

I

Considering the Enduring Questions and Necessary Features of Divine Providence

THE CONTROL OF GOD AND THE COMFORT OF THE BELIEVER

What comfort, joy, and strength believers receive from the truths of divine providence. Nowhere else are we given such assurance that the One who perfectly knows the past, present, and future, the One whose wisdom can never be challenged or excelled, the One whose power reigns and accomplishes all that he wills, governs all the affairs of creation, fulfilling in all respects what he alone knows is good, wise, and best. What may seem to us as "accidents" are no such things in the universe governed by the providence of the true and living God. Prayers may be directed to this mighty and reigning King knowing that while he tenderly and compassionately hears the cries of his people, he "sits" in the unique position of knowing perfectly what is best and possessing unthwarted power to bring to pass what he wills. The world is not spinning out of control; in fact, not one atom or despot or demon acts in any respect to hinder the fulfillment of what God has eternally ordained. To know this God, and better to be known by him (Gal. 4:9a), is to enter into the security and confidence of a lifetime of trust in his never-failing arms.

I am writing at 35,000 feet, on a flight that I wondered seriously whether I would make. Oh, how I longed to get aboard this plane, since it would take me home after a week away. But when my previous flight left nearly an hour late, and since the airline's representative told me that this, my connecting flight for home, was on time and wouldn't wait for our plane's late arrival, I began dreading a Saturday night in some unknown hotel instead of returning to the arms of my wife. And not only did I long to be home, but I also was scheduled to teach the first lesson in our church's high school and middle school combined classes the next morning. Now, I thought, I'll have to find a last-minute substitute and miss the opportunity to lay out the vision of the brief series on "relating to God" that I so wanted to share with our youth.

But knowing that God reigns over all, I prayed! "No matter what any airline's agent says, Lord, the fact is: you and you alone have ultimate control over what happens. If you choose, you can do something to ensure that I get on that flight home. I know you can! But if you choose for me to spend this night waiting, I'll accept this also from your good and wise hand. Bless Jodi tonight, if this happens, and please prepare the best person to teach in the morning," I prayed.

Jodi and Rachel (my wife and daughter at home) were also praying, and my how God did graciously answer. When my delayed flight arrived, I learned that my connecting flight—which, as I was told just one hour earlier, had been scheduled to leave on time—now also had been *delayed just long enough* for me to board. What had happened? In that hour, between when I was told it would leave on time and now when I boarded this delayed flight home, a "computer malfunction" occurred in Atlanta delaying several Delta flights nationwide by about a half hour, the gate attendant informed me. I smiled, looked heavenward, and gave praise to the God who reigns. Imagine that. Bringing about a computer glitch in order to answer the prayer of one of his tired and earnest children. What a God! And what providence is this!

Obviously, God does not always choose to answer such prayers in such a remarkable manner. But he does always reign over all that occurs, with just as much specific and meticulous detailed attention as is obvious in this case.[1] The providence of God assures us that the universe is not spinning out of control, that human history is not unfolding contrary to

---

[1] Concerning this account, someone might well ask, "What if someone else experienced harm due to the delay of the connecting flight?" Clearly, the omnipotent God who is able to bring about computer glitches to delay a flight also is omniscient (all-knowing) and omnisapient (all-wise). We should not think of prayer as our talking God into doing something that he, in his infinite knowledge and wisdom, believes would be foolish yet he does it anyway because we pray fervently for it. Rather, we acknowledge that the God who knows best will grant what the prayer seeks only if he believes, all things considered, that answering the prayer would be best. As we will consider more in chapter 7, below, prayer is designed by God as a gracious instrument by which

God's purposes, and that God, ultimately, sustains and regulates all that he has made, to the glory of his great name, and in fulfillment of his perfect will. Yes, our God—the true and living God—reigns over all!

DEFINING DIVINE PROVIDENCE

While this book deals generally with the nature of God and the relationship between God and his creation, broadly understood, the focus clearly is on the nature of God's providential dealings with his human creation. Divine providence is at once a gloriously wondrous doctrine, and one full of puzzles and questions. Christians have struggled long and hard over the nature of God's providential dealings with his creation. So as we begin this investigation, it is important that the reader know just what I mean by the term "providence" as it applies to God's relational dealings with the created order. I suggest, then, the following definition of *divine providence:*

> God continually oversees and directs all things pertaining to the created order in such a way that 1) he preserves in existence and provides for the creation he has brought into being, and 2) he governs and reigns supremely over the entirety of the whole of creation in order to fulfill all of his intended purposes in it and through it.

Stating the definition of divine providence in this way shows its two fundamental parts, as conceived by most in the Reformed and Lutheran heritage: providence as preservation and providence as governance.[2] Given

---

he draws us into relationship with him, yet we never instruct God or force his hand. Therefore, we can be sure that when he answers a prayer like the one I prayed—"If you will, Lord, please do something to get me on that flight home"—in granting what the prayer seeks rather than denying it, God is doing what he knows is best, all things considered.

[2] See Heinrich Heppe, ed., *Reformed Dogmatics* (Grand Rapids, Mich.: Baker, 1950), 251-254, where he offers several standard definitions of providence from various Reformed scholastic theologians. Representative is this definition from John Heidegger: "God's providence (*pronoia*) is His outward work, by which He preserves all things created by His word, rules their movements, acts and passions, so wisely directs them all to their ends that He promotes all good things effectually and mercifully, the bad either severely restrains or holily permits, wisely orders, righteously punishes; in a word, controls everything for the glory of His own name and the salvation of believers" (cited in ibid., 253). For those in the Lutheran tradition, Heinrich Schmid, ed., *Doctrinal Theology of the Evangelical Lutheran Church* (3rd ed., revised; Charles A. Hay and Henry E. Jacobs, trans. [Minneapolis: Augsburg, 1875, 1899], 170-172), offers this summary definition meant to represent broad Lutheran post-Reformation theology: "I. Preservation is the act of Divine Providence whereby God sustains all things created by Him, so that they continue in being with the properties implanted in their nature and the powers received in creation. II. Concurrence, or the co-operation of God, is the act of Divine Providence whereby God, by a general and immediate influence, proportioned to the need and capacity of every creature,

these two complementary elements of divine providence, it may be helpful to see more clearly the understandings I will be utilizing of these aspects of this doctrine. *Providence as preservation,* first, may be defined as follows:

> God preserves in existence and provides for the needs of each aspect of the created order for as long as he purposes it to exist, and he protects all of his creation from any harm or destruction that stands outside his purposes for it (see Neh. 9:6; Matt. 6:25-34; Acts 2:25; Col. 1:16-17; and Heb. 1:2-3; James 1:17).

Providence as governance, second, may be defined as follows:

> God governs and reigns supremely over 1) all of the activities and forces of nature and natural law, and 2) all of the affairs of his moral creatures, in all cases accomplishing in them and through them (at times by divine concurrence) his eternal purposes—yet in neither realm does he govern in such a manner that it violates the integrity of creaturely moral responsibility and volitional freedom to choose and act according to the moral agent's strongest inclinations, nor does God's exhaustive governance justly implicate the impeccable and infinitely holy moral character of God by making him either the author or the approver of evil (see Deut. 32:39; Ps. 5:4; 135:5-7; Prov. 21:1; Isa. 45:5-7; Dan. 2:21; 4:34-37; Eph. 1:11; James 1:13; 1 John 1:5).

Much in these definitions will be explicated more fully in subsequent chapters of this book as we unfold God's providential dealings with his moral creatures. Throughout this discussion, I will often speak merely of "providence" or "divine providence" as shorthand for God's providence as governance; and whenever the meaning is otherwise, this will be specified. The reason for this is simple: most of the enduring questions and deepest concerns that relate to God's relationship with humanity have to do, in particular, with his governance of human beings and their affairs from his position as Creator and Sovereign Ruler of the uni-

---

graciously takes part with second causes in their actions and effects. III. Government is the act of Divine Providence by which God most excellently orders, regulates, and directs the affairs and actions of creatures according to His own wisdom, justice, and goodness, for the glory of His name and the welfare of men." Schmid's definition separates out "concurrence" as a distinguishable aspect of divine providence, whereas many Reformed and Lutheran theologians have seen concurrence as part of the mechanism of providence as governance. This latter approach is the one I have chosen to follow, as is evident from the definitions offered here.

verse. Our concern with providence, then, is largely focused on his providence as governance, and how we, his human creatures, live out our lives in the light of this divine governance.

ENDURING QUESTIONS OF DIVINE PROVIDENCE

Given these definitions relating to the doctrine of divine providence, we should consider next some of the deepest questions and puzzles that thoughtful Christians have endeavored to explore when considering the nature of God and his exalted rulership over the world in relation, in particular, to the outworking of human life. I do not intend to answer these questions at this point; much of the remainder of this book endeavors to address most of the issues here raised. But it may prove helpful to have in mind some of the enduring issues raised by this doctrine, to begin thinking even now of how Scripture may lead us to treat them. Consider, then, the following broad questions and the issues they raise:

1. *What is the relation of divine providence to human freedom?* Without doubt, this is the most frequently raised and one of the most persistently difficult questions to come up when one considers divine providence. Of course, behind this question are several others. Is God truly sovereign over the world he has made? And what is the nature of the sovereignty Scripture affirms and asserts that God has? Along with this, what is the nature of the volitional freedom granted by God to his moral creatures (angels and human beings)? What mechanism best explains just how God may reign sovereign over the affairs of human beings and yet those humans remain free in their choices and decisions? One might consider this question, then, as a sort of *mechanical question*. It asks how two things (i.e., divine providential governance and human freedom) can fit together, how the two work together so that one does not cancel out or negate the other. What does Scripture instruct us on both realities, and how do these two truths work together, in the outworking of God's relationship with his human creation?

2. *What is the relation of divine providence to moral responsibility?* While the previous question, more mechanical in nature, is vexing, this

question is even more deeply troubling. This *moral question* arises when one considers God's sovereign control over the created order, and it asks two related questions: How are moral creatures rightly held morally responsible for their actions when God is sovereign over the world? And how is God preserved from being blameworthy for moral wrongdoing that takes place, while also being fully praiseworthy for all the good that occurs under his sovereign governance? In short, why is it that God's moral creatures bear all the blame for all the evil that occurs in the world, while God receives all the praise for all the good done—even good done through the hands of his moral creatures? And how can this be, when God is sovereign over the world? Clearly, "the problem of evil" is an outgrowth of the basic question of the relation of divine providence to moral responsibility, but less often noted, what might be called "the problem of goodness" is also raised by this question. How can moral creatures do good, and receive reward for good done, when God is the source of all good done and God alone is to receive the glory for all good that occurs? Here we have, then, a web of issues, all of which pertain to the basic question of how divine providence and moral responsibility relate.

3. *What is the relation of divine providence to good and evil respectively?* Is there any meaningful sense in which we might understand the action of God in the world as asymmetrical? That is, must we see divine providence as requiring a singular manner of divine action, such that God's relation to good and evil must be understood as identical (i.e., God's sovereign control of good is executed in exactly the same way as his control over evil)? Or, can we, with most throughout the history of theology (including most in the history of Reformed theology), distinguish some meaningful sense in which God's relation to good is different in kind and manner from God's relation to evil? Can we speak meaningfully and rightly of God *permitting* certain actions to occur while at the same time understanding God as fully sovereign? If not, and if we must entertain a fully symmetrical notion of God's relation to both good and evil, how can God escape culpability for evil while he retains praiseworthiness for good? But if some sense of the divine permission of evil is accepted, what does this require of our understanding of divine providence? And just how should we understand the nature of the divine

permission? Are there different senses of "permission," and how do these correlate with different senses of "sovereignty"?

4. *What is the relation of divine providence to natural law?* Here, the issues are more remote, since they do not involve persons and their moral choices and actions—except for God and his choices and actions as they relate to forces of nature and his sovereign regulation of natural law; and except for us in the sense that we are deeply affected by what laws of nature are established and what forces of nature do in our world. At one level, one can ask whether natural law is even a meaningful concept, if God is sovereign in a meticulous sense over all that occurs in the universe. Is natural law real? Or, does God regulate all things in a direct manner, giving merely the appearance of laws of nature functioning within the structure of the created order? Or, does God build into the universe what we have come to call "laws of nature," which (laws) he permits to operate essentially according to the properties of these very laws themselves? If so, what regulation does he exert over these laws of nature? What control does he have over the effects these laws of nature have as they bring about both great good and horrible devastation to human life and well-being? Is God "sovereign" over tornadoes, floods, hurricanes, droughts, famines, birth defects, and so forth, which bring untold pain and suffering to sentient life in this world? And yet, is God not also sovereign over the sun and rain that cause crops to grow, the changing seasons of the years, "normal" and healthy childbirths, and bodies that heal themselves from cuts and scrapes and bumps and bruises? What, then, is God's relation to natural law and forces of nature, both beneficial and harmful to human life?

5. *What is the relation of divine providence to salvation?* Clearly, at the center of biblical revelation is redemptive history, that is, the unfolding of the purpose of God to save a people from sin and condemnation, to the glory of his name (Eph. 1:3-14). And questions of divine providence's interface with salvation are manifold. No one doubts the fact that God has sovereignly planned to save his people, but when one considers the implementation of the plan, and its application in the lives of all who make up the company of the redeemed, then many questions arise that relate God's providence to human action and responsibility at

many different levels. For example, how shall we understand God's election of those whom he will save? Is election unconditional, so that God unilaterally chooses those whom he will save? Is the coming of just some and not others to Christ the outworking of God's prior unconditional electing purpose? Or is God's election conditioned upon the foreseen faith of those who, when hearing the gospel, choose to come? Does God choose those whom he knows, in advance, will choose him? And what about sanctification? What is the relation between God's sovereign dealings with his people and their growth in holiness? Can his people renounce him? Can they resist his working? Can God guarantee that those whom he has chosen to save will be saved in the end? If so, how should we understand our role in our sanctification and ultimate, final salvation? In short, is the outworking and not merely the plan of redemptive history regulated by the providence of God? And if so, to what extent and with what certainty are God's saving purposes accomplished? And how do our choices and actions accord with the outworking of those purposes?

6. *What is the relation of divine providence to practical expressions of the Christian faith, such as prayer, evangelism, and Christian service?* So many areas of the Christian life call us, God's people, to responsible action. We are commanded to pray, to witness to the gospel of Christ, to use our gifts to build up the body of Christ. The commandments contained in the teaching of Jesus and the New Testament epistles are numerous, and it is clear that God's people are to take them seriously. But how should we understand this commanded obedience in light of God's providence over all? Is prayer meaningful if God is sovereign? Is evangelism necessary if God is sovereign? Is Christian service to believers and unbelievers alike really a work for which we are responsible, if God sovereignly regulates all of his created order? How should we understand the outworking of the Christian faith in light of the providence of God?

7. *What is the relation of divine providence to the very nature and character of God?* Among some of the most important questions to arise out of recent discussions about process theology, open theism, and versions of classical theism have been questions about God himself. As God

relates to the world he has made, how should we think about his relation to space, time, and change? Attributes of God such as omnipresence, eternity, and immutability (and related attributes such as simplicity, impassability, omniscience) have brought about a renewed interest and attention to these complex and difficult areas of study. Should we think of God as eternally timeless and nonspatial and hence removed altogether from any literal temporal, spatial presence and interaction with created persons? If not, do we infringe on the perfection and transcendence of God? How can we best account for biblical teaching both on the transcendence and on the immanence of God? How can God eternally exist apart from all created reality while also dwelling fully and comprehensively among this created realm? What rethinking of God's very nature is required as we consider the reality of the God-world relationship required by the doctrine of divine providence?

NECESSARY FEATURES OF A RESPONSIBLE BIBLICAL MODEL OF DIVINE PROVIDENCE

In light of this understanding of what divine providence is and some of the main questions it raises, how should we conceive of the divine-human relationship? My purpose in much of this book is to address just this question. But here, at the outset, I would like to lay out ten features of a doctrine of divine providence that I believe are essential in formulating the doctrine such that it is faithful to all that Scripture teaches while also showing itself to be glorious and richly relevant to us, God's moral creatures. What follows here, then, anticipates much of what will be presented throughout this book with greater development.[3]

1. *Exhaustive and Meticulous Divine Sovereignty.* First, I begin with an unqualified commitment to the exhaustive and meticulous sovereignty of God. Passages such as Deuteronomy 32:39; Psalm 135:5-6; Isaiah 45:5-7; Daniel 4:34-35; Romans 9:6-26; and Ephesians 1:11 lead me to conclude that the God of the Bible, the true and living God,

---

[3] The following ten features of a model of divine providence were presented, in an altered form, in Bruce A. Ware, "Robots, Royalty and Relationships? Toward a Clarified Understanding of Real Human Relations with the God Who Knows and Decrees All That Is," *Criswell Theological Review* N.S. 1/2 (Spring 2004): 197-203.

has ultimate and specific (or exact, or precise, or detailed, or meticulous) control over all that occurs. The "spectrum texts"[4] of Scripture indicating God's control over death as well as life, sickness as well as healing, poverty as well as riches, disaster as well as peace, show the full spectrum of life over which God has complete control. While I realize that it is extremely important how we talk about the mechanics, as it were, of the exercise of this control, I believe that faithfulness to God's Word requires our full and unqualified assent to God's exhaustive and meticulous control over all. As Paul summarizes this truth, God "works all things according to the counsel of his will" (Eph. 1:11).

2. *Compatibility of Divine Sovereignty and Human Freedom.* Second, the kind of freedom and moral responsibility we ascribe to human beings must be compatible with God's meticulous sovereign control. I see two main reasons for this: 1) the nature of the divine sovereignty, as just discussed, requires that any and every aspect of the created reality, including human freedom and moral responsibility, adhere with it; 2) a compatibility of meticulous divine sovereignty and human freedom is required by Scripture's teaching. Passages such as Genesis 45:4-8; 50:20; Isaiah 10:5-19; Habakkuk 1:6-17; Acts 2:23; 4:27-28; Romans 9:6-26 demonstrate that God's sovereign control must be compatible with the choices and actions that human beings perform, and this must occur in such a way that humans fully carry out what they desire most to do and that they are fully responsible in so doing. To give just one example, the men who put Christ on the cross will not be able to plead "not guilty" at the Great White Throne judgment by pointing to Acts 2:23 and claiming, "See here, You say Christ's crucifixion was by Your predetermined plan and foreknowledge, so we are off the hook!" No, Christ was put on the cross by the hands of godless men, says Peter; hence, they are guilty. To cite just one other support here for the compatibility of divine sovereignty and human freedom, the doctrine of verbal plenary inspiration is virtually inexplicable without this understanding. John Feinberg argued in his essay years ago that the only way fully to account for every word of Scripture, every grammatical con-

---

[4] I earlier labeled these sorts of passages with the term "spectrum texts" in Bruce A. Ware, *God's Lesser Glory: The Diminished God of Open Theism* (Wheaton, Ill.: Crossway, 2000), 150, 204.

struction, every syntactical arrangement as both fully God's Word and fully human is by appeal to compatibilism.[5] I simply do not think that William Lane Craig's appeal to middle knowledge here works;[6] I have often wondered, when considering his proposal, if God could succeed with a one hundred percent success rate on Scripture using middle knowledge, why don't we see that kind of record reflected more in other aspects of his governance of the world (e.g., how many people, through-out the world today, have responded to his offer of salvation)?

3. *Freedom of Inclination, not Freedom of Indifference.* Third, human freedom that is compatible with God's meticulous sovereignty, then, cannot be libertarian or contra-causal freedom[7] but must instead truly be a freedom of one's strongest inclination, desire, and volition. That is, our freedom consists in our choosing and doing according to what we are inclined most, or what we desire most, to do. I remain fully unpersuaded by the case made for libertarian freedom. If an action is free *if,* when the action is performed and all things being just what they are, the agent could have done otherwise, then there is no choice-spe-cific reason for the action. Granted, the agent no doubt has a reason or reasons when he acts. But, if all things being just what they are (i.e., all those reasons are in place exactly as they are), he could have done other-wise, then it follows that any reason or set of reasons for why the agent did what he did would be the identical reason or set of reasons for why, instead, he might have done otherwise. More simply, no choice-specific reason or reasons can be given for any so-called "free" choices or actions that we do. Of course, this reduces all "free" choices and actions to arbitrariness and removes from us the bases for why we choose and act. Compatibilist freedom, on the other hand, insists that regardless of what struggles we go through in making our choices or deciding what action

[5] See John Feinberg, "God Ordains All Things," in David Basinger and Randall Basinger, eds., *Predestination and Free Will: Four Views of Divine Sovereignty and Human Freedom* (Downers Grove, Ill.: InterVarsity Press, 1986), 34-35.

[6] William Lane Craig, "'Men Moved by the Holy Spirit Spoke from God' (2 Peter 1:21): A Middle Knowledge Perspective on Biblical Inspiration," *Philosophia Christi* 1 (1999): 45-82.

[7] The view of freedom held in the Arminian tradition and elsewhere is often called 'libertarian freedom' and sometimes called 'contra-causal freedom.' The latter term refers to the notion that when we cause one thing to happen by the choice we make, we could have chosen otherwise, and hence, we could have "caused contrary" to what in fact we caused to occur by the choice we made. Freedom, then, is contra-causal; it is constituted by our ability to cause either one thing or its contrary to take place whenever we make a choice.

to perform, in the end, when we choose and act, we do so from prevailing desires which explain exactly why *this* choice and not another is made. This obviously means, however, that when we choose, all things being just what they are, we *must* choose as we do! This constitutes our freedom exactly at this point: we do what we most want. So, compatibilist freedom commends itself to me both because it alone accords with divine sovereignty and fits Scripture's teaching about divine-human concurrence of action, and also because it explains and accounts for human choice and action where libertarianism simply cannot do so.

4. *Asymmetrical Divine Agency in Regard to Good and Evil Respectively.* Fourth, the mechanism by which we conceive of God's control over and supervision of human affairs must involve asymmetrical aspects, one of which works in a direct and immediate fashion, causing particular events and actions to occur (e.g., creation, regeneration), but the other of which works in an indirect and permissive manner, allowing human activities or natural conditions to proceed as they are, all the while able to change those if what he sees would come from them stands in conflict to his wise and good purposes (e.g., the regular functioning of the laws of nature, ongoing unbelief and rejection of Christ by the non-elect). Perhaps we could call the first manner of divine activity "direct-causative" divine action and the second, "indirect-permissive" divine action. Notice that the second kind of divine action is not, in fact, inaction; i.e., it properly is "action." Why? Simply because, as Paul Helm makes clear in his volume on the providence of God,[8] this form of permissive divine will is one in which God permits *specifically* and *only* those aspects of the natural order or human actions which he could, were he to choose to, prevent. And, since he permits specifically and only what he could prevent, therefore he actively chooses to allow just these items when he is fully capable of having brought about others instead.

Having made clear this distinction, the main point, however, is that God's control requires both kinds of divine actions. It seems to me that the strain in Calvinism that has been reluctant to embrace the "permissive will of God" simply rejects one of the very conceptual tools neces-

---

[8] Paul Helm, *The Providence of God,* in Contours of Christian Theology, series ed. Gerald Bray (Downers Grove, Ill.: InterVarsity Press, 1994), 101-102, 172.

sary to account for God's moral innocence in regard to evil. Surely, more is needed than just this manner of the divine activity, but I don't see how we can proceed if God's sovereign dealings in matters of good and evil are, in fact, symmetrical.

5. *Compatibilist Middle Knowledge.* Fifth, this indirect-permissive divine action functions with human compatibilist freedom, avoiding coercion and allowing humans to do what they most want to do, by God's utilizing a Calvinist version of middle knowledge. I'll call it "compatibilist middle knowledge," knowledge of what compatibilistically free creatures *would* do, which is middle between God's knowledge of merely what *could* be and his knowledge of specifically what *will* be. Both Terrance Tiessen[9] and John Frame[10] have, in recent years, urged this concept, even if not with the same terminology. I agree fully with these men and others who argue that Molinist middle knowledge, predicated on libertarian human freedom, is not possible. How can God know what a free agent *would* do in some state of affairs if, all things being just what they are, the agent can do A or not-A? Knowing and controlling the circumstances in which free creatures act only exerts control over the range of possible choices, but in no way does it indicate just what choice would in fact be made. And, as seen earlier, since these libertarianly free choices have no choice-specific reasons for them, neither God nor the agent could know why he chooses specifically and exactly what he does. How, then, is God to know what an agent *would* choose?

But if we really do make our choices for prevailing reasons, if the conditions (both internal and external) surrounding a particular choice present to us the individually necessary and jointly sufficient conditions for making just the choices we do, if choices and actions are actually effects of sufficient causal factors—if this is so, then it follows that God can know what choices *would be made* by knowing just exactly the set of conditions (i.e., all factors which together form the set of individually necessary and jointly sufficient conditions) that gives rise to particular choices and actions. So, he can envision an agent in one situation, and

---

[9] Terrance L. Tiessen, *Providence and Prayer: How Does God Work in the World?* (Downers Grove, Ill.: InterVarsity Press, 2000), 289-336.

[10] John M. Frame, *The Doctrine of God* (Phillipsburg, N.J.: Presbyterian & Reformed, 2002), 150-152, 500-505.

knowing all the factors true in that situation can know from these factors what choice the agent *would make here,* and he can envision a slightly different situation, and again, in knowing all the factors true in that situation he can know what the agent *would do,* instead, *there.*

6. *Divine Omnipresence and Omnitemporality.* Sixth, relationship with God requires that God be involved with us in our time and space. Here, I will only say that I agree fully with the proposal John Frame has put forth in his *The Doctrine of God.*[11] Again, I might choose to use different terminology, but I affirm the concepts he advocates. It makes eminent sense to me to understand God, in himself and apart from creation, as both nonspatial and nontemporal, but then to see that when God creates the heavens and the earth, creating necessarily then both space and time, God "fills" the creation he has made. So we rightly speak of God as omnipresent, meaning that God really is here and everywhere present, while he is, in himself and apart from creation, nonspatial. So likewise, we should speak of God as omnitemporal, meaning that God is every-time present. God really is with us, in space and time, in all of life.

7. *Divine Immutability and Mutability.* Seventh, relationship with God requires vibrant conceptions of both God's immutability and his mutability. I have argued for this elsewhere,[12] and I'll only say here that it seems clear to me that God's ontological and ethical immutability requires that God be relationally mutable, so that when the moral situation with which God is in relation changes, so too does God "change" in relation to that changed situation in ways called forth by his immutable character and promise. For example, when a sinner repents, God's disposition toward that person changes, from wrath and impending condemnation to one of peace and acceptance. This is a change in God—not of his essential attributes and character, but of his disposition, relation, and attitude.

8. *Necessary and Contingent Divine Qualities.* Eighth, relational mutability requires that we understand God as having some kinds of

---

[11] Ibid., 543-575.

[12] Bruce A. Ware, "An Evangelical Reformulation of the Doctrine of the Immutability of God," *Journal of the Evangelical Theological Society* 29 (1986): 431-446.

contingent qualities. He should rightly be said to "respond" to situations that arise. His anger toward sin really does arise as the sin is committed, and his acceptance really is extended to those who repent. We should not understand all of God's qualities as absolute, but understand his relationship with the world he has made to involve, by his relational mutability, some contingent qualities.

Here, then, I would also urge a distinction between categories of the divine attributes: essential and contingent (or accidental, to use Aristotle's term) attributes. God, as triune and eternal, has infinite essential qualities of holiness, love, power, knowledge, and many more. But shall we say of all of God's qualities that they are equally eternal and essential? Again, it seems that creation, and particularly the entrance of sin into the creation, calls forth qualities of God that are expressions of eternal and essential qualities but that are themselves also contingent and conditional qualities occasioned by the world to which God is now related. For example, shall we think of God as eternally merciful? In the Trinity, apart from creation, to whom is God merciful? If mercy is favor shown to one who is destitute, needy, helpless, and hopeless, how can mercy be expressed within the Trinity? The same can be said of grace and wrath. It seems that these are qualities that express God's essential attributes of love and holiness, respectively, but they are conditioned by God's relationship with a sinful world, and hence come to be in time and are, therefore, contingent.

9. *Uniqueness of "Real Relationality" with God.* Ninth, relationship with God, because it is with God, departs in some respects from the kind of relationships we have with others. For example, I don't assume with any person I talk with that he or she is always right. But with God, I dare not assume anything else than that he is always right! Won't this require that my relationship with God will be different than my relationship with anyone else? If, as Isaiah 40 tells us, no one can counsel the Lord, then I ought not relate to God by trying to correct him or straighten him out. Rather, I seek to know what his will is and do it. Or to take another example, I do not assume with any other person that I must do absolutely everything that he or she tells me to do. But with God, must we not relate to him by acknowledging before him that we should do only and always what is his will for us to do? We can try to

determine what a "real" relationship with God is by insisting that the only kinds of real relations are the ones we have with other human beings; but since God is unlike us in so many ways, it stands to reason that our relationship with him will likewise be different in many ways, and yet it is no less a *real* relationship.

As an example of this, consider Jesus' repeated statements that he spoke only as the Father taught him, that he did only what the Father wanted him to do, that he always did what pleased the Father (e.g., John 8:26-32). Now, someone might conclude from these types of expressions that there was no *real* relationship between Jesus and the Father; Jesus was a robot, a puppet! He didn't have a mind of his own! But such a reaction would simply reveal a failure to realize that Jesus was relating here with *God*. And relationship with God will be different than relationship with any other person, but it can be just as real.

10. *The Glory of God Alone Is the Ultimate Purpose for the God-World Relationship.* Tenth, the glory of God is the end of human life, as it is the end or purpose for the universe as a whole. Indeed, pride of place goes exclusively to the glory of God, not to human satisfaction, and certainly not to charting one's own course, or to human attainment. If it's not all about me, but it is *all about God*, then we ask humbly how we fit into his wise and glorious plan rather than refashioning God to fit better into the kind of life we might wish to design for ourselves. Humbly accepting what God has designed, and being at peace with this as good, wise, and glorious, allows us to submit to God and, at the same time, be free to be exactly who God has made us to be.

STRUCTURE AND ORGANIZATION OF THE BOOK

With this overview now in mind, we proceed to look more closely at various aspects of God's nature, especially his relationship with the created order. The chapters that follow divide into two main sections, first theological, and second practical. Part One, "Foundational Theological Bases for Divine Providence," includes four chapters. Chapter 2 begins with a broad consideration of the importance of understanding God as both transcendent and immanent, as fully self-sufficient and as mercifully self-relating (i.e., freely choosing to relate to others). But the order here is crucial, and that balance is needed in our understanding of God will be made clear.

With this broad framework established, chapter 3 considers God's providential rulership *over* creation, focusing on the first three features of divine providence summarized above. Questions of divine sovereignty and human freedom and moral responsibility will be examined, and a case will be made for a compatibilist understanding of freedom, that is, a freedom, of inclination.

Chapter 4 considers God's rulership *through* creation, focusing on the fourth and fifth features of providence summarized above. This chapter examines the nature of divine concurrence by which God's will is sometimes carried out through the free and responsible agency of human beings. That God's relationship to good and to evil, respectively, must be asymmetrical will be demonstrated, and how the use of compatibilist middle knowledge assists in this discussion will also be examined carefully.

Chapter 5 discusses God's providential rulership *with* creation, completing our consideration of the sixth through tenth features of divine providence summarized earlier. Here, dynamics of the divine-human relationship will be examined. We will consider the importance of how God's relation to space and time figures into the real relatedness he has with his created beings. Special attention will also be given to the kinds of mutability and contingency that this divine relationship requires, along with what is both immutable and necessary in God. We'll explore how this relationship is in some ways like human relationships but also observe the sheer uniqueness of this relationship among all beings in the universe. The beauty and richness of the divine-human relationship shows how right it is that glory be given to God alone for making, sustaining, and empowering all that occurs, for the everlasting good of his people and for the honor of his name.

Part Two, "Practical Christian Relevance of Divine Providence," shifts attention to some of the ways in which this doctrine of divine providence affects the outworking of our Christian faith. Chapter 6 explores the experience of living *behind* God, as it were, in the veil of often unknown reasons for the suffering God calls his children to endure, for the evil that pervades life this side of the fall. There are, indeed, reasons for suffering, though they are often hidden from our view. Without this assurance, we lose hope, but because of it, we gain strength and passion to live faithfully through whatever God designs our lives to experience.

Chapter 7 considers living *before* God as we seek to move forward in life in trust and hope in God, as expressed chiefly in fervent, Spirit-prompted prayer. Great intimacy of relationship occurs as we live before him, depending on him and seeking his mind and will for our own.

Chapter 8 celebrates living *under* God as we experience his lavish goodness providing all we need for the joy and privilege of service. The generosity of God, here, is really beyond all human comprehension, and so we learn how wise and good it is to live under the God who provides and empowers all, for our good, and to his glory alone.

Chapter 9 concludes our study of God and his providential relation to creation. Brief consideration is given to how far many who claim to know and follow God actually are from God as he truly is. Those granted the privilege of handling the things of God in pulpits and class-rooms must resolve to stand faithful, upholding the true biblical vision of God, commending his glorious excellency and majesty, and caring only for God's approval and the growth in faith of God's people. Being "trustworthy stewards" is our calling, and it is a serious but joyful task.

Chapter 10 presents as an appendix a paper first delivered at the 53rd Annual Meetings of the Evangelical Theological Society, Colorado Springs, November 15, 2001, and published in the *Journal of the Evangelical Theological Society* in June of the following year. This paper inquires whether open theism is a viable evangelical model of divine providence. I give here twenty-six implications of the open view which are intended to show clearly that the open view fails as a viable model and should be rejected by the orthodox, evangelical church.

May God grant continued humility before him and his Word so that we may understand more clearly and accurately his design for our relationship with him. May the truthfulness of his self-revelation guide us, and may we make it our goal to be faithful to him and to his Word, no matter the cost to our lives and well-being. May God alone be praised, and may be his people be richly blessed.

PART ONE

Foundational Theological Bases for Divine Providence

2

Framework for Understanding God and Creation: God's Transcendent Self-Existence and Immanent Self-Relatedness

INTRODUCTION

With deep appreciation and respect for the historical heritage of the Christian faith and with ultimate allegiances pledged to Scripture alone, we need to consider how best to conceive of a framework for understanding the doctrine of God. In Scripture, which is God's own self-revelation, he portrays himself both as *transcendent,* as existing in the fullness of his infinitely glorious tri-Person unity and apart from the finite spatio-temporal created reality he freely brought into existence, but also as one who chooses to relate *immanently* as he freely enters into the realm of the creaturely existence that he designed and made. To think of God correctly, then, we must establish our framework for understanding God as containing both of these key elements—both the *transcendent otherness* of God in himself, apart from creation, and also the *immanent nearness* of God with every aspect of the created order. And it is in this latter aspect, in the immanent nearness of God to the created order, that we understand the place of the doctrine of divine providence. For in his immanence, he protects and provides for all of creation, according to his will and purpose (i.e., providence as preservation), and with immanent nearness and meticulous oversight he reigns over the heavens and earth that he has made, accomplishing fully his plans and designed ends for all of creation (i.e., providence as governance).

Having noted that the doctrine of divine providence resides, as it were, within the outworking of the immanence of God, we nonetheless would distort both our understanding of divine providence and our understanding of God himself were we to rush to his immanence without taking due care to comprehend, first, something more of his transcendent excellence and independence from the world. The immanence of God can only be rightly understood in light of his (prior and continuing) transcendence; but we also err in understanding God if we focus exclusively on his transcendence and neglect his immanence. In fact, this has been a significant problem in much of the history of the doctrine of God. Some have spoken of God in one way or the other (either as transcendent dominantly, or as immanent dominantly), and the result of this "preference" for one mode of the divine existence over the other has led, even if unwittingly, to distortion. Therefore, as we consider a framework that can best serve us in understanding God as he is, as he has revealed himself, we must endeavor to avoid talking of God's transcendence in ways that would jeopardize and diminish his real immanent interaction and relationship with the world; yet we also dare not speak of his immanence in ways that would cloud or weaken the fullness of his independence and infinite richness apart from the world.

Another way to say this is that we need methodological balance in our doctrine of God. As just noted, a tendency in this area of study—as seen both in classical and in modern portrayals of God—is to emphasize one side of what might be thought of as this transcendence-immanence duality, such that the contrasting side is consequently downplayed, perhaps even undermined. Here, a methodology is employed in which a particular set of features is singled out and given primacy in relation to all else that is said of God. Perhaps we could call this approach "duality reductionism." It works from the assumption that *one* conception of God should be given normative status as the "prime datum," i.e., a fundamental and axiomatic conception or item of information that must itself stand uncontested, and under which all other conceptions must be adapted and conformed. This one normative conception, then, is used methodologically as a control on all other relevant information; it regulates all other relevant conceptions in such a way that their own rightful and legitimate meanings are not allowed expression but instead are made to conform to the prime datum's own content and meaning. Although

often motivated from what are legitimate concerns regarding our understanding of God, the adoption of this approach inevitably (even if unwittingly) produces distortions of God's own self-disclosure for the sake of
the cherished position given to one primary and normative conception.

In order to provide a framework, then, for a correct biblical understanding of God, a framework also necessary to understand the God-
creation relationship (providence) rightly, it may be helpful to examine
briefly the forms of duality reductionism that appear in both classical
and modern approaches to God. Both approaches, it seems to me, are
in need of evaluation because in both cases the same methodological
problem is evident, even though each comes from the opposite direction.
Nevertheless, whether duality reductionism favors God's transcendence
or his immanence, the result is something less than a faithful representa-
tion of the God of the Bible.

Consider, then, a brief overview of both classical and modern methodological imbalances in their respective doctrines of God, and then we
shall offer a summary portrait of God's transcendence and immanence
from Scripture. This framework, rightly constructed, will permit us
greater confidence and insight as we then move to consider various features of God's providential relationship with the world he has made.

METHODOLOGICAL IMBALANCE IN CLASSICAL AND CONTEMPORARY DISCUSSIONS OF GOD

Most of us, no doubt, are very familiar with the modern critique of
classical theism along these lines. Theologians such as Barth, Brunner,
Moltmann, Rahner, Hartshorne, and Pinnock have often asserted that
the traditional view of God emphasizes so much his metaphysical perfection—a perfection defined abstractly as absolute infinity, simplicity,
timeless eternity, strict immutability, etc.—that as a result, his relational
involvement within a finite, temporal, and changing world must be qual-
ified and weakened so as to be virtually meaningless.[1] Stated differently,

---

[1] For some selected critiques of classical theism's stress on God's abstract absoluteness, see e.g.,
Karl Barth, *Church Dogmatics*, ed. G. W. Bromiley and T. F. Torrance (Edinburgh: T. & T. Clark,
1956–1975), II/1, 440-677, esp. 491-496; Emil Brunner, *The Christian Doctrine of God*, vol. 1
of the *Dogmatics,* trans. O. Wyon (Philadelphia: Westminster, 1950), 151-156, 241-247; Jürgen
Moltmann, *The Crucified God,* trans. R. A. Wilson and J. Bowden (New York: Harper & Row,
1974), 87-92, 207-219; Karl Rahner, *Foundations of Christian Faith: An Introduction to the Idea
of Christianity,* trans. W. Dych (New York: Seabury, 1978), 212-228; Charles Hartshorne, *The*

the modern allegation is that classical theism has made the conception
of God's absoluteness and abstract perfection its prime datum. Hence,
God's relatedness to the world is conceived not as real but as only ratio-
nal; God's creation of the world affects him none whatsoever but only
expresses in time what by divine reason he has decreed and known from
all eternity; God's coming into the world in Christ makes no impression
on the divine passionless and impassible nature while affecting only, but
greatly, the human nature of Jesus.

Concerning the modern critique of classical theism, I think it can
be shown that it has overstated the case and failed to acknowledge the
emphasis in the vast majority of classical theologians on God's relational involvement in this created world. Aquinas, for example, has
been wrongly understood as holding to God's absoluteness entailing
his static immobility. To the contrary, Aquinas vigorously affirms that
God is actively involved first as Creator and then as ongoing Sustainer
of all there is.[2] Likewise, the major theologians of the church have
consistently stressed God's activity in the world as Creator, Sustainer,
and Savior while insisting that this involvement can in no way lessen
his own eternal and immutable perfection.

While it is the case, then, that the modern critique has not always
been fair to classical theism's own stress on God's activity in the world,
I find some element of truth in the heart of this modernist complaint.
While it is undeniable that classical theists have affirmed God's active
and relational involvement in the world, the question remains of what
really it means to say that *God relates to the world* or that *God is
involved in the world* when first and foremost it has been established
that God, as the supremely perfect One, is absolutely unchangeable,
timelessly eternal, and altogether unaffected by the affairs of a creation
in time and space. If indeed he cannot exist in time and cannot in any

---

Divine Relativity: A Social Conception of God (New Haven, Conn.: Yale University Press, 1948);
"The Dipolar Conception of Deity," *Review of Metaphysics* 21 (1967): 273-289; and Clark
Pinnock, *Most Moved Mover: A Theology of God's Openness* (Grand Rapids, Mich.: Baker,
2001), 65-79.

[2] Aquinas, *Summa Theologiae*, Blackfriars trans. (New York: McGraw-Hill, 1964), IA., q. 9, 2:
"Now just as bringing things into existence depends on God's will, so also preserving them in
existence. For he preserves them in existence only by perpetually giving existence to them, and
were he therefore to withdraw his activity from them, all things, as Augustine makes clear, would
fall back into nothingness." See also R. Garrigou-Lagrange, *The One God: A Commentary on the
First Part of St. Thomas' Theological Summa*, trans. B. Rose (St. Louis and London: B. Herder,
1946), 267-270.

way change, then his relations to the world *must* be conceived solely as relations of reason on the side of God (i.e., relations forever in the eternal knowledge and will of God but which are not real in him nor have a true effect upon him), and his involvement in the world must be only according to his eternal decree while leaving unaffected his timeless and simple Being. Such an imbalance in which regulatory primacy is accorded God's metaphysical perfection and absolute transcendence, then, precludes any *real* involvement of God with the world he has made. Relations between God and the world may still be spoken of, but they can only be real for the world and never real for God.

In turning now to modern discussions of God, we find that while these approaches have been critical of classical theism's form of duality reductionism, they often have erred, nonetheless, in a similar manner. With their stress just the opposite from traditional theism, modern theologians tend to emphasize so much the immanent and relational involvement of God with his creation that the meaning of God's transcendent excellence and independent self-existence is, at times, weakened and diminished. Where in classical theology the conception of the divine transcendence tended to dominate that of his immanence, in modern theology, immanence regulates transcendence.

Take, for example, process theology's explicit attempt to conceive of God as "dipolar." According to Hartshorne, God is distinguished from all else in that whereas all other reality is related only to a portion of the universe, God is related to "all that is, in all its aspects."[3] God's immanence, then, is absolute and unqualified; hence, God is, for Hartshorne, both absolute and relative, transcendent and immanent, immutable and changing. God is, in short, "dipolar." While this sounds promising as a means to overcome the excesses of classical theology and to uphold God's transcendence and immanence, in the end it fails. What is difficult in Hartshorne's claim that the process God is truly dipolar is the fact that the concrete God—the one *really existing* God, as Hartshorne conceives God to be—is altogether relative and immanent. God's absoluteness and transcendence is a mere abstraction of what God is in his concrete pole. In the attempt to distance himself from classical theism's metaphysically removed and altogether transcendent God, what

---

[3] Hartshorne, *Divine Relativity*, 76.

Hartshorne has done, in essence, is to propose a God whose actual and concrete existence is altogether immanent. Transcendence is lost when such "transcendence" is true only as an abstraction from God's real and supremely relative nature.[4]

Perhaps the most compelling reason offered by various moderns for taking the divine immanence as primary is that God's revelation has come supremely in Jesus Christ. At first glance, this seems only right, but as shall be argued, this procedure is problematic for the doctrine of God. Karl Barth is representative of a major line of thought in modern theology stressing the primacy and near exclusiveness of God's revelation in Christ for all we know of God:

> The fact is sure that God constantly turns to us, whether He seems near or far, whether He speaks to us in silence and in secret or whether He addresses us openly, whether He blesses us or punishes us, kills or makes alive. . . . But we are sure of this fact only because God is Jesus Christ and Jesus Christ is God; only because the divine immanence in all its varied possibilities has its origin in Jesus Christ and therefore its unity in Him, but only in Him, in the diversity of its actions and stages. Therefore we cannot be sufficiently eager to insist, nor can it be sufficiently emphasized in the Church and through the Church in the world, that we know God in Jesus Christ alone, and that in Jesus Christ we know the one true God.[5]

Karl Rahner is another who lays great stress on our conceptions of God stemming from the incarnation. The starting point for what we know of God is not some abstract notion of perfection but the fact that the Word *became flesh*. The humanity the Logos became is, for Rahner, "that which ensues when God's self-utterance, his Word, is given out lovingly into the void of god-less nothing. . . . If God wills to become non-God, man comes to be, that and nothing else, we might say."[6] For Rahner, the *kenosis* and incarnation are of paramount importance in our understanding God. As King and Whitney say of Rahner's view, in Jesus

---

[4] For a further critique of Hartshorne's dipolar theism, see Bruce A. Ware, "An Exposition and Critique of the Process Doctrines of Divine Mutability and Immutability," *Westminster Theological Journal* 47 (1985): 175-196.

[5] Barth, *Church Dogmatics*, II/1, 318.

[6] Karl Rahner, *Theological Investigations*, 20 vols. (London: Darton, Longman & Todd, 1961–1972), 4:116.

we see "God's ultimate act of self-expression, God's very own finite reality in which he becomes."[7]

Enthusiastically we affirm with Barth and Rahner that God is revealed in Jesus Christ, and further, that God is revealed in Jesus Christ with an immediacy unparalleled by any other revelation. In significant ways Jesus explained God to the world (John 1:18) and displayed his glory (John 1:14) in a manner hitherto unknown. Especially one thinks of the cross of Christ where the meaning and manifestation of God's wisdom and power (1 Cor. 1:18-25), mercy and righteousness (2 Cor. 5:21; 1 Pet. 3:18) are heightened beyond all humanly comprehensible bounds. There is no question, then, of the centrality, supremacy, and finality of the revelation of Jesus Christ.

But on the other hand, Jesus Christ should not be viewed as the *exclusive* revelation of who God is. When Jesus came and revealed God, there was already a deep understanding of the true and living God through two millennia of his word and action expressed among his people Israel. Isaiah 40–66 shows, for example, the richness with which God's self-revelation had been apprehended. Jesus' disclosure of God neither conflicts with nor supplants all this prior revelation—it only intensifies it beyond any previously imagined bounds—and it does not lessen the importance of all that God had previously revealed to and through his people, Israel.

In the opening of his epistle, the writer to the Hebrews attests to the truthfulness and supremacy of God's revelation in Jesus Christ while also acknowledging the rich history of revelation already given when Jesus comes: "Long ago, at many times and in many ways, God spoke to our fathers by the prophets, but in these last days he has spoken to us by his Son" (Heb. 1:1-2a). As the book of Hebrews develops, it becomes eminently clear that the writer seeks to exalt God's revelation in Christ Jesus above all former revelation; and this is only right. Even so, one must not fail to recognize the abundant revelation of God prior to the incarnate life and ministry of our Lord, which revelation is necessary to gain as complete a picture as possible of the living God who has spoken. And even in the glad acknowledgment that all revelation ultimately points to the life, ministry, and saving work of Christ (cf. Luke 24:27, 44), we

---

[7] J. N. King and B. L. Whitney, "Rahner and Hartshorne on Divine Immutability," *International Philosophical Quarterly* 22 (1982): 202.

must still rightly insist on the importance of founding the doctrine of God on all relevant expressions of his self-disclosure.

Furthermore, when Jesus takes on human nature to reveal God, though he really does reveal who God is, we must realize that his revelation in this form *necessarily hides* from our view something of God that God might in other ways make known to us. Paul's explanation of the *kenosis,* the self-emptying of Jesus (Phil. 2:5-11), expresses this point. Whatever else this passage means, it is clear that in his taking the form of a human and a servant, Jesus willingly put aside the demonstration or manifestation of some portion of his intrinsic divine nature in order to be offered up "by the hands of lawless men" (Acts 2:23) as a perfect sacrifice for human sin. Or consider also the interesting juxtaposition of texts in John's Gospel: in John 1:14 we read that "the Word became flesh and dwelt among us, and we have seen his glory, glory as of the only Son from the Father"; but then in John 17:5 Jesus prays, "And now, Father, glorify me in your own presence with the glory that I had with you before the world existed." So, while Jesus *reveals* the glory of his Father (John 1:14), something of that intrinsic and eternal glory is *hidden* and will be restored only when Jesus once again is in the presence of his Father (John 17:5). The revelation of the glory of God in the incarnation also involves, necessarily and simultaneously, a hiding and veiling of the fullness of that very glory.

Thus, there is no questioning the supreme revelation of God's heart in the incarnate Son. But one must also recognize that God's revelation, in certain other of its features, extends beyond that revealed in Jesus. The reason for this is not that Jesus does not reveal God (he does!) but that by the very nature of Jesus coming in human form to carry out the mission the Father commanded him to fulfill, certain other truths about God's nature were necessarily hidden from our view. One must take into account, then, God's revelation *in toto*—the words and deeds of God expressed to Israel, the church, and in Jesus Christ as recorded by the writers of Scripture.

The problem that can arise for the doctrine of God when certain features of God's immanent revelation in Christ are singled out as primary can be illustrated through Moltmann's theology of the cross. Moltmann argues that "Christian theology is essentially compelled to perceive God himself in the passion of Christ, and to discover the passion of Christ in

God."[8] Thus, for Moltmann, the source for Christian theology's understanding of God is not in any sense independent of Jesus but is precisely in and through his suffering and death on the cross. God, then, is a God who actively suffers for his creatures out of a sense of deep love for them. This leads Moltmann even to suggest that God is in need of the world, for as One who *is* love, he cannot "be without the one who is his beloved."[9] For Moltmann, then, the prime datum that dominates all our thinking on the divine nature is the passionate and suffering love of Jesus for the creatures, whom he in a real sense needs.

The question may be rightly raised whether it is justifiable to single out one aspect of revelation (even as important an aspect as the cross of Christ) and elevate it to the status of such a primary and regulatory conception. Is it not possible that God's revelation extends beyond a given single feature? And if God's revelation is in fact larger, might it not be wiser to allow facets of his self-revelation to inform each other rather than selecting a certain portion as holding interpretive primacy over all else?

Orthodox theology has maintained that God's "revelation is, as his self-disclosure, the manifestation of his essence."[10] And it has upheld this while recognizing at the same time that "God's essence transcends his revelation."[11] There is no conflict here; God is who he is in his revelation, but God is infinitely beyond this limited self-disclosure. In a like manner, one must recognize that God's revelation in Christ Jesus is truly a revelation of God's essence, but there is no conflict if we immediately acknowledge that the full content of his self-disclosure to humans is broader than that given in Jesus and that his own nature surpasses even the total revelation he has offered to his creatures. And what is said here of God's revelation in Jesus Christ applies to any limited portion of his revelation. As revelation, it is true as it stands and is not in conflict with

---

[8] Jürgen Moltmann, *The Trinity and the Kingdom,* trans. M. Kohl (San Francisco: Harper & Row, 1981), 22. The reader may also refer to the comment by D. G. Attfield ("Can God Be Crucified? A Discussion of J. Moltmann," *Scottish Journal of Theology* 30 [1977]: 48) concerning Moltmann's view: "The cross is to be determinative of the divine nature, the yardstick of the attributes postulated of the deity."

[9] Ibid., p. 58. For a similar reason Hartshorne too holds that God needs the world. As a God who is love, it is inconceivable, so Hartshorne thinks, that there not be a creation that he assists and from which he receives value. See Hartshorne, *Divine Relativity,* 156; and "Dipolar Conception," 274.

[10] Otto Weber, *Foundations of Dogmatics,* 2 vols., trans. D. L. Guder (Grand Rapids, Mich.: Eerdmans, 1981–1983), 1:399.

[11] Hendrikus Berkhof, *Christian Faith: An Introduction to the Study of Faith,* trans. S. Woudstra (Grand Rapids, Mich.: Eerdmans, 1979), 106.

the whole of God's revelation, but it must be recognized that God has said more than this alone.[12]

If evangelical theology is to avoid the distortions that occur in either form of duality reductionism, it must resist the tendency to elevate facets either of the divine transcendence (as in some forms of traditional theology) or of the divine immanence (as in some modern theologies) to the level of regulatory primacy. In the former case one may so stress God's lofty and independent perfection that his caring involvement in the world seems an illusion; in the latter case God's intimate love for his needy creatures may be forced to overshadow his transcendent self-existence independent of the world. In both cases the same methodological error has, wittingly or not, been committed: the error of interpreting the whole strictly from a part and thus reducing one or the other central truth about God to its alternate. God's *full* self-revelation must be accepted by evangelical theology with the deep conviction that all of what God has disclosed of himself is important for our understanding, and that no part of it should be granted the regulatory function of a prime datum in its doctrine of God.

THE GOD OF THE BIBLE: TRANSCENDENT SELF-EXISTENCE AND IMMANENT SELF-RELATEDNESS

In an endeavor, then, to formulate a framework for understanding correctly the true and living God, we need to examine his self-disclosure as recorded for us in Scripture. Whether or not we are justified in giving regulatory primacy to any aspect of God's nature will depend, not on *a priori* considerations either of God's distinction from all created reality or of his intimate care for what he has made, but solely on how God has chosen to reveal himself.

Sensitive readers of the Bible have long noted that the God presented therein is one who stands both as the unique, holy, and eternal self-existent Being, and as the one who seeks and establishes intimate relations with his own creatures. In brief, God is both transcendent and

---

[12] Since I have called attention elsewhere to open theism's own distinctive diminishing of the divine transcendence and its overstress on divine immanence, I will not do so again here. Please see Bruce A. Ware, *God's Lesser Glory: The Diminished God of Open Theism* (Wheaton, Ill.: Crossway, 2000), 144-148, the section titled, "An Unbalanced and Excessive View of God's Immanence."

immanent,[13] both self-existing and self-relating, independent of all created reality and intimately involved within the history of the world. Isaiah 57:15 expresses this well:

> For thus says the One who is high and lifted up,
>   who inhabits eternity, whose name is Holy:
> "I dwell in the high and holy place,
>   and also with him who is of a contrite and lowly spirit,
> to revive the spirit of the lowly,
>   and to revive the heart of the contrite."

Or, consider a similar conception expressed in Isaiah 66:1-2:

> Thus says the LORD:
> "Heaven is my throne,
>   and the earth is my footstool;
> what is the house that you would build for me,
>   and what is the place of my rest?
> All these things my hand has made,
>   and so all these things came to be," declares the LORD.
> "But this is the one to whom I will look:
>   he who is humble and contrite in spirit
>   and trembles at my word."

The conceptions of the divine transcendence and immanence form part of the very fabric of Old Testament theology,[14] and New Testament writers only intensify both aspects as they understand the incarnation as the coming of the eternal God ("In the beginning was the Word," John 1:1; and "before Abraham was, I am," John 8:58) to dwell among humans ("the Word became flesh and dwelt among us," John 1:14).[15] A correct

---

[13] For an insightful discussion of both transcendence and immanence, see John M. Frame, *The Doctrine of God* (Phillipsburg, N.J.: Presbyterian & Reformed, 2002), chapter 7, "Transcendence and Immanence," 103-115.

[14] Walther Eichrodt, *Theology of the Old Testament,* 2 vols., trans. J. A. Baker (Philadelphia: Westminster, 1961), 1:205: "Both in the new formation of its own divine names and in the selection it makes of those which it has inherited or which have been imported from without, the faith of Israel demonstrates an unmistakable tendency to emphasize both *the mighty immanence and the exalted transcendence* of the deity." Cf. B. W. Anderson, "God, OT View of," *The Interpreter's Dictionary of the Bible (IDB),* vol. 2, 419-423.

[15] Donald Guthrie (*New Testament Theology* [Downers Grove, Ill.: InterVarsity Press, 1981], 76) speaks of these two elements as the "loftiness and tenderness" of God, of which both are integral

framework for understanding the living God must be informed by both
of these major conceptions if it hopes to be faithful to the biblical witness to God.

But furthermore, as we shall see, these complementary truths of
God must be understood in proper order. As these texts themselves
indicate, the divine transcendence must be conceived first in order for the
beauty and glory of the divine immanence likewise to be apprehended
correctly. Recall that it is the high and holy One who *also* dwells with
the contrite (Isa. 57:15); it is the One whose expanse cannot be contained by the heavens and the earth who *also* dwells with the humble
(Isa. 66:1-2). Yes, God is both transcendent and immanent. But marvel
that the God who is fully and infinitely transcendent would choose to
become immanent. Marvel that the One who stands eternally independent of the world should choose to relate so intimately with those of this
world. So, to understand better both aspects of God's existence and to
see them in proper relation, we turn now to examine—and worship—
the transcendent and immanent God of the Bible.

God's Transcendent Self-Existence. God's transcendence can only
be rightly understood, as Scripture makes abundantly clear, in light of
the fact that God exists eternally independent of the world, as the One
who is fully self-sufficient in his own infinitely perfect self-existence.
Throughout the Bible, God is understood as qualitatively distinct from
and superior to humankind. Quell points out that the Hebrew term for
deity, 'ēl, "is the simplest term for what is divine as distinct from what
is human. . . . The 'ēl, is thus a being which is completely different in
nature from man, so that there can be no comparison."[16] The Lord
asserts through the prophet, "I am God and not a man, the Holy One
in your midst" (Hos. 11:9), and the whole of Scripture confirms this
qualitative distinction. Yahweh's transcendent purity forbids Moses
from looking on him lest he die (Ex. 33:20), and before his awesome
holiness even the seraphim of the throne room of God hide their faces

to New Testament theology. Cf. C.F.D. Moule, "God, NT," *IDB,* vol. 2, 430-432; and
J. Schneider, "God, Gods, Emmanuel," *New International Dictionary of New Testament
Theology (NIDNTT),* vol. 2 (1976), 74-76.

[16] G. Quell, *"theos," Theological Dictionary of the New Testament (TDNT),* vol. 3 (1965), 83.
See also F. M. Cross, *"theos," Theological Dictionary of the Old Testament (TDOT),* vol. 1
(1974), 242-261; and H. Ringgren, *"elohim," TDOT,* vol. 1 (1974), 267-284.

(Isa. 6:2). The psalmist distinguishes God from even the most powerful of men, noting that, in contrast to God, even those who are exalted on earth shall die like men (Ps. 82:6-7; cf. Isa. 31:3).

The prominent conception of the unique holiness of God accents also his distinction from all lesser reality. Eichrodt comments:

> 'Holy' describes the character of God as it has been made known to this people; and, as understood in the priestly conception of God, this means *him who is unapproachable because of his complete 'otherness' and perfection when compared with all created things.*[17]

The Song of Moses captures well the fundamental idea of God's holiness when it asks rhetorically:

> Who is like you, O LORD, among the gods?
>> Who is like you, majestic in holiness,
>>> awesome in glorious deeds, doing wonders? (Ex. 15:11; cf. 1 Sam. 2:2).

God is unique; there is no one like him (Isa. 44:6-8; 45:5, 18, 21-22; 46:5-11). His thoughts are not our thoughts, nor are his ways our ways (Isa. 55:8-9). Truly the greatness of the Lord is, as the psalmist declares, unsearchable (Ps. 145:3).

God's utter transcendence is also expressed when his eternal existence is contrasted with all created reality. Abraham Heschel points out that Genesis 1:1 does not begin by saying "God created the heavens and the earth," but rather, *"In the beginning,"*[18] thus acknowledging from the outset the eternal existence of God that transcends the entire created and contingent order. The supreme existence of God is assumed by biblical writers; it is taken as a given fact which then explains the existence of all else. Furthermore, as Vriezen observes, there is never even any argument in the Scriptures against the notion that God's existence might be contingent along with that of the world.[19] That God could have had a beginning or could come to an end would be to the

---

[17] Eichrodt, *Theology of the Old Testament,* 1:273.

[18] A. J. Heschel, *The Prophets,* 2 vols. (New York: Harper & Row, 1962), 2:45, emphasis in original.

[19] T. C. Vriezen, *An Outline of Old Testament Theology,* 2nd ed. (Newton, Mass.: Charles T. Branford, 1970), 328-329.

biblical writers unthinkable (cf. Deut. 33:27; Ps. 41:13; 90:1-4; 102:25-27; Jer. 10:10; 1 Tim. 1:17).

Not only is God's transcendence displayed in his utter distinction from all lesser contingent reality and in his eternal self-existence, but the transcendence of God finds full expression in the conception of God's absolute self-sufficiency. God exists eternally by his own will and nature, and his existence is of such a quality as to contain intrinsically every quality in infinite measure. The eternal existence of God is the eternal existence of *all perfection, infinitely and intrinsically possessed, within the eternal triune nature of God.* Just as it is unthinkable from a biblical point of view that God could ever not be, so too it is unimaginable that God could ever receive some quality, some value, some knowledge, some power, some ability, some perfection that he previously lacked. The apostle Paul echoes the Old Testament prophets' understanding of God when he writes:

> For who has known the mind of the Lord,
>   or who has been his counselor?
> Or who has given a gift to him
>   that he might be repaid?

> For from him and through him and to him are all things. To him be glory forever. Amen (Rom. 11:34-36; cf. Isa. 40:12-28).

If God were ever in need of food, says the psalmist, he would not inform his creatures, for the world and all it contains is his (Ps. 50:7-12). His greatness so surpasses the created realm that the earth itself is the mere footstool for his feet (Isa. 66:1). The God of the Bible, the true and living God, is in need of nothing from any created being; quite the opposite, whereas he is not dependent on anything whatsoever, all else is dependent entirely on him. Concerning God's unqualified self-sufficiency, the apostle Paul declares:

> "The God who made the world and everything in it, being Lord of heaven and earth, does not live in temples made by man, nor is he served by human hands, as though he needed anything, since he himself gives to all mankind life and breath and everything" (Acts 17:24-25).

As the supreme Creator of the world and everything in it, and as the sole Giver of "everything" that is given to "all mankind," God, then, possesses within himself all that is, and absolutely nothing can exist independent of him that could contribute in some way to enrich his very being or enlarge his possessions. God is supremely independent of the world, and hence he simply does not need the world he has made. His transcendence is revealed most clearly by his independent and infinite self-sufficiency. He possesses within himself, intrinsically and eternally, every quality in infinite measure. As Karl Barth rightly comments:

> God is not dependent on anything that is not Himself; on anything outside Himself. He is not limited by anything outside Himself, and is not subject to any necessity distinct from Himself. On the contrary, everything that exists is dependent on His will.[20]

God utterly transcends all lesser reality, then, in that he alone exists eternally and of necessity, and his existence encompasses the fullness of all value and perfection entirely within itself. Any and all other existence, goodness, perfection, power, holiness, beauty, or whatever value one might mention is strictly derivative in nature, as coming to be from the eternal God who alone has all such perfection infinitely and intrinsically. The question of Paul to the Corinthians, "What do you have that you did not receive?" (1 Cor. 4:7), is appropriate in regard to all finite beings. The thought that somehow we frail creatures of his making may somehow contribute value to or fill some void within the divine nature is utterly abhorrent to biblical thought. God stands supreme and above all as the one who exists in his fullness, independent of all. And our finite existence bears testimony, not to any human capacity to be anything in itself, much less to some supposed ability to add anything to God, but only to God's gracious will in creating out of nothing all that is and in granting to all his creation each and every quality it possesses.

The doctrine of process theologians and others whereby God is understood as the eminent recipient of value apprehended from the world is here utterly rejected. Surely one may wish to imagine that God so benefits intrinsically from human existence and activity, but the self-revelation of God, as given in Holy Scripture, simply will not bear this out. The

---

[20] Barth, *Church Dogmatics*, II/1, 560.

fundamental (but misguided) religious intuition that underlies this doctrine of the divine dependence is that if God is viewed as self-sufficient and thus in no need whatever of humankind or other contingent reality, then surely it must make no difference to God whether we exist at all or whether we are happy in our existence.[21] As Heschel expresses this view: "If God is a Being of absolute self-sufficiency, then the entire world outside Him can in no way be relevant to Him."[22] Heschel rejects the independence and self-sufficiency of God and argues instead:

> Biblical religion begins with God addressing man, and His entering into covenant with man. God is in need of man. A Supreme Being, apathetic and indifferent to man, may denote an idea, but not the living God of Israel.[23]

There can be no doubt, as we shall see more clearly momentarily, that God cares deeply and intimately for humankind. The full range of God's self-disclosure bears witness to this truth. But where we must part ways with those who advocate the divine dependence is in the implicit or explicit logic of their argumentation: that *because* the true and living God is personal and intimately involved in the world, this entails a denial of his self-sufficiency. This, simply put, is a *non sequitur*. Surely one might imagine that if a Being were in fact utterly self-sufficient (as has just been described), then one might naturally wonder of what concern the world would be to him. After all, the world and all it contains can in no way benefit his inherent excellence, for indeed that excellence is infinite and hence eternally and intrinsically incorporating of all value and perfection. Admittedly, then, one might naturally be led to conclude that God is indifferent concerning the world—when it is first shown that he is absolutely self-sufficient. But while the conclusion of God's indifference may follow naturally from his self-sufficiency, it does not follow necessarily, nor does it follow rightly. As we turn next to the immanent

---

[21] Hartshorne writes: "If God be in all aspects absolute, then literally it is 'all the same' to him, a matter of utter indifference, whether we do this or do that, whether we live or die, whether we joy or suffer. This is precisely not to be personal in any sense relevant to religion or ethics" (*Divine Relativity*, 143). In another place, Hartshorne speaks of the essence of "true religion" to be found in humans "contributing value to God which he would otherwise lack" ("The Dipolar Conception of Deity," *Review of Metaphysics* 21 [1967]: 274).

[22] Heschel, *Prophets*, 2:12.

[23] Ibid., 2:15.

self-relatedness of God, let us bear in mind this discussion and return to it again in wonder and awe at the glorious reality that God is both infinitely self-sufficient and lavishly loving.

God's Immanent Self-Relatedness. This brief exposition of the transcendence of God may lead us to wonder whether God truly and meaningfully cares to relate to the world he has made. After all, he needs nothing he has made, so why should he be concerned with a relationship with any part of it? Yet, we begin our inquiry into the divine immanence by noting that Scripture itself lays great stress upon God's free and active personal involvement in the world and in human affairs in particular. The Bible itself gives particular importance to the divine immanence, as numerous biblical scholars have pointed out. A. W. Argyle comments:

> The emphasis of the Bible falls upon God's activity, God's initiative, God's approach to man preceding man's approach to God. Both in the Old Testament story and in that of the New, He is an intensely personal God who visits His people, and hears and answers their prayers.[24]

Distinctive of the biblical witness to God as over and against both near-Eastern and Greek conceptions is this fundamental conviction that the one and only true God has involved himself personally at every level of his created order.[25]

Mention need be made of only some of the major themes of biblical revelation to illustrate the extent to which the God portrayed in the Bible is a God intimately concerned with and actively involved among his creatures. Take, for example, the prominent emphasis throughout Scripture on God as Creator.[26] The Scriptures proclaim from beginning to end that God, as the Levites declare, has made "heaven, the heaven

---

[24] A.W. Argyle, *God in the New Testament* (London: Hodder & Stoughton, 1965), 11.

[25] H. H. Rowley ("The Nature of God," chapter 2 in *The Faith of Israel* [London: SCM, 1956], 48-73) has observed that it is not Israel's belief that God exists or that God is one or even that God is powerful, omnipresent, and wise that distinguishes her conception of God from the Gentile world. Rather, it is her conviction that God is personal (p. 57) and moral (pp. 61-68), i.e., intimately involved with Israel in a moral relationship, that sets her conception of God apart from all others. On God's personal and active involvement in history, see also Eichrodt, *Theology of the Old Testament,* 1:206-210; Vriezen, 162-164; and J. Schneider and C. Brown, "God, Gods, Emmanuel," *NIDNTT,* vol. 2 (1976), 66-76.

[26] On the doctrine of creation and God as Creator, see, e.g., B. W. Anderson, "Creation," *IDB,* vol. 1, 725-732; W. Foerster, "*ktizō, ktisis, ktisma, ktistēs,*" *TDNT,* vol. 3 (1965), 1000-1035; H. H. Esser and I. H. Marshall, "Creation, Foundation, Creature, Maker," *NIDNTT,* vol. 1

of heavens, with all their host, the earth and all that is on it, the seas and all that is in them" (Neh. 9:6; cf. Gen 1:1-31; Ps. 89:11; 121:2; 124:8; Isa. 42:5; 44:24; Acts 14:15; Rev. 4:11). By his free word, all that is receives its existence (Ps. 33:6; Heb. 11:3). And that is not all. One learns within the very creation account of Genesis 1–2 that this God who speaks into existence all that exists created humankind uniquely in his own image (Gen. 1:26-27). Man, as male and female, participates from the beginning in relationship and fellowship with God as God grants humankind lordship over the earth (Gen 1:28-30) and as God reveals the conditions of obedience necessary for ongoing personal relations (Gen. 2:16-17).[27]

But when one has spoken of the relationship between God and humans only in terms of Creator-creature, one has only scratched the surface of the intimacy and depth of this relationship. The full impact of the revelation of God's immanent self-relatedness can be seen only in light of humanity's sinful rebellion against God, and God's indefatigable and self-sacrificing determination to restore and refashion that relationship to its intended fullness. Thus, while the fundamental basis of God's self-relatedness with humankind is seen in his role as Creator, the depth and breadth of the seriousness with which God intends to relate himself to this contingent other is understood only when God is seen, in addition, as Redeemer.

The notion of covenant[28] reveals the heart of God with respect to the creatures who willfully turned from him. By means of various covenants, God expressed his desire to relate once again with fallen humanity. Especially significant is the special relationship God established with Abraham (Gen. 12:1-3; 15:7-21), a relationship that

---

(1975), 376-389; E. Jacob, *Theology of the Old Testament* (New York: Harper & Row, 1958), 136-150; Eichrodt, *Theology of the Old Testament*, 2:96-117; Barth, *Church Dogmatics*, 3/1-4; and Weber, 1:463-501.

[27] Cf. Bruce A. Ware, "Male and Female Complementarity and the Image of God," *Journal for Biblical Manhood and Womanhood* 7/1 (Spring 2002): 14-23; also as a chapter in Wayne Grudem, ed., *Biblical Foundations for Manhood and Womanhood* (Wheaton, Ill.: Crossway, 2002), 71-92.

[28] See, e.g., G. E. Mendenhall, "Covenant," *IDB*, vol. 1, 714-23; J. Behm and G. Quell, "*diatithēmi, diathēkē*," *TDNT*, vol. 2 (1964), 104-134; J. Guhrt and O. Becker, "Covenant, Guarantee, Mediator," *NIDNTT*, vol. 1 (1975), 365-376; Jacob, pp. 209-217; G. von Rad, *Old Testament Theology* (2 vols.; trans. D. M. G. Stalker; New York: Harper & Row, 1962–1965), 1:129-135; D. R. Hillers, *Covenant: The History of a Biblical Idea* (Baltimore: Johns Hopkins, 1969); William J. Dumbrell, *Covenant and Creation: An Old Testament Covenantal Theology* (Exeter, U.K.: Paternoster, 1984); and Craig Blaising and Darrell Bock, *Progressive Dispensationalism* (Grand Rapids, Mich.: Baker, 1993), 128-211.

promised not only the emergence of a peculiar nation which had privileged communion with God but also the future blessing of all the families of the earth through Abraham's own seed (Gen. 12:3). God's concern to relate himself once again in global dimensions is expressed in covenant form to Abraham and, of course, is revealed supremely in God's sending of his own Son to all the world (John 1:29; 3:16) as the fulfillment of this early pledge to Abraham (Gal. 3:14).

Furthermore not only has God created certain beings capable of relationship with him, and not only has he offered himself in covenant to them (the free pledge of his commitment to his people), but beyond this God has acted in history to bring restoration to his fallen and sinful creatures. That is, God has expressed his great love and concern for humanity supremely in his acts of salvation. Redemptive history is prominent in the Old and New Testaments. In Old Testament theology, the high point of God's loving commitment to his special people Israel is demonstrated in the exodus. It is at this point in the history of Israel that God reveals his covenant name (Ex. 6:2-3), a name that forever captures the special relationship that God causes to exist between himself and Israel.[29] Roland de Vaux suggests that Yahweh, the name of God revealed to Moses in Exodus 3, speaks in a dual sense both of the supreme existence of God and of his specific existence *for* the people of his choosing.[30] The context of Exodus 3 emphasizes God's hearing and seeing the people's distress (Ex. 2:23-25; 3:7-9) and his uncompromising commitment to bring them release from bondage (Ex. 3:16-22). The God of the exodus is the God who cares deeply for his people's welfare and acts powerfully on their behalf. This commitment of God to be pres-

---

[29] On the name of God revealed to Moses, see, e.g., D. N. Freedman, "The Name of the God of Moses," *Journal of Biblical Literature* 79 (1960): 151-156; R. Abba, "The Divine Name Yahweh," *Journal of Biblical Literature* 80 (1961): 320-328; R. de Vaux, "The Revelation of the Divine Name YHWH," in *Proclamation and Presence: Old Testament Essays in Honour of Gwynne Henton Davies,* ed. J. I. Durham and J. R. Porter (Richmond, Va.: John Knox, 1970), 48-75; B. Childs, *The Book of Exodus* (Philadelphia: Westminster, 1974), 60-70; and R. B. Allen, "What Is in a Name?" in *God: What Is He Like?* ed. W. F. Kerr (Wheaton, Ill.: Tyndale, 1977), 107-127; Henry O. Thompson, "Yahweh," in *The Anchor Bible Dictionary,* vol. 6, David Noel Freedman, ed. (New York: Doubleday, 1992), 1011-1012; and D. N. Freedman, M. P. O'Connor, and H. Ringgren, "Yahweh," in *TDOT,* vol. 5, 500-521.

[30] de Vaux, "Revelation of the Divine Name YHWH," 65-75. He writes: "The care of the people is of prime importance: Yahweh sends Moses to lead them out of Egypt and orders Pharaoh to let them go, and it is for their good that he reveals his name. The consequence is implicit: Israel must recognize that Yahweh is for her the only one who exists and the only saviour. This is not a dogmatic definition of an abstract monotheism, but the injunction of a practical monotheism, and henceforth Israel will have no other God but Yahweh" (72).

ent with his chosen ones no matter the obstacles resounds from the miraculous exodus of Israel from her bondage in Egypt. God actively seeks restored relationship with those whom he has made.

If the exodus reveals God's heart of love and his willingness to act powerfully for his people, the New Testament events of the incarnation and cross emphasize the same concerns of God but now at the highest level imaginable. The intensity and immensity of God's concern for a fallen humanity is nowhere more visible than at the cross of Christ. Moltmann is surely right in saying, "God is not greater than he is in this humiliation. God is not more glorious than he is in this self-surrender."[31] It may be added: God is not more desirous of relationship than he is in this estrangement. The cry of Jesus, "My God, my God, why have you forsaken me?" (Matt. 27:46) is undoubtedly one of the most incredible expressions ever uttered. That the Father would (and could!) forsake the Son—all to bring restoration to a forsaken humanity—is surely the epitome of the expression of God's inexhaustible love. The God of the Bible seeks relationships with those whom he has freely made, and the cross of Christ serves to implore us never to think lightly of the intensity of this desire within the heart of God as expressed supremely here. God went to the greatest lengths possible to satisfy his wrath against sin and bring fallen humans back to himself. The depth of his desire to be related anew to his rebellious creatures is, as manifested above all in the cross, truly beyond all human comprehension.

Though only brief mention has been made of some of the highlights of divine revelation pertaining to the relatedness of God to humanity,[32] the point is clear: the God of the Bible is one who actively seeks to be in intimate relationship with those whom he has freely made. His love for the world is unconditional and inexhaustible, so that although we had willfully turned from him, bringing condemnation on ourselves, he deliberately sought us out even at great personal cost (Rom. 5:6-8). God's immanent self-relatedness is surely one of the great marvels of his self-disclosure, and in response we can only rightly bow before this

---

[31] J. Moltmann, *The Crucified God: The Cross of Christ as the Foundation and Criticism of Christian Theology*, trans. R. A. Wilson and J. Bowden (New York: Harper & Row, 1974), 205.

[32] Besides the themes mentioned, one could also point to such important features as God's restoration of his people after their captivity, the prophetic witness to God's great holy love for Israel, the promised sending of the Holy Spirit as humans now become the temples in which God dwells, the eschatological promise of everlasting fellowship in the presence of God—all this and more illustrates the intense desire of God, as revealed by him, to relate himself with his creatures.

gracious God in humble and thankful adoration for such boundless love (2 Cor. 9:15).

Relation of God's Transcendent Self-Existence and Immanent Self-Relatedness. Having considered both God's transcendent self-existence and his immanent self-relatedness, how, then, shall we draw the two together? The incredible and humbling testimony of God's self-revelation is that God is *both* self-sufficient (i.e., transcendently self-existent) *and* wholly loving (i.e., immanently self-relating). Although he eternally exists, independent of all else, in the infinite fullness of all goodness, truth, righteousness, and every other perfection, and although he possesses no deficiency or lack which could be supplied by any finite reality, nevertheless, he has freely willed to bring into being a contingent order to which he has voluntarily pledged his intimate and most personal involvement. In an important passage, Barth expresses this point well in contrast to theistic positions that connect God necessarily to a finite order:

> The right understanding of the freedom of God's will excludes all those views which seek to represent the relation between God and the reality distinct from Himself as a relation of mutual limitation and necessity. In the first instance this includes all pantheistic and panentheistic systems, according to which the existence of this other reality belongs in some way to the essence and existence of God Himself. The reason why God gives them real being and why from eternity they are objects of His knowledge is not that God would not be God without their actual or even possible existence, but because He wills to know them and to permit them to be actuality. As real objects of His will, and therefore already as real objects of His knowledge, they are distinct from Him. He is not conditioned by them. They are conditioned by Him. They have not proceeded from His essence. On the contrary, He has called them and created them out of nothing. He was not obliged to do this. He did not do it to satisfy some need in His own being and life. The eternity and necessity of the divine will do not involve the eternity and necessity of its objects. With whatever necessity God acts in Himself, He is always free in relation to these.[33]

---

[33] Barth, *Church Dogmatics,* II/1, 562.

The creation of the world was not necessary to God; as the eternal self-sufficient One, he did not (and could not) choose to make a finite order to add somehow to his inherent and infinite fullness of perfection. And yet he willed to create the world (Rev. 4:11), and in his free willing to create, he also committed his very self in personal relatedness to what was not God, to what he knew would reject him and rebel against his perfect will. Though he needed none of what he made, yet he brought it to be and made it the object of his special care.

If we felt the strain and ultimate inability to comprehend fully each of these two truths central to a proper understanding of God—the transcendent self-existence of God, by which he stands eternally independent of the world, possessing the infinite fullness of all perfections within his own nature, intrinsically; and the immanent self-relatedness of God, a relatedness expressed supremely in the cross, in God's relentless love that pursued its beloved in the face of open and willful rebellion—we now must acknowledge our complete wonder and amazement at an even greater mystery, one that is exposed only when these two grand truths of God are brought together: *the God of the Bible loves and seeks us out with such eagerness and persistence when he himself stands in no need whatever of the objects of his love.* His love, then, is unconditional without qualification. It is, as C. S. Lewis puts it, "bottomlessly selfless by very definition; it has everything to give and nothing to receive."[34] Surely one of the most amazing facets of God's self-revelation is this truth: though God does not need us, he loves us; and though we can do nothing for him, he does everything for us. That God is utterly complete in the fullness of perfection, and that he has brought into being what he need not have made and has pledged to it his deepest personal love—this is undoubtedly at the very heart of the self-revelation of God to his creatures.

THE TRANSCENDENCE-IMMANENCE FRAMEWORK AND THE PROVIDENCE OF GOD

I have endeavored to make the case that duality reductionism in the doctrine of God should be avoided and that a methodology proper to the God of the Bible should hold together the divine transcendence and

---

[34] C.S. Lewis, *The Problem of Pain* (New York: Macmillan, 1961), 38.

immanence. Both are crucial to a correct biblical understanding of God, while clearly the transcendent self-existence of God must be comprehended first in order to appreciate and understand correctly the nature of God's immanent self-relatedness.

Support for this conviction has been both negative and positive. Negatively, we have seen that classical and modern approaches to the doctrine of God have, in many cases, been marked by a stress on one side or the other of the transcendence/immanence duality, reducing the alternate side to virtual meaninglessness. Whether God's transcendence is so heightened in order to sustain his distinction from all finite reality, or whether his immanence (especially in Christ) is emphasized in order to underscore his intimate relatedness in love for all else, in either case what is lost is the substance of the alternate truth of God, and so our conception of God becomes essentially distorted.

Positively, we have seen that Scripture's record of God's revelation to Israel and in Christ expresses with equal stress both God's transcendent self-existence and his immanent self-relatedness. Clearly no scriptural warrant can be found to give either of these major truths a regulatory primacy by which one effectively cancels out or minimizes the other. Furthermore, only when both truths are taken together are we in a position to appreciate more fully the significance of each. Transcendence and immanence, then, need to stand toward each other in ways that complement rather than contradict each other. God's transcendence must be upheld, but in ways that agree with and support meaningful immanence; immanence must be upheld, but in ways that agree with and support meaningful transcendence.

With this methodological principle now understood and this overall framework for understanding the God-world relationship in mind, we conclude this chapter by inquiring what bearing this discussion has on our continuing development of the God-creature relationship. Consider a few of the implications from this framework understanding of God for our further reflection on the providence of God.

First, in light of God's transcendent self-existence and infinite self-sufficiency, we must resist the temptation to imagine God's relationship with the world as somehow contributing to meeting some deficiency in God himself. To put this differently, the dependence relationship between God and the world is asymmetrical: we (the world) depend on

God for absolutely everything; God depends on the world not one bit. As the Giver of every good and perfect gift (James 1:17), and as the One from whom, through whom, and to whom are all things (Rom. 11:36), we simply must accept in humility the staggering truth that God does not need us or anything we have to offer. That he wants us and uses us (more on this in due course) is true, to be sure! But that he does so, in light of his self-sufficiency, is nothing short of stunning. Our doctrine of providence, then, must never stray from the framework established here as seen in the transcendence and immanence of God.

Second (and following from the first), we must settle this issue up front: because it is true that every quality in existence resides in God intrinsically and infinitely, then no one other than God deserves honor and glory—period (Isa. 42:8). If what is truly beautiful is worthy of honor (and it is), then God alone deserves all honor, for all beauty resides ultimately, infinitely, and intrinsically in him alone! If true wisdom is worthy of honor (and it is), then God alone deserves all honor, for all wisdom resides ultimately, infinitely, and intrinsically in him alone! And what is said here of beauty and wisdom could be reproduced over and again, for every quality that exists, all of which reside in God alone ultimately, infinitely, and intrinsically. The universe displays the glory of God (Ps. 19:1), since all that it is simply echoes and reflects the glory of its maker. Hence, the story of providence is all about God in the ultimate sense. His glory, and not the glory of any other, is center stage in this story. We (sinners) must come to terms with the fact that God is central and all-encompassing, and that we exist by his will and good pleasure for reasons that have to do with the display of his glory. It neither can be otherwise nor should be otherwise. And our role in the providential outworking of God's purposes is to see more clearly how we exist and live to the glory of his name—to whom belongs *all* glory and honor.

Third, as we consider the divine-human relationship proposed within our doctrine of divine providence, it stands to reason that we should expect this relationship to look different in certain respects from the kinds of relationships we have with one another. No other person, apart from God, has no intrinsic needs! No other person cannot be given something that is not already his! No other person can love entirely unconditionally, since all finite beings have needs to be met, and our relationships serve, to some degree, as the means by which others benefit us while we seek to benefit them. Not so with God. Therefore, our framework conception of God, established when seeing correctly God's transcendence and immanence, leads us to anticipate that aspects and features of the divine-human relationship will stand apart from any other relationship we may have or that we may conceive. We must resist the temptation, here, to "pull God down" to our level and domesticate him in the ways in which we conceive any "real" relationship to be. Rather, we must allow God to define the terms of our relationship with him, and follow his lead in understanding what a real relationship with God actually is and how a real relationship with God actually works.

Last, a probing question arising out of this framework understanding of God is this: since God did not need to create the world, yet knowing that the world he would create would be filled with unspeakable suffering, devastation, ruin, and evil, why would he choose, nonetheless, to create? At this point, open theists offer the most facile of answers: God created "blind," as it were, not knowing the evil that would come until his free creatures brought it about. This answer reminds me of Esau's selling his birthright for a bowl of stew, for here God's "innocence" in regard to evil is secured at the cost of making God a dupe and a fool. The only way this view can be maintained is that it is the logical entailment of another conviction which itself is considered deeply precious and unthinkable to deny: the libertarian freedom of us, God's moral creatures. Due to our love affair with libertarian freedom, we come with birthrights in hand, ready to trade. But the truth of the matter is both more complicated and more glorious. Just how God creates a world that, in time, incorporates evil, and then exerts providential control over it, sets the stage for one of the most intriguing of all of the mysteries of God. We shall work hard to explore the extent to which God's self-revelation would encourage us to understand God's relation to good and evil, and we shall be prepared for when we must stop. Secret things there are, indeed. But the things revealed are for us and our children forever so that we may do all the words of the law (Deut. 29:29). May God grant vision to his children in order that we may see his providential hand at work, from the divinely willed rise of evil to its sure and certain willed end. To the glory of God, this story will be told, and perhaps we all will be surprised and delighted how God, in the end, solves the problem of evil. No doubt we will marvel, and no doubt we will be corrected. So, let us let God be God in his providential dealings with his creation, for only then will we understand the fullness of God manifested in the outworking of his infinitely wise and good plan, to the glory of his name.

3

Ruling Over Creation:
Divine Sovereignty and Human Freedom
(Features 1–3)

IN THE BEGINNING . . . GOD!

We observed in the previous chapter that while both the divine transcendence and divine immanence are equally crucial for understanding the God-creature relationship, and while both must be held together in a balance in which neither is allowed to diminish or cancel out the other, yet to understand God correctly we must (with Scripture) begin with the divine transcendence. The God who eternally *is,* is the God who then chooses to create and to enter into relationship with the world he has made. The divine immanence is made far more meaningful, and can rightly be understood, only when we comprehend the astonishing truth that the God who relates to us is the God who stands apart from creation, in the fullness of his infinite and eternal glory and perfection, needing no part of what he has made, yet longing to give himself to this very world that contributes nothing to his own existence or fullness. In this sense, then, transcendence takes priority over immanence. God in himself (*Dei in se*) both precedes and grounds God in relation (*Dei in re*) to the created order. The nearness and love of God are only magnified when we understand that these are extended to us from the God who exists eternally in the infinite fullness of his own intrinsic beauty, truth, joy, goodness, holiness, and all perfection.

In a similar way, when we now consider the divine-human relationship more specifically, we realize that of the two parties—God and us—priority must be given to God. God is Creator; we are his creatures. God is infinitely rich and full; we are weak, empty, and in need of being filled. God is fully independent and self-sufficient; we are deeply dependent and desperately needy. God's life, existence, and perfection are intrinsic to him; our lives and every quality we possess are derivative. Yes, the priority in this relationship belongs to God, not us.

And when we inquire, further, just what in particular is *true of God* that he would like us to be clear about in seeking to understand the God-creature relationship aright, the answer we receive over and again from Scripture is that God wants us to understand that he is God, he is Creator, he is Lord. Indeed, he is the Sovereign Ruler of the universe. Consider again Paul's first words to the philosophers in Athens when he sought, by their invitation, to tell them about the God whom they worshiped as "unknown," who is (ironically) the one and only true and living God. Notice here where Paul begins and what he asserts:

> "The God who made the world and everything in it, being Lord of heaven and earth, does not live in temples made by man, nor is he served by human hands, as though he needed anything, since he himself gives to all mankind life and breath and everything" (Acts 17:24-25).

Clearly, what is of utmost importance to the apostle Paul in understanding the true and living God is that he is the Creator of all that is, he is Lord over all he has made, he is the Giver of every good thing to every creature under his universal rule. And of course, this only picks up and brings forward the theology of Genesis 1–2, where God is Creator of the heavens and earth, and by virtue of being Creator, he has rightful rulership over all he has made. In his kindness, he extends to human beings the privilege of ruling on his behalf,[1] but this never diminishes the absolute sense in which God, and God alone, possesses rightful rulership, authority, and power over the whole of creation. We might even put the creation theology of Scripture this way: to create is to own, to own is to possess inherent rights to rule, and to rule manifests God's absolute claims upon the whole of what he has made. We stand (or better, bow) before God, then, as creatures who owe to God our unquali-

---

[1] In chapter 8 we will give much more attention to the notion of God's gracious kindness in extending to his creatures the privilege of service.

fied allegiance, uncompromising obedience, earnest thankfulness, loving devotion, and adoring worship. We do so because God is our Creator and Lord, as he is the Creator and Lord of all that is. Therefore, his rulership rights are universal, absolute, uncontested, and uncontestable. He is Lord of heaven and earth, and this we *must see* if we are to understand the God-human relationship correctly.

A FORK IN THE ROAD AT THE START

It seems that at the very starting point of understanding and developing the nature of the God-creature relationship, we in the broad evangelical community find ourselves at a crossroads. Though evangelical Christians of all theological persuasions acknowledge that unfolding the subject of the God-human relationship requires that we endeavor to make sense of two sets of truths, as it were—truths about God and truths about us—we differ over which set of truths, functionally, takes priority. Those in the broad Reformed tradition will follow along the lines that I am suggesting here: that our understanding of God must take priority over what we say next about the nature of human life and our relationships with God and others.

But from the very outset, those in the broad Arminian tradition take a different fork in the road, and by this they pursue a very different path. Whether they acknowledge this explicitly or not, their clear tendency is to begin with understanding the nature and significance of human life. We need to see, they argue, that human persons are created as free beings, whose freedom consists precisely in their God-given power of contrary choice. "Libertarian freedom," as it is often called, proposes that at the very moment of choice, we are free in making that choice if (and only if) in choosing what we do, we could have chosen otherwise. So we are free when choosing A if, at the moment of this choice, we could instead have chosen not-A, or B. And if this is not the case, then we are not genuinely free.[2] Therefore, they assert, we must begin with the nonnegotiable "truth" about human life that asserts 1)

---

[2] For a discussion of libertarian freedom by an advocate of this notion of freedom, see David Basinger, *The Case for Freewill Theism: A Philosophical Assessment* (Downers Grove, Ill.: InterVarsity Press, 1996), 26, where he writes that proponents of libertarian freedom "believe that given the conditions preceding any voluntary decision, more than one decision must be possible—the person making the decision must be in a position to chose differently."

that we are free, and 2) that our freedom is libertarian—lest we have no freedom at all.

Furthermore, not only do Arminians (broadly speaking) hold that the only real and genuine freedom is libertarian, they also propose that only libertarian freedom grounds the moral significance of our lives, our choices, and our actions.[3] If we are not free to do otherwise, then how can we be held accountable for what we choose and do, they argue. If human life truly involves, at its core, morally significant choices that are judged right or wrong, good or evil, loving or spiteful, and if the choices and actions we do in this world really matter and make a difference, then human persons must make their choices and perform their actions as free agents. But since libertarian freedom is the only kind of real and genuine freedom there is, it follows that human moral significance requires that human beings possess libertarian freedom. This, it seems to the Arminian mind, is nonnegotiable and undeniable, so that whatever else we say theologically, we cannot call into question the nature and reality of libertarian freedom. Therefore, we must begin here.

This starting place for those in the broad Arminian tradition has some very significant consequences. Most notably, because we must accept the libertarian freedom of human beings as a virtual axiomatic truth, therefore, when we proceed to consider the nature of God and his relationship with the world, we must shape our understanding of God so as not to jeopardize or threaten our previous commitment to libertarian freedom. Because we are so sure that we are free and that our freedom is libertarian, it simply follows that we cannot hold other ideas, including ideas about God and his relationship with the world, that conflict with and contradict the axiomatic truth of libertarian freedom.

The necessary result of this uncontestable adherence to libertarian freedom is, in part, a view of God's lordship and sovereign rulership over the universe that is strikingly different from the view held by most in the Reformed tradition. Allow me to illustrate this with two versions of Arminianism.

First, classic Arminianism insists that it upholds the sovereignty of

---

[3] Ibid., 33.

God, and of course, it does. But how it conceives of God's sovereignty is notably different from how sovereignty is understood by Reformed theologians, and the heart of the difference has to do with the Arminian commitment to libertarian freedom. Since (notice this is a given from the outset) we human beings possess libertarian freedom, then the kind of sovereignty God exercises is the full freedom and ability to grant to his moral creatures some of the control over what happens that otherwise would have been his. That is, God is sovereign in relinquishing control to us.[4] No one forced God to do this; rather, he does so by his own good pleasure and free (yes, libertarianly free) will. He could have chosen otherwise, but in fact he did choose to grant moral creatures true freedom by which he allowed them to do what they pleased, and he could not control how they used their free wills.

And of course, the problem of evil in the Arminian tradition is usually said to be solved right at this point. God gives us freedom, without which we could not be moral beings or choose to love or obey or worship. But he cannot give us this freedom to accomplish the good he longs for us to do without it being possible, also, for us to use this gift of freedom to do evil.[5] After all, our freedom is the power of contrary choice. If we choose good (which God intends for us to do), we might instead have done evil (which God wishes that we did not do). But God cannot be blamed for the evil we do, since we do it, not he. All God did was to give us the libertarian freedom (with the intention that we use it for good) by which we freely choose to do evil. God, then, is sovereign in bestowing libertarian freedom, in relinquishing some of the power that would otherwise be his exclusively, but in so doing he cannot control what we do with our freedom.

When one considers the number of libertarianly free choices and actions carried out from the garden of Eden to this day, it is staggering to contemplate how vast and broad and immense is the domain of free human choice over which God exerts (can exert!) no control whatsoever. Of course, he can limit the range of our choices, and he can use his persuasion in an endeavor to steer us in the right direction; but the one thing he cannot do—by definition—is to control our libertarianly free choices

---

[4] Jack W. Cottrell, "The Nature of Divine Sovereignty," in Clark Pinnock, ed., *The Grace of God, the Will of Man: A Case for Arminianism* (Grand Rapids, Mich.: Zondervan, 1989), 108.
[5] Alvin Plantinga, *God, Freedom, and Evil* (Grand Rapids, Mich.: Eerdmans, 1977), 30.

and actions. Although Arminians call this sovereignty, it is vastly different from what those in the Reformed tradition understand Scripture to
teach regarding God's lordship over all.

Second, the stepchild of classic Arminianism, open theism, has
gone one (huge!) step further. Not only does the sovereignty of God
need to be understood in a way that conforms altogether to libertarian
freedom (hence, they agree fully here with their Arminian brothers and
sisters), but now the *knowledge* of God must also be revised in order
not to conflict with this precious and prized truth. As open theists argue,
because we have libertarian freedom, it is possible for us at any moment
of genuine choice to choose one thing or another. We have, that is, the
power of contrary choice. But if it is the case that God knows precisely
and exactly the very choices that we will make in every single instance
in our lives, and if it is the case that God's knowledge (*qua* knowledge)
cannot be mistaken, then it follows that we will make exactly and only
those choices that God knows we will make, and thus we are not free
to do otherwise—that is, we are not free to do other than what God
knows we will do.[6] Hence, they argue, if we continue to affirm with
the entirety of the church throughout its history that God knows the
future meticulously and exhaustively, then it follows that we simply are
not, and cannot be, free. As a result, not only must our conception of
divine sovereignty bow to the demands of libertarian freedom, but also
our conception of God's omniscience must be reformulated, in order
for God's knowledge not to conflict with our libertarian freedom. God
knows, according to open theists, everything past and everything present, but he cannot know the future free choices and actions of his moral
creatures. As noted a moment earlier, when one considers the number
of libertarianly free choices and actions carried out from the garden of
Eden to this day, it is staggering to contemplate how vast and broad
and immense is the domain of free human choice that God, according
to this view, does not and cannot know, and over which God exerts no
control whatsoever.

It seems clear, then, that open theism only extends further the
same kind of approach taken in Arminianism generally. When the
starting place for understanding the God-world relationship is the

---

[6] Gregory A. Boyd, *God of the Possible: A Biblical Introduction to the Open View of God*
(Grand Rapids, Mich.: Baker, 2000), 121-123.

uncontested reality of libertarian free will, then God must be understood in a manner that "fits" our freedom. Yes, classic Arminians and open theists differ on the question of whether exhaustive definite foreknowledge conflicts with libertarian freedom—classic Arminians deny, whereas open theists affirm, the conflict—but both follow the same fundamental methodology. We begin with what we know to be true about human beings. We know that we are free, and we know that the only true freedom is libertarian freedom. Therefore, all else that we say about God and any other theological subject must be understood in a manner that accords with, and does not contradict, libertarian freedom.

THE EXHAUSTIVE, METICULOUS SOVEREIGNTY OF GOD

Rather than looking at God and the God-world relationship through the lens of libertarian freedom, Reformed thinkers have insisted that we must start with God himself. We must listen to God's self-revelation to learn both the nature of his sovereignty and the nature of the volitional capacities we have as human beings. We agree with those in the Arminian tradition that there cannot ultimately be a conflict between the nature of divine sovereignty and the nature of human volition, but we do not use libertarian freedom as a criterion in conceiving what divine sovereignty can or cannot be. The sole criterion for understanding the nature of divine sovereignty is simply this: whatever God tells us in Scripture about his lordship and sovereign rulership over the universe is what we should believe, because this alone can be the infallible truth about his sovereignty. So, what has God revealed to us in Scripture about the nature of his sovereign rule?

From the beginning of the Bible to the end (quite literally), readers are constantly encouraged, in account after account, to think of God as in control of what takes place in this world. And this control extends to the large (Acts 2:23; 4:27-28) and the small (Prov. 16:33), both to all that is good (Ezek. 36:24-28) and all that is evil (Isa. 10:5-15), and it encompasses occurrences in nature (Ps. 104; 147:15-18) as well as the free choices and actions of people (Prov. 21:1). While never minimizing either the genuineness of human choosing nor the moral responsibility attached to human choice, Scripture presents God as having ultimate and exacting control over just what happens.[7]

Ephesians 1:11. One of the most sweeping summary statements of God's sovereign control over all things is found in Ephesians 1:11: "In him [Christ] we have obtained an inheritance, having been predestined according to the purpose of him who *works all things according to the counsel of his will*" (emphasis added). Notice first that this statement occurs in the opening section of Ephesians (1:3-14) where Paul extols God for the many blessings that have been brought to us by the Father through his Son. What begins this list of blessings for Paul are the dual truths that God has chosen us in Christ before the foundation of the world (1:4) and that he predestined us for adoption through Jesus Christ, out of his love, according to his will, and to the praise of his glorious grace (1:5-6). It is nothing short of astonishing that when Paul brings to mind reasons for why God should be praised, election and predestination are the first and second items he proposes.[8] How is this instructive? Simply in that for Paul, apart from the sovereign will of God in choosing us to be saved, and in predestining us to become his children, our salvation would never have happened. But because God has so ordained, we are assured that God will bring about what he has planned.

In Ephesians 1:11, Paul makes explicit the theology of divine sovereignty that underlies the entirety of this opening section (1:3-14). Not only have we been predestined to adoption (1:4-5), but with that adoption also comes an inheritance that we have also been predestined to receive (1:11). As if to anticipate the question from his readers, "But can we be sure that we'll receive this inheritance of our adopted sonship?" Paul presents the grounding that guarantees that all those in Christ will have it. The inheritance is pledged to us according to (i.e., grounded in) God's predestined purpose that we will have it, and in turn this purpose is grounded in God himself who works all things accord-

---

[7] For an insightful and scripturally saturated discussion of God's sovereign control of all things, see John M. Frame, *The Doctrine of God* (Phillipsburg, N.J.: Presbyterian & Reformed, 2002), 47-79 (chapter 4, "God's Control: Its Efficacy and Universality").

[8] See my forthcoming chapter, "Divine Election to Salvation: Unconditional, Individual, and Infralapsarian," in Chad Brand, ed., *Five Views of Election* (Nashville: Broadman & Holman, forthcoming).

ing to the counsel of his will. That is, God is ultimate and sovereign over all, as demonstrated by the fact that *God's will encompasses all things* that occur in the universe, and his will is efficacious in that *God works all things in fulfillment of his purpose.*

If we wonder whether "all things" in 1:11 really refers to absolutely everything, we need only look back to 1:10 where "all things" are united in Christ, "things in heaven and things on earth." Yes indeed, "all things" means "absolutely everything." And because our predestination to receive the inheritance is included in the purpose of God that is fulfilled as all things are accomplished according to what God has willed, therefore we can be sure that all those in Christ will surely and certainly receive this inheritance.

Those who hold to a universal and efficacious understanding of God's sovereignty are sometimes accused of falsely generalizing from selected instances of God's control to argue for his universal control.[9] In Ephesians 1, of course, the generalizing comes from the pen of the apostle Paul himself, not from some unwarranted logical inference made by Reformed theologians. For Paul, the greatest security he can offer his readers of the certainty of God fulfilling all that he has promised to all who are in Christ is this: God "works all things according to the counsel of his will" (Eph. 1:11b). Nothing is left out, and all things occur as God has willed. If this is what Scripture teaches, then we need to acknowledge it and then work out our understanding of human volition and moral responsibility in ways that accord with this central truth and with the rest of biblical teaching.

Spectrum Texts. Consider next a set of biblical teachings offering overwhelming support for the exhaustive and meticulous sovereign rulership of God. One of the most important and most compelling of all biblical themes demonstrating God's comprehensive sovereign control is the teaching found in a number of "spectrum texts."[10] These are passages that indicate in sweeping language that God controls both sides of the spectrum of life's occurrences, both those actions and events con-

---

[9] Boyd, *God of the Possible,* 25, 29.

[10] I discussed these texts by this name previously in Bruce A. Ware, *God's Lesser Glory: The Diminished God of Open Theism* (Wheaton, Ill.: Crossway, 2000), 150, 204-207.

sidered pleasant and good and those considered harmful and evil. Consider the force of these five passages (emphases added):

> "See now that I, even I, am he, and there is no god besides me; I *kill* and I *make alive;* I *wound* and I *heal;* and there is none that can deliver out of my hand" (Deut. 32:39).

> "The LORD *kills* and *brings to life;*
>   he *brings down to Sheol* and *raises up.*
> The LORD *makes poor* and *makes rich;*
>   he *brings low* and he *exalts*" (1 Sam. 2:6-7).

> Consider the work of God: who can *make straight* what he has *made crooked?* In the day of *prosperity* be joyful, and in the day of *adversity* consider: *God has made the one as well as the other,* so that man may not find out anything that will be after him (Eccles. 7:13-14).

> "I am the LORD, and there is no other, besides me there is no God; I equip you, though you do not know me, that people may know, from the rising of the sun and from the west, that there is none besides me; I am the LORD, and there is no other. I form *light* and create *darkness,* I make *well-being* and create *calamity,* I am the LORD, who does all these things" (Isa. 45:5-7).

> Who has spoken and it came to pass, unless the Lord has commanded it? Is it not from the mouth of the Most High that *good* and *bad* come? (Lam. 3:37-38).

Most Christians would affirm without hesitation that God has control over the good that happens; after all, James 1:17 tells us that "every good gift" is from the Father of lights. So, it is not surprising or troubling to read in these passages that God makes alive, God heals, God raises up, God makes riches, God exalts, God brings about days of prosperity, God makes straight, God forms light, God makes well-being, and God brings about what is good. But what is amazing and instructive about these texts is that they attribute to God, in the same breath, human realities on the opposite side of the spectrum. Not only does God make alive, but God kills; not only does God heal, but God wounds. Indeed, God is said to make poor, to bring low, to make crooked, to bring about adversity, to create darkness, to create calamity, and to bring about what is bad.

It is not my purpose here to deal with the moral implications of these biblical statements, since I discuss this issue in some detail in the next chapter. Here, though, it is important that we simply allow the Scriptures to register in our thinking by letting these texts instruct us regarding the extent of God's sovereign control. Even if we cannot answer satisfactorily just *how* God controls good and evil without being morally compromised by his relation to evil, these texts affirm unambiguously *that* God so controls both. How could we miss the point? The parallel nature of these claims of God's control of both good and evil (e.g., "I kill and I make alive," Deut. 32:39) makes it simply impossible to remove from God what he insists on and asserts as true: that God controls the full spectrum of human experiences, both good and evil.

In fact, to deny God's control of both is to deny the very "Godness" of God and to remove from him his own stated basis for claiming to be the one and only true and living God. Perhaps Isaiah 45:5-7 shows this clearest. Notice the buildup in 45:5-6 preceding God's claims to control all in 45:7. No reader should be able to miss the point: *"I am the* LORD, and there is no other, *besides me there is no God;* I equip you, though you do not know me, that people may know, from the rising of the sun and from the west, that *there is none besides me; I am the* LORD, and *there is no other"* (emphasis added). Then, amazingly, following this repeated emphasis on "I alone am God!" comes God's own declaration of what he as God—the true God and the only God—is like: "I form *light* and create *darkness,* I make *well-being* and create *calamity,* I am the LORD, who does all these things" (Isa. 45:7, emphasis added).

And notice three features of this text that underscore the intentional and deliberate force of the language used. First, the stronger verbs indicating God's control are used, not for "light" and "well-being," but for "darkness" and "calamity." In both cases, God (through the prophet) uses the term *bārā',* a term used uniformly throughout the Old Testament only with God as its subject.[11] This, of course, is the verb used in Genesis 1:1 ("In the beginning God created [*bārā'*] the heavens and the earth"), and it indicates a work of creation that only God is able to

---

[11] Thomas E. McComiskey, *"bārā',"* in *TDOT,* vol. 1, 127-128.

do. That *bārā'* would be used for "darkness" and "calamity" instead of with their positive counterparts only underscores the fact that God does not want us to yield to the intuition to relinquish from him responsibility for these kinds of actions. Just the opposite; God's responsibility for them is both stated and emphasized with the choice of this verb.

Second, the term translated as "calamity" is the Hebrew word *rā'* and is by far most often translated "evil" (also sometimes "bad," "harmful," or "wicked"). There is no stronger Hebrew term than this one for all that is ruinous and disastrous and wicked, both from the vantage point of human experience and as seen from God's own perspective.[12] That God, through the prophet, would make his claim to exclusive deity here by affirming, "I, God, create evil/wickedness/calamity" is nothing short of astonishing. Are we to accept what God tells us, or not? Since God has stated that his own unique deity is made manifest by his control of both well-being (Hebrew *shālôm*) and calamity (Hebrew *rā'*), we are obligated simply to believe what God tells us and accept this as the truth about the extent of his sovereign rulership.

Third, lest the reader might have mistaken the main point of these verses, Isaiah 45:7 concludes with God asserting, "I am the LORD, who does all these things." That is, God does not do just *some* of these things, but God does *all* (Hebrew *kol*) of these things. The buildup in verses 5-6 ("I am the LORD, and there is no other, besides me there is no God") is matched, then, by the conclusion here ("I am the LORD, who does all these things"). That God wants us to understand his own deity, his own "Godness," as possessing the power and authority to control all that occurs, both good and evil—this much is simply undeniable, from this text.

Are we to call God a liar? Are we to say, "But no, God certainly does good, but just as certainly he does *not* do evil. God gives light and peace and well-being, yes; but he surely has nothing to do with darkness or calamity or evil." If we were to think this, we would simply be denying the teaching of this passage of Scripture, in which God has bent over backwards, it seems, to make it clear that *he does both!* If we're interested in removing God from control of the evil that happens in our world, evidently God does not share this concern. In fact, the opposite

---

[12] G. Herbert Livingston, *"rā'a'*," in *TDOT,* vol. 2, 854-857.

clearly is the case. To remove from God his control of evil (along with good) is to deny his being the one and only, true and living, God.

Control of the Nations. Besides the "spectrum texts" of Scripture, many other passages instruct us that God controls what happens in human history and that his will and purpose cannot be thwarted. In particular, a number of texts speak of God's control of the nations of this world, i.e., of their rise and fall, their successes and defeats, their boundaries, their wars, in short, what they do and cannot do. Psalm 33:8-11 provides a sample of Scripture's teaching concerning God's governance of the nations:

> Let all the earth fear the LORD;
>   let all the inhabitants of the world stand in awe of him!
> For he spoke, and it came to be;
>   he commanded, and it stood firm.
>
> The LORD brings the counsel of the nations to nothing;
>   he frustrates the plans of the peoples.
> The counsel of the LORD stands forever,
>   the plans of his heart to all generations.

The contrast could not be plainer. While God speaks and what he says certainly comes to pass, and while his counsel stands forever, unshakable and permanent, the nations' plans are frustrated by the Lord, and all of their counsel comes to nothing. Psalm 2:4 gives us a glimpse of how seriously God takes the nations' collective striving against him: "He who sits in the heavens laughs; the Lord holds them in derision." So much for free will creatures causing God to be frustrated and keeping him from being able to accomplish his will! And Isaiah 40:15 provides some rich metaphors for understanding just how puny and trivial the nations' power and wisdom is in comparison with God's: "Behold, the nations are like a drop from a bucket, and are accounted as the dust on the scales." And the prophet continues in 40:17: "All the nations are as nothing before him, they are accounted by him as less than nothing and emptiness." How much power and wisdom do the nations have that could in any way rival God or add to the infinite fullness of his omnipotence and omnisapience? The answer in 40:15 might indicate that they at least have some, albeit inconsequential; a drop of water is at least a drop, and dust on the scale is at least something. But 40:17 ends all pretense and puts the nations—the collective totality of humanity taken together—in their proper place. In comparison to God, their mass of knowledge, wisdom, and power is "as nothing before him . . . less than nothing and emptiness." How audacious to think that we human beings can resist, threaten, or jeopardize the will of God. The God of the Bible, the true and living God, simply cannot fail to accomplish his will, and the nations are subject fully to him, not he to them.

The great Nebuchadnezzar, king of the mighty Babylon, has given one of the greatest tributes to God's universal and uncontested sovereignty in all of Scripture. After Nebuchadnezzar was humbled for his pride and arrogance, God once again brought his reason back to him, and he was moved to praise and honor God, saying:

> "for his [God's] dominion is an everlasting dominion, and his kingdom endures from generation to generation; all the inhabitants of the earth are accounted as nothing, and he does according to his will among the host of heaven and among the inhabitants of the earth; and none can stay his hand or say to him, 'What have you done'?" (Dan. 4:34b-35).

With language reminiscent of Isaiah 40:17, Nebuchadnezzar speaks of the inhabitants of the whole earth, before God, as "accounted as nothing." Now surely this statement in isolation from its context could be misleading; it could be taken to mean that God cares nothing for the nations, that he considers them as of no value or worth to him. But this is not the point. Rather, when one looks at the next statement, one can now see what Nebuchadnezzar means to communicate: "all the inhabitants of the earth are accounted as nothing, and *he does according to his will* among the host of heaven and among the inhabitants of the earth" (Dan. 4:35, emphasis added). The point is this: the inhabitants of the earth can simply do nothing to thwart, jeopardize, or sabotage God's will or to keep God from doing what he has planned. It is in this sense that they are "accounted as nothing." Despite what the nations plot or plan or devise or scheme, God does exactly as he wills "among the host of heaven and among the inhabitants of the earth," so that the fulfillment of his will is universal in scope. As we learn from Genesis 1:1

and on throughout the Bible, the expression "heaven and earth" is a reference to the whole of the universe that God has made. So, not only are the nations fully unable to thwart God's will, God in fact fulfills his perfect will in every place throughout the universe—including, obviously, among all the nations, peoples, and individuals that populate the world. And Nebuchadnezzar ends with this astonishing conclusion: "none can stay his hand or say to him, 'What have you done'?" (Dan. 4:35b). That is, no one can keep God's hand from doing what God chooses and wills, and no one can rightly charge God with wrongdoing or call into question the wisdom and rightness of his actions. God's power, his will, his authority, his wisdom, his knowledge all render any check to the power of his hand or any affront to the rightness of his plan strictly impossible. God's will is done, for God is God.

Perhaps some specific examples of God's control over nations will help make these generalized truths more concrete in our minds. Consider first the astonishing promise and prediction of God to Moses of what will happen when Moses returns to Egypt and requests permission of Pharaoh to take the Israelites three days' journey to sacrifice to the Lord (Ex. 3:18). God says to Moses:

> "But I know that the king of Egypt will not let you go unless compelled by a mighty hand. So I will stretch out my hand and strike Egypt with all the wonders that I will do in it; after that he will let you go. And I will give this people favor in the sight of the Egyptians; and when you go, you shall not go empty, but each woman shall ask of her neighbor, and any woman who lives in her house, for silver and gold jewelry, and for clothing. You shall put them on your sons and on your daughters. So you shall plunder the Egyptians" (Ex. 3:19-22).

Notice two features of this prediction. First, God states categorically that Pharaoh will not let Israel go, and therefore God will stretch out his hand to perform the wonders he has planned. In the next chapter, God expanded on this prediction, saying to Moses, "When you go back to Egypt, see that you do before Pharaoh all the miracles that I have put in your power. But I will harden his heart, so that he will not let the people go. Then you shall say to Pharaoh, 'Thus says the LORD, Israel is my firstborn son, and I say to you, "Let my son go that he may serve me.'" If you refuse to let him go, behold I will kill your firstborn son'" (Ex. 4:21-23). Clearly, then, God knew that Pharaoh would not let Israel go, even after nine of the ten plagues occurred that were about to be unleashed on Egypt. God knew this (Ex. 3:19-20) because he controlled what response Pharaoh would have to the request to let them go (Ex. 4:21). God's hardening of Pharaoh's heart expresses God's full control over just how, and when, and under what conditions Pharaoh finally would let Israel go. But clearly God controlled Pharaoh all the way to the end, even ensuring that the final plague—death to the firstborn throughout Egypt (Ex. 4:23)—would be accomplished. God's deliverance of Israel as the angel of death "passed over" the Israelites' homes with blood spread over their doorposts was planned by God and carried out with certainty, in part, by his control of Pharaoh.[13]

Second, not only does God control Pharaoh, the king of Egypt, he also controls vast numbers of common people throughout the entire nation, for he predicts that when the Israelite women ask the Egyptians for silver, gold, and clothing, these Egyptians will give it to them; the Israelites "shall not go empty" (3:21), but they "shall plunder the Egyptians" (3:22)! Just imagine how astonishing this situation is. After nine plagues have occurred in which the people of Egypt have been afflicted over and again by the God of Israel while the Israelites have been spared, nonetheless, when the Israelites ask the Egyptians for their gold and silver and clothing, the Egyptians willingly give it to them! You would think that if the Egyptians despised Israel prior to the plagues, surely now they would hate them with a vengeance. But God is in control, and just as predicted, we read in Exodus 11:3, "And the LORD gave the people favor in the sight of the Egyptians," and the people gave bountifully to them, just as God said they would.[14] We read,

---

[13] Just how God accomplishes this hardening of Pharaoh's heart without himself absolving Pharaoh of moral culpability for his own denials to let the people go, and without God's incurring guilt for the disobedience of Pharaoh, will be discussed below as we consider "compatibilist middle knowledge" as one means God may use for such control. But, that God controls, and that Pharaoh is responsible, are both clear from this text. For further helpful discussion of this and other such biblical instances of God's hardening of people's hearts, see John Piper, "Are There Two Wills in God?" in Thomas R. Schreiner and Bruce A. Ware, eds., *Still Sovereign: Contemporary Perspectives on Election, Foreknowledge, and Grace* (Grand Rapids, Mich.: Baker, 2000), 113-116.

[14] Psalm 105:25 notes that at an earlier time, after Joseph had died, God had turned the hearts of the Egyptians to hate the Israelites ("He turned their hearts to hate his people"). So, God regulates whether the Egyptians hate or favor Israel. Ultimately, he controls both.

now after the final plague of death, that "the people of Israel had also done as Moses told them, for they had asked the Egyptians for silver and gold jewelry and for clothing. And the LORD had given the people favor in the sight of the Egyptians, so that they let them have what they asked. Thus they plundered the Egyptians" (Ex. 12:35-36). Does this text not encourage the reader to conclude that God controls kings and common people? He controls the destiny of nations. He controls the outcome of history. Surely, the God of the Bible reigns as the sovereign ruler of all, accomplishing his will without failure, frustration, or defeat.

A second specific example of God's control of the nations comes from the apostle Paul's sermon in Athens. After asserting that the true God is Creator of all, Lord of heaven and earth, and the self-sufficient Giver to all of life and breath and everything, he then says of God:

> "And he made from one man every nation of mankind to live on all the face of the earth, having determined allotted periods and the boundaries of their dwelling place" (Acts 17:26).

If Paul had said merely that God made from one man every nation of mankind, one might think of this simply in the sense of God creating Adam, from whom all nations and peoples have come. This would not require, necessarily, any divine regulation of which nations would arise; it would simply mean that all nations have come from Adam, whom God had made. But, as is apparent, Paul says more. Perhaps for the very purpose of specifying the nature of divine sovereignty of which he had already spoken—"Lord of heaven and earth" (Acts 17:24)—Paul now makes clear that God's sovereign control is such that God has determined both the time periods in which the nations of the world would exist and the geographical boundaries they would inhabit. It makes one wonder how many kings and armies throughout history, setting out to conquer another people's territory, realized that as they did this, they were fulfilling the determined will of God, who set in advance just what nations would exist, how long each would survive, and exactly what borders would encircle the land that each would possess, in each stage of its existence. To accomplish this, God must be in control of the small and the great, the decisions of kings and the will of the people. He must both know and control precisely what whole civilizations invent and produce and develop. He must control their monetary and military strength. He must regulate uprisings and revolutions and reactionaries. In short, God must control the entirety of what takes place in the nations of the world in order to determine their "allotted periods and the boundaries of their dwelling place" (Acts 17:26). Yes, God is sovereign, and his sovereignty is both exhaustive (covering the whole sweep of history) and meticulous (every detail is planned and regulated).

HUMAN FREEDOM THAT IS COMPATIBLE WITH EXHAUSTIVE, METICULOUS DIVINE SOVEREIGNTY

Since God is sovereign over all that occurs in human history, we must seek, then, to understand the nature of human freedom in a way that accords with that divine sovereignty. And since the Scriptures that teach us about God's sovereignty also teach us about the nature of human volition, we anticipate understandings of both that are consistent with each other. Whether we can understand fully how they fit together is another question. But that both teachings of Scripture are true, and that both are consistent when taken together, is our expectation from the outset. All Scripture is God-breathed, and hence we should seek to understand the unity, truthfulness, and coherence among all of its teachings, including its teachings on divine sovereignty and human freedom.

But not only does the Bible's teaching on the nature of human volition need to be *consistent* with its teaching on divine sovereignty, our human volition must be manifested in a manner that is *compatible* with this strong understanding of divine sovereignty. Human freedom, in a word, must be compatibilistic. That is, exhaustive and meticulous divine sovereignty must be compatible with the actual and real manner by which human freedom operates. God's control of all that occurs, including his control of human choice and action, must be compatible with the nature of human freedom, rightly understood.

This raises the question, then, of just what Scripture teaches about human freedom and whether it gives indication of a compatibility between human freedom and divine sovereignty. We'll consider first the nature of our freedom as human beings, and secondly we'll examine some of the biblical evidence for human freedom being compatible with exhaustive and meticulous divine sovereignty.

Human Freedom as a Freedom of Inclination. Probably the single most important biblical conception relating to the question of human freedom is the notion that we human beings perform our choices and actions out of what we desire in our hearts. That is, what we want most, what our natures incline us most strongly to—this is the pool out of which the stream of our choices and actions flows. Jesus uses a different metaphor:

> "For no good tree bears bad fruit, nor again does a bad tree bear good fruit, for each tree is known by its own fruit. For figs are not gathered from thornbushes, nor are grapes picked from a bramble bush. The good person out of the good treasure of his heart produces good, and the evil person out of his evil treasure produces evil, for out of the abundance of the heart his mouth speaks" (Luke 6:43-45).

Our wills function, according to Jesus, as agents of our hearts. Out of the abundance of our hearts, we choose to speak what we will. If our hearts are filled with love for fishing or golf or computers or cars, of this we will speak. That is, there is a necessary connection between character and conduct, heart and hands, desires and decisions. Our choices and actions and words and plans betray what we are on the inside. A good tree bears good fruit, and a bad tree bears bad fruit. Our wills give expression to the nature and character of our hearts.

Given this, what then constitutes our freedom as individuals? While more will be said about this shortly, clearly what has just been described above is not true of libertarian freedom. If, as Arminians propose, our freedom consists in the power of contrary choice, then quite unlike what Jesus has taught us, regardless of our hearts and characters, we are always free to choose either good or evil. But Jesus indicated just the opposite: that a good tree cannot bear bad fruit, and a bad tree cannot bear good fruit. In other words, our volition expresses the precise kind and quality of our character. So, our freedom cannot consist in the power of contrary choice, but rather it consists in the power to choose according to what we are most inclined to do. We are free when we choose and act and behave in accordance with our strongest desires, since those desires are the expressions of our hearts and characters.[15] In a word, we are free when we choose to do what we want.[16]

But it stands to reason that if we choose to do what we want, then at the moment of that choice, we are not "free" to do otherwise. That is, if I want an apple, not an orange, and if my freedom consists in choosing to do what I want, then I'm free to choose the apple but I'm not free to choose the orange. Freedom, then, is not freedom of contrary choice but freedom to choose and act in accordance with what I most want. It is, as Edwards called it, our "freedom of inclination," i.e., we are free when we act in accordance with what we are most strongly inclined to do.[17]

When are we not free? Our freedom would be rendered inoperative if we were forced or coerced to act in ways contrary to what we most wanted. If, for example, a man were to grab you on the street, hold a gun to your head, and take your wallet out of your pocket, then you would not be free when you surrendered your wallet to him. Coercion by which you cannot act according to your strongest inclination or deepest desire precludes true freedom. But influences in your life that stop short of being coercive do not have the same effect. Consider a different scenario: imagine walking down the same street as before, but this time being approached by your wife, who requests some money to finish her Christmas shopping. In this case you may surrender your wallet as before, but you may do so freely. That is, under the circumstances, you

---

[15] See also Jonathan Edwards, "A Careful and Strict Inquiry into the Modern Prevailing Notions of the Freedom of the Will," in *The Works of Jonathan Edwards*, 2 vols. (Edinburgh: Banner of Truth, 1974), 1:5, 30.

[16] A question sometimes raised here is this: We may be free when we choose to do what we want, but are we free to decide what kinds of things we will want or desire? I believe that the most responsible answer is, yes and no. Yes, we are free to seek to change our desires. Much of Scripture admonishes just this. We are encouraged to love God more, to see sin for the evil and destructive power that it is, to long for the pure milk of the word, etc. We are constantly being called in Scripture to "want to want" something different than we do in our sinful flesh. In fact, part of our hope that sanctification in the believer's life will take place comes precisely as we long for renewed desires that conform us more and more with the will and ways of God. But, no, we do not have control over all of the factors that play into our having just the desires we have. Everything from the ways in which we were raised, the features of our own genetic makeup, the places we've lived, and the people who have influenced us—these factors and many, many more indicate that there are limits to how much we can redirect the desires of our hearts. And here is where God's role to work in our hearts to give us hearts of flesh instead of hearts of stone (Ezek. 36:26) becomes so precious. Only God can work in us so that our deepest desires are changed. And, unless God so works, sinful men and women simply cannot change the deepest longings of their sinful natures. So, it seems clear that the answer to whether we are free to decide what our strongest desires are is complex; in some sense, yes, but in another sense, no.

[17] Edwards, "Careful and Strict Inquiry," 21.

do what you most want to do. In the previous case, you were forced to surrender your wallet contrary to what you most wanted, and hence, you were not free; in the latter case, you were influenced to surrender your wallet, but the influence of your wife's request only acted on your will in such a way that you did what you most wanted, and hence, you acted freely. Human freedom, then, is consistent with a multitude of influences and contributing factors involved in bringing about our strongest inclination at any given moment, but human freedom is ruled out in the presence of coercion.

Before considering our next question, it is important to point out briefly how deeply practical and powerful this conception of human freedom is. If, as we've argued here, our freedom consists in our choosing to act according to our strongest desires or inclinations, then it stands to reason that we can change our behavior only when our strongest desires and inclinations change. Character transformation is the key to behavior modification. And, of course, this is why Scripture is so consistently concerned with the renewal of our minds, our hearts, our characters, and our inner persons. Only as the Spirit of God works in us to transform our deepest desires will we choose and act in ways, increasingly, that are pleasing to the Lord. What hope there is here. We can be assured, as Jesus himself indicated, that as the Spirit and the Word transform our characters so that we become good trees, the fruit we bear will evidence the new "trees" that we are. Unlike libertarian freedom, which bifurcates character from conduct (with its insistence on freedom as a supposed power of contrary choice), here we take great strength and direction from the fact that as God works to make us increasingly holy and Christlike, we will live out what we love. Character matters, and it holds the key, ultimately, to living the transformed lives that God calls and empowers us to live.

Compatibility of Divine Sovereignty and Human Freedom. Can a strong sense of divine sovereignty rightly be seen as compatible with human freedom? Yes, so long as our freedom is, as argued above, a freedom of inclination. Recall first that, whereas innumerable influences may be consistent with our freedom to choose to do what we most want to do, coercion, on the other hand, precludes our freedom. Given this, is it not possible for God to influence us in some direct but noncoercive ways, and to be involved in the vast number of other influences upon us, in such a way that when we make our choices, influenced as we are in all of these various ways, we do exactly as we most want to do? If so, then we must conclude that God's influences on us are, in principle, compatible with our acting freely, since we do, in the face of those influences, what we most want to do.

Let's take this one step further. Is it not possible also for God to know just what impact certain influences will have upon our decisions, so that prior to our choices and actions, God can know the precise choices and actions that we in fact will make and do? That is, God may know that certain influences will result in our acting in one particular way but that with a different set of influences, we will be inclined to choose and act in a different way. Therefore, by knowing the sorts of influences that incline our wills or give us the strongest desires, he can know in advance what choices we will make.

Finally, is it not clear that God is able not only to know what impact a certain set of influences will have upon our decisions, but that since he is God, he is able to adjust and regulate the influences that come into our lives, so that by controlling the influences he can regulate the choices we will make? Yet, when we make those choices, since we choose and act according to our deepest desires and strongest inclinations, we act freely. Therefore, the picture is complete: God's sovereign control of human choice and action is fully compatible with our freedom in choosing and acting in accordance with our strongest inclinations and deepest desires.

There are many biblical examples of this very compatibility. Text after text in Scripture indicate situations in which human beings do precisely what they most want to do, and they are both free and responsible for their actions. But at the very same time, what those humans freely choose to do, in turn, accomplishes precisely what God has ordained and determined that they do. We could easily fill a whole book discussing examples from Scripture of the compatibility of divine sovereign regulation of human choices with the human freedom and moral responsibility in making those very choices.[18] Perhaps just one example will suffice.

---

[18] At least one book already has been filled on this subject. For an excellent discussion of many Old Testament passages, and passages from John, illustrating compatibilism, see D. A. Carson, *Divine Sovereignty and Moral Responsibility: Biblical Perspectives in Tension* (Grand Rapids, Mich.: Baker, 1981).

Isaiah 10:5-19 presents us with one of the most striking examples of compatibilism in all of Scripture. As this section begins, God describes Assyria as "the rod of my anger; the staff in their hands is my fury!" (v. 5). The point seems to be, as it is confirmed immediately, that Assyria is carrying out God's will and performing God's work. Assyria is God's very rod and staff by which God is accomplishing his will. And so it is. In the following verses we hear God saying, "Against a godless nation *I send him,* and against the people of my wrath *I command him,* to take spoil and seize plunder, and to tread them down like the mire of the streets" (v. 6, emphasis added). Our preliminary hypothesis has now been confirmed. God sends Assyria to do his work, he commands Assyria to carry out his will. Assyria, then, is God's tool ("rod" and "staff") performing precisely what God commissions ("send" and "command") this nation to do.

And just what is this work that God sends and commands Assyria to do? In a word, the answer is: divine judgment against God's own people, Israel. God had warned Israel that should she disobey his word and turn from following him, he would bring judgment upon her. In part, this judgment would come in the form of other nations defeating Israel, taking her away in exile and plundering her cities and lands (e.g., Deut. 28:25-26, 36-37, 47-50, 63-65). Of course, such a warning is totally ineffectual unless God can control what nations do! For God to make good on his word that he will send other nations against Israel to plunder her and take her children into exile, God must be able to control the nations so that when Israel disobeys, he can actually fulfill what he has said. Isaiah 10 provides us with one picture of just how God, indeed, is able to carry out the warning he gave to Israel. He controls Assyria so much that the devastation that he brings upon Israel is, most importantly, *God's work* of judgment, even though Assyria is the tool executing the judgment. As Assyria plunders and destroys, he does exactly in accord with what God has willed and ordained.

Given this, some might conclude that Assyria cannot, then, be acting freely. But this clearly is not the case. We read in Isaiah 10:7, "But he [Assyria] does not so intend, and his heart does not so think; but it is in his heart to destroy, and to cut off nations not a few." Notice particularly the phrase, "it is in his heart to destroy." In other words, Assyria is doing exactly what he wants to do when he plunders and destroys

God's people, Israel. Assyria has no clue that he is being used as a tool of God to perform the will of God—hence, the opening phrase of 10:7, "But he does not so intend"; i.e., Assyria has no idea that he is acting as God's tool or that he is carrying out the will of God in what he does. Rather, Assyria simply is doing exactly as he most wants, out of the deepest desires of his heart, and so Assyria acts freely.

One more feature needs to be mentioned. What motivates Assyria to bring this devastation upon Israel is his own haughtiness, pride, and arrogance. His boasting of his superiority is recorded in Isaiah 10:8-11. How lofty an opinion Assyria has of himself, and oh how pathetic all other nations are in comparison. But here is God's response to Assyria:

> When the Lord has finished all his work on Mount Zion and on Jerusalem [i.e., God's work of judgment done by Assyria upon his people, Israel], he will punish the speech of the arrogant heart of the king of Assyria and the boastful look in his eyes. . . . Shall the axe boast over him who hews with it, or the saw magnify itself against him who wields it? As if a rod should wield him who lifts it, or as if a staff should lift him who is not wood! (Isa. 10:12, 15).

Although God has raised up Assyria to be his tool of judgment against his people, and although Assyria is carrying out precisely what God commanded and sent him to do, nevertheless, when Assyria is finished carrying out God's ordained will, God will punish Assyria for the arrogance and the evil intentions of his heart. Although Assyria carries out God's will, Assyria acted freely (i.e., he did what he most wanted to do) and from his heart when he acted with pride and wickedness toward Israel. Therefore, God's prior determination to raise up and use Assyria is fully compatible with Assyria's own freedom of will to do what he wanted, from the depths of his heart, to do. And this was a work that, at the very same time, fulfilled exactly what God ordained that he do. Exhaustive, meticulous divine sovereignty is here fully compatible with human freedom consisting of people doing what they most strongly desire to do.

THE FAILURE OF LIBERTARIAN FREEDOM

We've seen now that the sovereignty God possesses is a strong understanding of sovereignty in which he exerts exhaustive, meticulous control over all that occurs in creation. Further, we've seen that this view
of sovereignty is fully compatible with human freedom understood as a
freedom of inclination, a freedom in which we are genuinely free when
we choose in accordance with our strongest inclination or deepest desire.
When we act according to our characters in an uncoerced fashion and
choose and do what we most want, we are free, and this is compatible
with God's control over those influences that affect the formation of
what we most want. Scripture demands this understanding, as we have
just seen in the example from Isaiah 10 with Assyria doing what was
in his heart to do, all the while fulfilling exactly what God willed and
ordained that he do. We turn now to a discussion of why libertarian
freedom fails as a viable model of human freedom. Essentially, it falters
on both philosophical and biblical grounds.[19]

Philosophical Objection. First, consider the philosophical objection.
You'll recall that libertarian freedom proposes that we have the power
of contrary choice. That is, an agent is free when making a choice, if in
choosing A, all things being just what they are at the moment of choosing, he could instead have chosen B, or not-A. In other words, when he
chose A, he could have chosen otherwise.

This view clearly has a sort of intuitive appeal. It just seems to
many people that this matches their experience. When they choose one
thing, it was in their power to choose something different, they reason.
For example, after dinner last evening, I took my family to a nearby ice
cream store, and each of us stood at the counter looking over the selection. Eventually each of us made our choice, but we had other options,
and it seems as though we could have chosen differently than we did.
What's wrong with this notion?

The philosophical problem comes here: if at the moment that an
agent chooses A, with all things being just what they are when the choice
is made, he could have chosen B, or not-A, then it follows that any rea-

---

[19] See also Frame, *Doctrine of God,* 138-145, where Frame discusses eighteen objections to
libertarian freedom.

son or set of reasons for why the agent chooses A would be the *identical reason or set of reasons* for why instead the agent might have chosen B, or not-A. That is, since at the moment of choice, all factors contributing to why a choice is made are present and true regardless of which choice is made (i.e., recall that the agent has the power of *contrary* choice), this means that the factors that lead to one choice being made must, by necessity, also be able to lead just as well to the opposite choice. But the effect of this is to say that there can be *no choice-specific reason or set of reasons* for why the agent chose A *instead of* B, or not-A. It rather is the case, according to libertarian freedom, that every reason or set of reasons must be *equally explanatory* for why the agent might choose A, *or* B, *or* not-A. As a result, our choosing reduces, strictly speaking, to arbitrariness. We can give no reason or set of reasons for why we make the choices we make that wouldn't be the identical reason or set of reasons we would invoke had we made the opposite choice! Hence, our choosing A over its opposite is arbitrary.

This Arminian notion of libertarian freedom is often referred to as a "freedom of indifference" in contrast to the Reformed notion of a "freedom of inclination." In the former, we are strictly indifferent to whether we choose A or not-A, since the reason or reasons we have for one are identical to the reason or reasons we have for the other. Imagine this in a concrete situation: the reasons that the murderer had for pulling the trigger must be, on grounds of libertarian freedom, exactly and precisely the same were he, instead, to have refrained from pulling the trigger. If this is the case, then we cannot know "why" he committed the murder, i.e., why he chose to pull the trigger *instead of* not. There is no accounting, then, for human moral choice, and our actions become fully inexplicable. Philosophers might put it this way: while necessary conditions surely can be present in order for us to be able to choose what we do (e.g., the *necessary* conditions of our being alive, and being present where we are, and having these particular options set before us, may all be present), yet none of those conditions can either be individually or jointly *sufficient* for why we choose what we do. There simply cannot be any choice-specific explanation for why we choose one thing over another, and this renders libertarian freedom fully inadequate as an explanatory model for human freedom and human volition.

The freedom of inclination proposed here, on the contrary, argues that we always do what we most want to do, and hence there always is an explanation (i.e., a choice-specific explanation) for the particular choices that we make. To illustrate the difference, let's consider my family's trip to the ice cream store. Our older daughter, Bethany, looked over the selection and finally decided to order one scoop of peanut butter chip. Now, was it in her power to choose otherwise? The answer is yes and no—yes, before her eyes was spread an array of options, and had her strongest inclination been directed toward a flavor other than the one she chose, in this case, she would have chosen otherwise. For example, if she had overheard another customer say, "the peanut butter chip looks different than it normally does," this may have influenced her to consider another option more seriously, resulting in her having a strongest desire for a different flavor. But no, at the moment of her choice, all things being just what they were (e.g., she did *not*, in fact, overhear anyone question whether the peanut butter chip ice cream was as good as normal, but instead she *did* remember how much she enjoyed it on another occasion), the factors that went into her choosing the flavor she chose were such that these factors produced in her a "strongest inclination" for peanut butter chip ice cream *over* any other flavor. So, she chose the flavor that she most wanted—i.e., at that moment, with those factors being what they were, she could not have chosen otherwise because she acted according to her strongest desire.

How different this would be if libertarian freedom were considered. Instead, at the moment that Bethany selected peanut butter chip, all things being exactly what they were at that moment, she could just as well have chosen, say, black raspberry. But if this were the case, then it follows that any reason and any set of reasons for why she chose peanut butter chip would be the *identical* reason or set of reasons for her choosing, instead, black raspberry. In this case, there simply would be no explanation at all for why she chose peanut butter chip *instead of* black raspberry. Her choice, in this case, would be both inexplicable and arbitrary.

It is clear, then, that while libertarian freedom has an intuitive appeal, on analysis it fails to account for why we choose (specifically) what we do, whereas compatibilist freedom—the freedom of inclination—can and does account fully for why we make the choices we make. With compatibilist freedom, in the broad sense we can choose otherwise since, had the factors been different, we might have been led to form a different "strongest inclination" for what we choose. But narrowly viewed, at the moment we make our choice, we do the one (and only one) thing that we most want, and in this sense, we could not do otherwise. Only if this is the case can we ascribe motive and give meaningful explanation to our moral actions. Libertarian freedom, the freedom of indifference, falters exactly here.

Biblical Objection. Second, and more importantly, libertarian freedom simply cannot account for the human volition and moral responsibility that we see in Scripture. Consider again the example of God and Assyria in Isaiah 10. If the Assyrians had libertarian freedom, then they would, by definition, possess the power of contrary choice such that if they chose to wage war against Israel, it would always be in their power to refrain from doing so. But if this were the case, how could God "send" and "command" Assyria to do the very thing that they chose to do? Obviously, this is impossible, as Arminian theologians have long agreed. A strong view of divine sovereignty—the understanding of exhaustive, meticulous sovereignty defended above—clearly is incompatible with libertarian freedom. If the Assyrians have libertarian freedom, God cannot control what they do. But the main problem is that imagining them as having libertarian freedom conflicts with what the passage teaches. The only kind of freedom that is compatible with strong divine sovereignty is the freedom of inclination. Libertarian freedom fails in accounting for how both God and the Assyrians are said to act as recorded in Isaiah 10.

What is true in Isaiah 10 is true throughout Scripture. Over and over again we are faced with situations in which God ordains what human persons carry out freely. But libertarian freedom simply is incompatible with such divine ordination of human free choices, and therefore it fails as an explanatory model for accounting for the kind of freedom we possess.

Consider some other biblical accounts and ask whether libertarian freedom can account for what we see. Recall, for example, the promise discussed earlier by God that he would cause the Egyptians to look with favor on the Israelites, so that when the Israelites asked for their silver, gold, and clothing, the Egyptians would give it to them (Ex. 3:21-22; 11:2-3; 12:35-36). Now, the force of this passage is not merely that God *knew* that the Egyptians would oblige when Israel asked them for their possessions. As remarkable as this is, God states more strongly that he will *"give this people favor* in the sight of the Egyptians" (3:21, emphasis added) so that when asked, they will give of their belongings. Considering this, could we say that the Egyptians, at the moment that Israel asked them for their gold, silver, and clothing, had the "power of contrary choice"? To say so is to say that God could not do what he claimed he would do, that is, *guarantee* that the Egyptians would in fact give of their belongings. After all, he promised, "So *you shall* plunder the Egyptians" (3:22). No, libertarian freedom simply fails as an explanatory model of human freedom in light of this account. Rather, the freedom the Egyptians had was the freedom of inclination, such that God knew that they would do the one (and only one) thing that they most wanted to do. And God so worked in their hearts so that what they wanted most to do was to give of their belongings to the Israelites. Only compatibilist freedom, and not libertarian freedom, can account for this remarkable historical event.

One thinks most notably of the cross of Christ, where we are told by Peter that Christ was "delivered up according to the definite plan and foreknowledge of God" and yet he was "crucified and killed by the hands of lawless men" (Acts 2:23). Could God have guaranteed that Christ would be crucified if those who crucified him had possessed libertarian freedom? After all, those who put Christ on the cross, in this case, could have done otherwise. The cross might not have happened! But we know that God not only knew (merely) that Christ would be crucified, he ordained it. In answer to the question, "Who put Christ on the cross?" the most significant answer, biblically and theologically, is not, "wicked men put him there." While that is true, the most important answer is this: "God, the Father, determined and carried out his purpose to put his Son on the cross." This is at the heart of the gospel, is it not? God so loved the world that *he gave* his only Son. Indeed, the cross manifests the work of God to bring salvation to sinners as he offered his Son in our place, to die our death and pay for our sin. Yes, God put Jesus on the cross, and without this, we have no sure gospel. But then, could those human agents who physically nailed him there have had libertarian freedom? If so, God could not be ascribed as the one who, primarily and ultimately, put Christ there, for this simple reason: despite what influences God might have had upon them endeavoring to have his Son placed on the cross, those men would always have the ability to carry out placing him on the cross or not! They could have chosen otherwise. Hence, in that case, God could not be said to be the one, ultimately, who put his Son on the cross.

But that this is not the case is made abundantly clear by another statement by Peter. Consider carefully his words:

> "for truly in this city there were gathered together against your holy servant Jesus, whom you anointed, both Herod and Pontius Pilate, along with the Gentiles and the peoples of Israel, *to do whatever your hand and your plan had predestined to take place*" (Acts 4:27-28, emphasis added).

Given this statement by Peter, can we rightly say that those who put Christ on the cross *could have chosen otherwise?* If so, how could God have planned and predestined that Christ's crucifixion take place, such that "whatever" Herod, Pilate, the Gentiles, and the Jews did, all of it conformed to what God had ordained? No, again, libertarian freedom simply fails to account for what Scripture teaches. Where the "freedom of inclination" accords well and is compatible with God's strong sovereign control over creation, libertarian freedom, the "freedom of indifference," stumbles and proves altogether inadequate.

A final helpful example of the inadequacy of libertarian freedom comes from the doctrine of the divine inspiration of Scripture.[20] As evangelical Christians, we believe that all of Scripture—its very words, grammatical structure, syntactical arrangement—is the "outbreathing" of God himself. Paul says that, "All Scripture is breathed out by God" (2 Tim. 3:16). Scripture is entirely the word of God, in that every word of it is exactly what God wanted written.

But we also hold, as evangelicals, that human beings wrote the Bible. The Bible did not descend from heaven, nor was it dictated by God to human secretaries. Rather, as Peter puts it, "men spoke from God" as they wrote the very letters and narratives and historical accounts that they thoughtfully and carefully chose to write (2 Pet. 1:20-21). So, Scripture is simultaneously the word of God and the word of

---

[20] I first encountered this helpful argument in John Feinberg, "God Ordains All Things," in David Basinger and Randall Basinger, eds., *Predestination and Free Will* (Downers Grove, Ill.: InterVarsity Press, 1986).

men. Every word is exactly as God wanted it written, and yet every word was written by men who chose to write what they wanted.

Now, given this doctrine of the divine inspiration of Scripture, one must ask whether the freedom by which the authors of Scripture wrote was libertarian freedom. If so, for every word they wrote, they could have written differently, and God would have been unable to control the choices that they made. Let's just say, for the sake of argument, that even though God couldn't control what they wrote, nonetheless it just happened that every single word they chose to write was exactly the one God wanted them to write! Incredible, to be sure, but let's suppose that this is what happened. But if this had been the case, could we rightly say that Scripture is the product of *God's* outbreathing? Wouldn't we rather have to say that Scripture is entirely from men, but that God got very, very lucky insofar as it turned out just as he wanted it to be? But if that were so, Scripture really would not be inspired by God, even though it states exactly what he wants.

But let's think just one more moment whether it could be the case that, though God could not control what they wrote, the authors of the Bible nonetheless wrote exactly as God wanted. The problem with this view is that it stretches credibility to the breaking point. Just consider how many words there are in the Bible, and how many choices for other terms might have been available to biblical writers. Consider the various grammatical options, and the different syntactical arrangements that could have been used. Is it even close to reasonable to think that these men, with no control by God over what they actually wrote, made every single selection of words, grammar, and syntax so that the Bible written was *exactly* as God wanted? Clearly, this defies any reasonable basis for belief.

But if the writers of Scripture had, instead, compatibilist freedom (the freedom of inclination), then the divine inspiration of the Bible makes sense. Peter's larger statement in 2 Peter 1:20b-21 is this: ". . . no prophecy of Scripture comes from someone's own interpretation. For *no prophecy was ever produced by the will of man,* but men spoke *from God* as they were *carried along by the Holy Spirit"* (emphasis added). As "men spoke," they were moved by the Holy Spirit to desire to write just the things that they did write. This is so much the case that Peter makes clear, "no prophecy was ever produced by the will of man." Ultimately, what accounts for the Bible we have is not the will of humans to write it; rather "men spoke from God" so that as God moved them to write, they wrote exactly as God wanted them to write. They wrote as they wanted (freedom of inclination), and they wrote exactly as God wanted (God's sovereign control). Libertarian freedom fails to account for the divine inspiration of the Bible where compatibilist freedom succeeds.

One Major Objection Answered. We conclude with a brief response to what is probably the most common objection raised against compatibilist freedom by those advocating libertarian freedom. Essentially, the objection goes like this: the Bible is filled with commands and admonitions that put before us choosing right over wrong, good over evil, obedience over disobedience. Therefore, it must be the case that we are free to do one or the other; if we choose to disobey, we could have chosen to obey; if we choose the wrong, we could have chosen the right. Do not all of these moral commands and admonitions assume that we have the power of contrary choice, i.e., that we have libertarian freedom?

In light of the problems we have seen with libertarian freedom, however, we should consider carefully whether these commands of Scripture in fact assume our having libertarian freedom. I think it can be shown that no such assumption is present behind these commands. Consider with me the nature and force of these moral commands in Scripture, first for the unbeliever, and secondly for the believer.

First, for the unbeliever, the moral commands of Scripture are universally and necessarily met with a complete inability to do what is commanded. Both Jacob Arminius and John Wesley agreed with John Calvin, who in turn agreed with Augustine, on this point (although many in the Arminian tradition have departed from the view of the founders of Wesleyan Arminianism). These men all agreed that sin has resulted in human nature being unable, on its own, to do what pleases God or to obey (from the heart) the commands of God. Paul writes, for example, that "the mind that is set on the flesh [i.e., the unbeliever, who does not have the Spirit] is hostile to God, for it does not submit to God's law; indeed it cannot. Those who are in the flesh cannot please God" (Rom. 8:7-8). Because of sin, our natures are turned away from God, whether we recognize it or not, and until we are saved, we have no choice but to sin. There is, then, no "power of contrary choice" for the unbeliever, if what this means is the ability to do good *or* evil, right *or* wrong. No, the unbeliever is able only to sin, and is unable not to sin (cf. Rom. 14:23; Heb. 11:6). Apart from grace, this is the condition of the whole of the human race in Adam.

Now, this point is significant, because some commands in Scripture are clearly addressed to unbelievers. Jesus' first words recorded in Mark's Gospel constitute such a command. Jesus said, "The time is fulfilled, and the kingdom of God is at hand; repent and believe in the gospel" (Mark 1:15). But if unbelievers are unable, by nature, to do anything but disobey the command of God, can they be held responsible? Surely they are. Recall the teaching of John 3:18: "Whoever believes in him [Christ] is not condemned, but whoever does not believe is condemned already, *because he has not believed* in the name of the only Son of God" (emphasis added). Therefore two things are clear in regard to unbelievers and the nature of their freedom upon being faced with the commands of God: 1) they are unable by nature[21] to obey these commands (Rom. 8:6-8), and 2) they are responsible and accountable for the rejection of the command (i.e., their disbelief—John 3:18). So, while unbelievers do not have libertarian freedom (they cannot obey the command of God), they nonetheless do exactly what they, by nature, want to do upon hearing the gospel or being faced with the command of God. And since they act out of their natures in disbelief, doing exactly what they most want, they are free in this rejection of the gospel and they rightly are held accountable. Clearly, then, compatibilist freedom that advocates our freedom of inclination, and not libertarian freedom that advocates our power of contrary choice, is the kind of freedom possessed by unbelievers.

Second, what about believers? Believers have been given the grace by which they are saved (Eph. 2:8-9), and as a result they are new creatures in Christ (2 Cor. 5:17), they are recipients of the Holy Spirit (Gal. 4:4-6), and they are in the process of being transformed into the likeness of the risen Christ (2 Cor. 3:18; Col. 3:8-10). Does this mean, however, that believers have been granted, in their salvation, libertarian freedom?

---

[21] In light of what I've argued above, it should be clear that this inability of nature is a moral inability. That is, it is not that their nature physically or materially constrains them in such a way that they disobey, but rather that the moral disposition of their nature is repulsed by God's will and ways.

Some might imagine that this is the case, since now we have divine grace and Spirit empowerment to obey whereas before, apart from Christ, we could only disobey. But one of the problems with thinking that we now, as believers, function with libertarian freedom is that there really is no connection between our character transformation and our obedience. If, in our salvation, we have been granted the "power of contrary choice," then it is always the case, no matter what level of growth we've experienced in the Christian life, no matter how transformed our characters are or are not, that we are able to obey just as well as to disobey.

But the very reason that we are called to work at the transformation of our minds (Rom. 12:1-2) and the renewal of our characters (Col. 3:8-10) is precisely that as we *become* more like Christ, we *choose and act* more like Christ. In other words, we still act out of our natures, even as believers. It's just that now our natures have been regenerated and they are in the process of renewal. But if we fail to grow and fail to be more and more transformed, we will continue to choose and act out of natures still strongly inclined toward sin. We will do what we want most, and because we are not as transformed as we ought to be, we will want most to sin. But as we submit to the disciplines of the Spirit (e.g., Bible meditation, prayer, corporate worship, preaching, teaching), and as our characters undergo increasing transformation, our "want to's" change. We begin, more and more, choosing and acting according to our deepest desires, but these deepest desires now have changed. By the transformation of our characters, we long more and more to please the Lord, to obey his word, to follow his voice, and in all these ways we live out the true and transformed natures of our hearts.[22] Believers, then, act out of their natures just as unbelievers do. But by grace, believers are granted new natures that are in the process of transformation necessary to alter radically the deepest inclinations and strongest longings of our hearts.

This process will be completed one day when our characters are so fully transformed into the likeness of Christ that every desire of our hearts, all of our strongest and deepest longings, will always and only be to please the Lord. Praise God that our hope for eternity without sin is sure, in part, because the freedom we will have then, as the freedom

---

[22] David Peterson, *Possessed by God: A New Testament Theology of Sanctification and Holiness* (Grand Rapids, Mich.: Eerdmans, 1995), 115-137.

we have now, is not libertarian freedom in which we can do otherwise (free to sin in heaven?), but a freedom by which we act out of the deepest desires of our hearts, desires that are now fully conformed to the likeness of Christ. Only then can eternal life be secure. True human freedom, then, for the unbeliever, for the believer in the process of transformation, and for the fully glorified believer is at every step compatibilist freedom. We possess by God's created design a freedom of inclination, a freedom that previously chose *only to sin* when we were apart from Christ, but a freedom that will choose one day *only to obey* when we are conformed fully to the likeness of Christ. Praise God for the grace that takes us from bondage to sin into the freedom of the glory of the likeness of the risen Christ reproduced in our lives (Rom. 8:21-23). Divine sovereignty works, then, with our true human freedom—a freedom of inclination— to accomplish most importantly God's saving purposes, for our eternal good and to the praise of his glorious name.

4

Ruling Through Creation:
Divine-Human Concurrence
(Features 4–5)

AFTER THE BEGINNING . . . GOD AT WORK THROUGH GOOD AND EVIL

God's sovereignty in Scripture should rightly be understood as an exhaustive sovereignty, since he reigns over all that is in heaven and earth, and it is a meticulous sovereignty, since there is no detail in human or angelic life or in all of the natural order that is not included in the scope of his intentional, willful, purposeful plan for all of creation. But with this understanding of divine sovereignty must also come the careful delineation of how God relates to good and evil, respectively. To say that God controls both is true, and it is required by Scripture, as we saw in the previous chapter (e.g., Deut. 32:39; Isa. 45:5-7). But while God controls both *good and evil,* it is also true that God is *good but not evil.* And it is at this point that more careful thought must be given to the relation God has to good and to evil, respectively.

In wanting to preserve in our understanding of God his unqualified righteousness and goodness while also affirming his absolute control over evil, we are simply seeking to do what many Christian thinkers have done previously. Consider, for example, the Westminster Confession of Faith on the question of God's providence. Chapter 5, article I of the Confession reads:

I. God the great Creator of all things doth uphold, direct, dispose, and govern all creatures, actions, and things, from the greatest even to the least, by his most wise and holy providence, according to his infallible foreknowledge, and the free and immutable counsel of his own will, to the praise of the glory of his wisdom, power, justice, goodness, and mercy.

Article I, then, begins with the straightforward affirmation that "God . . . doth direct . . . all creatures, actions, and things . . . by . . . the free and immutable counsel of his own will." In other words, God possesses exhaustive and meticulous sovereignty over the universe that he has made, and this is stated without qualification or compromise.

But this chapter of the Confession is not content to leave the discussion at this point; rather it seeks to clarify something of just how God's control over everything is exerted in a way compatible with human freedom, and so that God's own holy and righteous character is not implicated in the control he has over evil. Consider articles II, III, and IV:

II. Although, in relation to the foreknowledge and decree of God, the first Cause, all things come to pass immutably, and infallibly; yet, by the same providence, he ordereth them to fall out, according to the nature of second causes, either necessarily, freely, or contingently.

III. God, in his ordinary providence, maketh use of means, yet is free to work without, above, and against them, at his pleasure.

IV. The almighty power, unsearchable wisdom, and infinite goodness of God so far manifest themselves in his providence, that it extendeth itself even to the first fall, and all other sins of angels and men; and that not by a bare permission, but such as hath joined with it a most wise and powerful bounding, and otherwise ordering, and governing of them, in a manifold dispensation, to his own holy ends; yet so, as the sinfulness thereof proceedeth only from the creature, and not from God, who being most holy and righteous, neither is nor can be the author or approver of sin.[1]

Much of what we'll consider here, then, has to do with how God exercises his rule *through* the created order. That he rules *over* creation

---

[1] Westminster Confession of Faith, chapter 5, "On Divine Providence."

is clear from the nature of his sovereignty as exhaustive and meticulous. But now we concern ourselves with the implementation of this rule in and through what he has made. Divine-human concurrence—the exercise of his rule through secondary agency within the created order—is here the framework within which our thinking and discussion will proceed.

The issues we propose to discuss in this chapter, then, involve two main areas. First, we'll consider God's relation to good and evil, respectively, and propose that this relation must be understood as fundamentally asymmetrical, since God's own nature is wholly good but not in any respect evil. And second, we'll explore the role that a modified version of middle knowledge—which I'll call "compatibilist middle knowledge"—may play in helping understand God's relation to and control of evil, in particular.

A word of caution is in order before we proceed. Since Scripture is our only final and absolutely authoritative source in understanding truths about God and his relation to the created order, two things are required of us. First, we must submit to and embrace all that Scripture does teach, despite its agreement or disagreement with the values and teachings of our culture. If the authority of Scripture means anything, it means that our mistaken ideas must change to conform to Scripture's teachings, and we must resist at every turn the temptation to conform Scripture's teachings to what seems so clear and true to us from our culture. Granted, this is easier said than done. Nonetheless, this must be our goal and earnest desire if we are to honor God and his Word in the process of our theological formulation. Second, we must also be ready to stop our theological formulations at the point that Scripture's revealed truth stops. We can violate the authority of Scripture as much by going beyond what it says into areas wherein Scripture is silent as we can by distorting and reshaping what it actually does say to fit the mindset of our culture. In other words, we must discipline our minds and our theology to conform to Scripture and to be content to say what it says and remain silent where it is silent. With that caution in mind, we proceed now to explore, as best we can from Scripture's own teaching, what we should think in the two main areas of this chapter.

GOD'S ASYMMETRICAL CONTROL OF GOOD AND EVIL

The absolute nature of God's control over all things in the created universe might lead some to think that we should not bother with going further. Rather, we should recall the very words God speaks concerning his exclusive deity and his control over evil in Isaiah 45:5-7, and this should be enough for us. God, through the prophet, says:

> I am the LORD, and there is no other,
>   besides me there is no God. . . .
> I form light and create darkness,
>   I make well-being and create calamity,
>   I am the LORD, who does all these things (Isa. 45:5a, 7).

And so it is. God does reign over good and evil, over light and darkness, and with this biblical teaching as with many, many other passages of Scripture, we concur that God controls everything that occurs in the created order. Everything!

But simply to leave the discussion here without further thoughtful inquiry is problematic. There are obvious moral questions that arise, insofar as it is difficult on the surface to see how God is not morally culpable for evil in the same sense that he is morally praiseworthy for good, if we simply (and only) say that God controls both equally. Granted, leaving the statement at this level—namely, God controls good and evil equally—is not wrong, nor does it contain necessarily a basis for charging God with moral responsibility for evil. Nonetheless, it does raise the question of the divine moral culpability for evil and provides no answer to it.

Someone might say, but this is not the first time that we have raised questions for which we find no answers in Scripture. For example, remember the Trinity! How can God be one essence yet three divine persons? And surely there are numerous areas where we must simply acknowledge the limits both of revealed truth (Deut. 29:29) and of our finite understandings and learn to be content not knowing what God has chosen to keep veiled.

But this issue is different. To leave the discussion simply at the level of affirming God's equal control of good and evil is problematic for a more important reason, and this is that Scripture itself reveals more on this issue, and hence we would be irresponsible to stop short of considering all that God wants us to know. Clearly, if we can err by presumptuousness in going beyond Scripture into areas of sheer human speculation, we also can err by negligence in failing to incorporate all that God has said, some of which may be difficult to understand yet crucial in seeing the bigger picture as God would have us see it.

What else, then, does Scripture reveal about God and his relation to good and evil? The answer here has to do both with Scripture's teaching about God's intrinsic moral nature, and clear indications of his manner in controlling good that differs from his manner of controlling evil. We'll consider each of these in order.

God Is Good, Not Evil. One of the difficult issues that Augustine had to deal with as a young believer was how to explain the presence of evil in a world created by a good (and only good) God. Years prior to his conversion, Augustine had been a follower of Manichean dualism, which proposed that good and evil were equal, eternal realities. Under such a system, explaining evil is just as easy as explaining good: both evil and good just exist, and they have so existed eternally. But when Augustine became a Christian, he had a major intellectual and spiritual problem. How could there be evil in a world when the Creator of the world is eternally good and not evil, and when the world he created was entirely good and in no respect evil (Gen. 1:31)? In time, Augustine proposed that since only good has eternal existence, evil must, in some way, be parasitic on good. That is, evil must be (he used two main concepts here) either a privation or absence of good, or it is the misuse and distortion of good. In other words, you don't need eternal evil to account for evil. All you need is good that goes wrong, good that is misused, or good that is rendered void—and in this way, evil comes about through what is good.[2]

We'll come back to the problem of evil shortly, but now our main concern is the beginning point of Augustine's inquiry. Clearly, he was correct in asserting that God is eternally good and not evil. And in fact, some of Scripture's teachings regarding the inherent and exclusive good-

---

[2] Augustine, *The Enchiridion on Faith, Hope, and Love,* trans. J. F. Shaw (Chicago, Ill.: Regnery, 1961), XI.

ness and righteousness of God need to be set alongside its teachings on the control that God has over both good and evil.

For example, recall again that in Isaiah 45:7 God says, "I form light and create darkness." But alongside this passage, consider also 1 John 1:5: "This is the message we have heard from him and proclaim to you, that God is light, and in him there is no darkness at all." How instructive! Although God controls *both light and darkness* (Isa. 45:7), God's own nature is exclusively *light and not darkness* (1 John 1:5).

Or, consider also God's claim, "I make well-being [Hebrew *shālôm*] and create calamity [Hebrew *rā'*], I am the LORD, who does all these things" (Isa. 45:7). But alongside this, consider Psalm 5:4: "For you are not a God who delights in wickedness [Hebrew *resha'*]; evil [Hebrew *rā'*] may not dwell with you." And in Habakkuk 1:13, God is distanced so much from evil that the prophet says, "You who are of purer eyes than to see evil [Hebrew *rā'*] and cannot look at wrong . . ."

So, while God controls both well-being and calamity (evil), he does not delight in wickedness, nor does any evil dwell in him, nor can he even look upon evil (i.e., approvingly). In short, God is good and not evil though he controls both good and evil. His eternal and holy nature is in no way compromised. He is not stained by evil nor does he approve of evil. Evil is contrary to God's holy, moral nature, and his disposition toward evil is always one of hatred and opposition whereas his disposition toward good is always one of approval and embrace. That God is good and is in no respect evil is part of Scripture's clear teaching that must be taken into account in dealing with the question of God's control of good and evil.

God's Asymmetrical Relation to Good and Evil. Because God's nature is good and not evil, and yet God has complete and absolute control over both good and evil, it seems that we must carefully consider God's relation to both good and evil, respectively. More specifically, it does seem incumbent upon us to view God's relationship to good and evil in asymmetrical terms in light of the fact that when God controls *good,* he is controlling what *extends from his own nature;* yet when he controls *evil,* he controls what is *antithetical to his own nature.*

GOD'S RELATION TO GOOD. In the case of good, God's own nature "breathes" goodness and exhibits goodness. No goodness—not even that goodness which is external to God—exists apart from God, for God is the giver of every good and perfect gift (James 1:17). In this sense, no goodness exists that is not God's goodness, since no goodness can have an origin anywhere other than in and by the very nature of God. Therefore, God's control over goodness must be through the mechanism of his own natural bestowing, out of his very nature, of the goodness that is produced. If no goodness can be produced apart from God's bestowing of it (Ps. 34:8-10; 1 Cor. 4:7; Acts 17:25; James 1:17), then all the goodness that occurs in the created order, including all goodness produced through human choices and actions, must flow from the very nature of God, as an extension of his own work and character.

Perhaps we should speak, then, of God's relation to goodness as being through a kind of *direct and immediate divine agency* in which there is a necessary correspondence between the character and agency of God and the goodness that is produced in the world. We might call this kind of divine agency "direct-causative" divine action, since it is strictly impossible for any goodness to come to expression apart from God's direct causation and as the outgrowth of his own infinitely good nature. Goodness, then, is controlled by God as he controls the very manifestation and expression of his own nature, causing all the various expressions of goodness to be brought into our world, whether goodness in nature or goodness revealed through human (secondary) agency.

And of course it stands to reason, then, that because all goodness produced in the world results from the direct-causative agency of God, including even (and especially!) that goodness that comes to be through human choice and action, God should rightly receive *all* the glory for the good that is done. This understanding makes sense, for example, of Jesus' statement in Matthew 5:16: "In the same way, let your light shine before others, so that they may see *your good works* and *give glory to your Father* who is in heaven" (emphasis added). One might indeed wonder, if these are *my* good works, why should the glory go to God and not to me? After all, this goodness came about from me! But the answer now is clear. Since the only way in which I am capable of bringing good into the world is as God bestows through me the goodness that is his alone, therefore, all the good produced and done (whether through me or not) is ultimately and exclusively the property of God, as it were. His goodness is shown, then, and not any that I (supposedly) had independent of God. Therefore, when God grants to me the privilege of bringing forth some of the goodness that is his alone, to him belongs all the glory and praise both because the goodness expressed is his and because it is his prerogative to share of his goodness, in and through me, to others.

Or consider God's work of regeneration and conversion in the life of a sinner. Before God worked savingly in our hearts, we were bound in slavery to sin (John 8:34; Rom. 6:17a), blinded to the truth of the gospel (Acts 26:18; 2 Cor. 4:4), spiritually dead (Eph. 2:1-3), and unable to do anything that pleased God (Rom. 8:6-8). But God, by his love and grace (Eph. 2:4-9), opened our blind eyes (2 Cor. 4:6) and awakened our dead hearts (Acts 16:14) so that we saw now the beauty and glory of Christ and turned in love to the Light that we formerly despised (John 3:19-21). What divine agency, then, shall we say brought about our regeneration and conversion? Clearly, God's own character of love, grace, mercy, and truth shone within us and caused us to believe and be saved. Therefore, the control that God exhibits in conversion must be through his direct-causative divine agency, by which aspects of his own nature are given expression in and through our lives as we embrace what is of him and make it our own. Therefore, no boasting may be done before God for our salvation, since all the good done originates from and is granted by God (1 Cor. 1:30-31; Eph. 2:8-9).

Similarly, all progress and fruitfulness in the Christian life must be by this same direct-causative divine agency. Consider Jesus' teaching in John 15 that unless the branch abides in the vine it cannot bear fruit, but when it abides and so draws life from the vine, it bears much fruit. Jesus applies this to the lives of his followers, saying, "I am the vine; you are the branches. Whoever abides in me and I in him, he it is that bears much fruit, for apart from me you can do nothing" (John 15:5). Jesus' agency, directly at work in and through us, bears his fruit through our lives. Hence, life lived in reliance on the power and risen life of Christ manifests in fruitfulness the very character qualities of Christ. Or, in parallel language, if we walk in the Spirit, we will bear the fruit of the Spirit—those character qualities of the Spirit of Jesus lived out in our lives (Gal. 5:16, 22-23).

And yet this direct-causative divine agency by which God's character is manifested in and through our lives is not a passive matter. We shouldn't take the "abiding" language of John 15 to imply passivity. Consider Paul's admonition to "work out your own salvation with fear and trembling, for it is God who works in you, both to will and to work for his good pleasure" (Phil. 2:12b-13). While it is God's work in us that causes both our willing and our working for God's good pleasure (note: there is nothing left for us to take independent credit for when both the *willing* and the *working* that we do are accomplished by God's work in us), nonetheless this occurs only as we lay hold of the mandate to trust and obey and serve God with all of our heart ("with fear and trembling"!). This is no independent work of ours, separate from the work of God in us, but as John Murray has put it, *"because* God works we work."[3] The work that God does, then, in the life of a believer to produce fruitfulness and growth is by his direct-causative agency, working in and through us from out of his very character of wisdom, truth, goodness, holiness, and love. And because it is altogether his work, to him belongs all the glory, honor, and praise (Eph. 1:6, 12, 14).

The relation of God to the good that occurs in the world, then, is a relation of direct-causative divine agency, a relation in which the goodness expressed in and through aspects of the created order, including his goodness and character made manifest through God's moral creatures, flows out of the very nature of God, and by his gracious will. To him belongs all the glory and praise for all good done, for God alone is the source and the empowerment of this good, and by his agency alone is his goodness made manifest in the creation at large, and in and through the lives of his moral creatures.

GOD'S RELATION TO EVIL. In the case of evil, however, we clearly have a very different situation. Since evil can never extend from the nature of God in the way that good does and must, evil quite clearly stands against God and is antithetical to his very character. And yet, as we saw in the last chapter, the "spectrum texts" of Scripture do not blush to present God's control over evil in equal if not (in some cases) even

---

[3] John Murray, *Redemption—Accomplished and Applied* (Grand Rapids, Mich.: Eerdmans, 1955), 149 (emphasis in original). Murray's larger statement is instructive: "God's working in us is not suspended because we work, nor our working suspended because God works. Neither is the relation strictly one of co-operation as if God did his part and we did ours so that the conjunction or coordination of both produced the required result. God works in us and we also work. But the relation is that *because* God works we work" (148-149).

stronger terms than his control of good. While evil never flows from the nature of God, it is in all cases controlled by the agency of God. But how shall we speak of the divine agency that controls evil?

Since God's control of evil does not extend from his own nature, it cannot be "direct" in the way his control of good is. That is, evil does not extend from God as good does, and hence, evil never is produced, as it were, "out of" God's own being and nature. Furthermore, God cannot will directly and immediately to cause evil, since all that God wills to do himself (immediately) is good (e.g., Gen. 1:31; James 1:13, 17), and it is impossible for him to do evil of any kind. But if God does not directly cause evil, and yet evil happens under his watch, as it were, must it not be the case that he permits the evil to occur that he could, in any and every instance, prevent?[4]

We referred above to the mechanism by which God controls good as his "direct-causative" divine agency; so here we can refer to God's control of evil as his "indirect-permissive" divine agency. While this indirect-permissive control of evil is no less exact, or meticulous, or comprehensive than his direct-causative control of good, nonetheless it is of a different kind. In God's control of evil through indirect-permissive agency, God's own character and nature are separated from the evil that is done. This stands in stark contrast to the union of his character and nature to all good that is done by the control he exerts over good through his direct-causative agency. So, while God controls both good and evil, and his control of both is equal in force and measure, his control of evil is also strikingly different in quality and in manner.

Is the notion of God "permitting" actions and events to occur a biblical idea? Consider these texts, where it seems clear that the biblical writers recognize and invoke this concept and way of speaking (emphases added):

> "Your father [Laban] has cheated me [Jacob] and changed my wages ten times. But *God did not permit him to harm me*" (Gen. 31:7).

---

[4] See Paul Helm, *The Providence of God,* in Contours of Christian Theology, series ed. Gerald Bray (Downers Grove, Ill.: InterVarsity Press, 1994) for a very helpful discussion of the divine permission in the Reformed sense as permission of what God could prevent.

"Whoever strikes a man so that he dies shall be put to death. But if he did not lie in wait for him, but *God let him fall into his hand,* then I will appoint for you a place to which he may flee" (Ex. 21:12-13).

. . . and they [the demons in the Gerasene demoniac] begged him, saying, "Send us to the pigs; let us enter them." So *he gave them permission.* And the unclean spirits came out, and entered the pigs. (Mark 5:12-13).

"In past generations *he allowed all the nations to walk in their own ways"* (Acts 14:16).

And when they [Paul and Silas] had come up to Mysia, they attempted to go into Bithynia, but *the Spirit of Jesus did not allow them* (Acts 16:7).

For I do not want to see you now just in passing. I hope to spend some time with you, *if the Lord permits* (1 Cor. 16:7).

And this we will do *if God permits* (Heb. 6:3).

One notices, then, that the language of divine permission is biblical, and the writers of Scripture evidently see no conflict between this language and conception and Scripture's other strong teaching on divine sovereignty. And, while some of these texts indicate a permission by God for good things to occur, some specify God's permission of evil. Exodus 21:12-13 is especially instructive, where God "let him fall into his hand" when, obviously, as omnipotent, God could have prevented this event from happening. Divine permission, then, is a legitimate category, and it has the advantage of indicating a way in which God retains full control of evil while not actively, directly causing it to occur.

Some may wonder further just how God's control of evil can be as exact and comprehensive as here claimed, since he does not actually bring evil about. Here, I will give part of the answer and reserve the remainder for our discussion of compatibilist middle knowledge. What needs to be understood here is that God is always able to permit only those occurrences of evil that he knows will serve his purposes and never thwart or hinder those purposes. He is able to do this because, for any evil that may occur, it is always in God's power to prevent that specific evil from happening.

Now, of course, one might say that this is also true for the God of Arminianism; this God, likewise, is omnipotent, and he also possesses the power to keep anything from happening that he would choose to prevent. Yet there is a significant difference between what might be thought of as the actual "functional power" of God in the world for the God of Arminianism and for the God of Reformed theology. The Arminian God has created the world with a sort of personal pledge that he will not violate the libertarian freedom of his moral creatures, except in the most dire of circumstances. Furthermore, he pledges also not to interrupt the normal processes of natural law and the forces of nature unless he deems it absolutely crucial so to do. Why? Simply for this reason, that if he grants libertarian freedom and natural law, but then constantly micromanages just *which* libertarian choices and *which* outworkings of natural law he will permit, then this trivializes the value of having given both libertarian freedom and natural law in the first place. No, the integrity of the whole design of God, by which he chose to make the world this way and not another, requires that since he gave libertarian freedom, he'll let it be used, and since he created natural laws, he'll let the forces of nature operate without interference. Of course, he reserves the right to interfere in the most extreme of emergencies, but in the vast majority of cases he chooses to permit both moral creatures and laws of nature to operate uninterrupted by himself, even when those moral creatures or natural forces end up inflicting enormous evil upon people.[5] So, in light of God's design for creation to operate by generally uninterrupted libertarian freedom and natural law, he is not "functionally" able to prevent the vast majority of evil from occurring.

How different this is with the Reformed understanding of God and his created design for the world. Here, God has full and absolute "functional" power to prevent any and every instance of evil that might occur, whether it is evil done by human volition or evil done by laws of nature. That is, because God has determined to exercise meticulous sovereign rulership over the world, this means that when it comes to regulating evil, God specifically permits only those instances of evil to occur that he judges, by his infinite wisdom and in light of his ultimate purposes, will advance and not hinder his designed ends for the world.

---

[5] Michael Peterson, *Evil and the Christian God* (Grand Rapids, Mich.: Baker, 1982), 111.

And how can he prevent specific instances of evil that might hinder his purposes? In regard to forces of nature, obviously God can change any natural occurrence that he chooses. As in the book of Jonah, God can bring about a storm at sea or cause it to cease; he can cause a fish to swallow a man or spew him out; he can cause a plant to grow or make it wither. Because God retains absolute authority over the laws of nature he has made, he permits those forces of nature to operate in every way advancing of his purposes but prevents or alters any and all such forces that would be contrary to those purposes. In regard to human volition, because the freedom given us is the freedom of inclination, God is able to control those factors influencing a person's strongest inclination or deepest desire, and by this he can control the choices and actions that a person will make or do. Therefore, God permits only those free moral choices bringing about evil that advance his ultimate purposes, but for any moral choice or action that might conflict with those purposes, God can alter or redirect the choice or action, or simply eliminate it altogether.

So, in the Arminian model, God's permission of evil is very *general* and *broad*. He creates a world with laws of nature and libertarianly free creatures, and he "permits" that they act as they will. By permitting this, he permits them to carry out evil (both natural evil and moral evil), but this permission is of the whole category of evil in general, not any specific instance of evil in particular. But in the Reformed model, God's permission of evil is *meticulous, specific,* and *particular*. That is, he does not permit evil in general, but he does permit each and every instance of evil that in fact occurs in human history. His permission here is specific, in that for any instance of evil (natural evil or moral evil), he possesses the power and absolute authority to prevent whatever action or event might conflict with the fulfillment of his purposes. So, while both Arminian and Reformed models may appeal to God's "permission" of evil, the Arminian model supports God's general permission of the class of evil, while the Reformed model supports God's specific permission of any and every particular instance of evil. In the Arminian model God cannot "functionally" prevent evil without preventing the whole possibility of evil through eliminating natural law and libertarian freedom altogether. But in the Reformed model, God can prevent any specific instance of evil, ensuring that no evil is gratuitous and that only those instances of evil occur that advance, not hinder, God's ultimate aims.

COMPATIBILIST MIDDLE KNOWLEDGE

One of the most perplexing questions that those in the Reformed tradition endeavor to address is just how God's permission of evil functions in light of his eternal decree by which he ordains all that will come to be. That is, if God determines all that occurs, in what meaningful sense does God permit some things to occur (especially, evil) while he actively brings other things to pass? Put differently, using the language suggested above, if God decrees or determines all that will come to pass in human history, how can the distinction be meaningfully maintained between God's direct-causative agency and his indirect-permissive agency? Is not the latter category really merely illusory, since God's determination of actions and events is comprehensive?

It has occurred to me over the past several years that one promising answer to this question may be provided if a modified version of Luis de Molina's notion of middle knowledge[6] were incorporated, here, within a fundamentally Reformed and compatibilist model of divine providence.[7] Molina, a Jesuit theologian in the post-Reformation period, argued that God has three logical moments of knowledge prior to creating the universe. God not only possesses knowledge of what *could* be, i.e., knowledge of all bare possibilities and logical necessities (what Molina calls "natural knowledge"), and knowledge of what *will* be, i.e., knowledge of all future actualities, or exact and detailed knowledge of the way the world, when created, will be (what Molina calls "free knowledge"), but importantly, God also possesses knowledge of what *would* be if circumstances were different from what they in fact will be in the actual world, i.e., knowledge of those possible states of affairs which would have become actual had circumstances other than those in the real world obtained (what Molina calls "middle knowledge").

One can think of middle knowledge as a subset of natural knowledge. That is, natural knowledge—knowledge of what *could* be—envi-

---

[6] Luis de Molina, *On Divine Foreknowledge,* Part IV of the *Concordia,* trans. Alfred J. Freddoso (Ithaca, N.Y.: Cornell University Press, 1988). For contemporary defenses of the middle knowledge view, see especially William Lane Craig, *The Only Wise God: The Compatibility of Divine Foreknowledge and Human Freedom* (Grand Rapids, Mich.: Baker, 1984); and Thomas Flint, *Divine Providence: The Molinist Account* (Ithaca, N.Y.: Cornell University Press, 1998).

[7] Terrance L. Tiessen, *Providence and Prayer: How Does God Work in the World?* (Downers Grove, Ill.: InterVarsity, 2000), 289-336.

sions all possibilities and all necessary truths. Imagine for a moment all
the possible places you *could* be at this moment instead of where you
are now. It only takes a few seconds to realize that you cannot possibly think of all the places you could be; the list is endless, and your
mind simply cannot envision so many possibilities meaningfully and at
once. But God can! God knows all the possible places you could be at
this moment (i.e., natural knowledge), and he also has known, from
eternity past, the actual place where you are at this moment (i.e., free
knowledge). But God not only knows all the places you *could* be, God
is also said to know the one particular place that you *would* be at this
moment if circumstances had varied even slightly in one particular way.
So, middle knowledge is a very small subset of natural knowledge. One
of the possible places you *could* be is the very place that you *would* be,
were circumstances different, even slightly, so that you were not where
you *now are*—and God knows all three.

According to this theory (sometimes referred to as Molinism),
God knows all possible states of affairs, and he also knows what free
creatures *would* do in various possible sets of circumstances. Although
God does not and cannot control what free creatures do in any set of
circumstances (they retain libertarian freedom in Molinism), he is able
to control certain aspects of the circumstances themselves and by this
he can regulate which choices and actions *actually* obtain from among
all those that are possible. Now while God can control these sets of
circumstances, he cannot necessarily guarantee that the choice or
action he wants a free creature to perform will be done. For example,
it just may be the case that, although God wants Sam to take a week's
vacation to attend a Christian retreat center where he would hear the
gospel, in no set of circumstances in which he envisions Sam deciding
his vacation plans will Sam freely choose to attend the retreat. But God
knows that while there are many sets of circumstances in which Sam
will not freely do what God wants (Sam's refusal to attend the retreat
being one grouping of these), there is at least one (or more) other set
of circumstances which, if God were to actualize it, would result in
Sam choosing freely to do as God wishes in other areas, and on other
issues. And God can choose to actualize one set of circumstances in
which Sam freely chooses what God wants. So, by middle knowledge
God exerts massively more providential regulative influence over the

world than is the case if God possesses only simple foreknowledge, yet he does so in a manner in which libertarian freedom is retained for God's moral creatures.

Despite the appeal of Molinism for some today, there are at least two significant problems with it, as seen from a Reformed perspective.[8] First, it is not at all clear *how* God can know by middle knowledge just what choices free creatures would make in various sets of possible circumstances. The problem here is that since freedom in the libertarian sense is defined as the ability, *all things being just what they are,* to choose differently, it is impossible to know what decision will be made simply by controlling the circumstances within which it is made. Because, all conditions being just what they are, one can choose otherwise, control of the conditions exerts no regulative power over the actual choice made within those conditions. Therefore, it is impossible to know what decision *would* be made just by knowing the conditions within which it is made. In short, nothing grounds God's knowledge of what free creatures would do in various possible sets of circumstances, and hence, God cannot know what middle knowledge advocates claim he knows: what free creatures *would* do in any and all possible sets of circumstances.

Second, Molinism's insistence on libertarian freedom is itself problematic. For reasons argued in the previous chapter, libertarian freedom simply fails as a viable understanding of human freedom for both philosophical and biblical reasons. Since libertarian freedom reduces human choosing to arbitrariness, and since libertarian freedom is fully incompatible with the strong view of divine sovereignty taught in Scripture, therefore the very notion that humans have the power of contrary choice (as understood in the libertarian model of freedom) simply must be rejected. Hence, the Molinist model as it stands cannot and should not be adopted by Reformed thinkers.

But notice that both of these objections are fundamentally objections to libertarian freedom. The second objection was so explicitly. But the first objection, at root, pointed out the impossibility of God knowing by middle knowledge what a free creature would do, if the type of

---

[8] Open theists would agree with the first of these two problems with Molinism, but they would deny that the second is a problem (since they affirm libertarian freedom), and they would object instead to Molinism being too deterministic in its overall framework and outcome.

freedom the creature had was libertarian freedom. That is, because there is not a necessary connection between the circumstances in which an agent was envisioned (by God) as performing a free action, and the actual free action that the agent would do, God cannot know what a free agent *would* do simply by knowing the circumstances related to his choice. So notice, the main problem that the Molinist model has, as conceived by Molina, is its insistence on libertarian freedom. Both because libertarian freedom fails on its own as a viable model, and because libertarian freedom precludes God from knowing what Molinism claims he knows about human choices by middle knowledge—for both reasons, libertarian freedom must be rejected.

But can middle knowledge be conceived, instead, with compatibilist freedom? I believe not only that it can, but that in so doing, we have a tool for understanding God's control of evil that accords with biblical teaching and illuminates biblical texts. In what follows, then, I shall first explain how middle knowledge works with compatibilist freedom, and second, I will develop briefly the help this may be in understanding God's relation to evil.

Middle Knowledge with Compatibilist Freedom. Traditional Molinism claims to account for God's middle knowledge, but as explained above, its advocacy of libertarian freedom renders such divine knowledge impossible. So, how would middle knowledge fare if compatibilist freedom replaced libertarian freedom? It appears that this exchange permits middle knowledge to work.

According to the notion of middle knowledge, God can envision a free agent in various sets of circumstances or states of affairs, and it is claimed that God knows what the agent would do in each differing state of affairs. The problem for traditional Molinism, with its commitment to libertarian freedom, is that since there is no necessary connection between knowledge of each state of affairs and knowledge of what the agent would in fact choose in each different setting, God could not know the agent's choice by knowing the circumstances. But what if there were a necessary connection between knowledge of a given state of affairs and knowledge of what the agent would choose in that particular setting? If this were the case, then God could know what the agent would choose by knowing fully the circumstances in which the agent would make his choice. That is, because in any one given set of circumstances envisioned by God, the agent in that particular setting, with exactly that particular set of factors present, would make one and only one choice—a choice that would be called for by just those circumstances in that setting— therefore, God could know with certainty the choice the agent would make by knowing precisely and exhaustively the setting in which the agent would make his choice. But what is this proposing if not that compatibilist freedom (freedom of inclination) replace libertarian freedom (freedom of indifference)?

Consider more specifically how middle knowledge might work if we assumed that human beings possessed compatibilist freedom— the freedom of inclination—rather than libertarian freedom. Recall that the freedom of inclination proposes that we are free when we choose according to our strongest inclination or deepest desire. In short, we are free when we do what we most want to do. This means that the circumstances and factors that influence our decisions result eventually in our having, at the moment of choice, *one* desire or inclination that stands above all others. The fact that we have *one* desire that is our *highest desire* explains why we make the *one choice* that we do, in that particular setting. Put differently, the set of factors in which the agent makes his choice constitutes a set of individually necessary and *jointly sufficient* conditions[9] for forming within the agent a strongest inclination or highest desire by which he then makes the one choice that is in accordance with that highest desire. And his freedom is then expressed when he chooses according to that highest desire.

What is different about this understanding of middle knowledge is that since freedom means that we always do what we most want, and since what we "most want" is shaped by the set of factors and circumstances that eventually give rise to one desire that stands above all oth-

---

[9] 'Necessary' conditions are those which must be present for the effect to occur; 'sufficient' conditions are those which, whether necessary or not, when present require that the effect occurs. As an example, consider the individually necessary and jointly sufficient conditions of combustion. Each of the following is necessary for combustion to occur: oxygen, fuel, friction/heat. But, the presence of either merely one or two of these necessary conditions will not produce combustion. Rather, all three have to be present for combustion to occur, and when all three are present combustion will occur. Therefore, we can say that oxygen, fuel, and friction/heat are the *individually necessary* (i.e., each must be present) and *jointly sufficient* (i.e., when all three are present the effect occurs) conditions for combustion.

ers, therefore God can know the circumstances giving rise to our highest desires, and by knowing these, he can know the choice that we would make, given those particular circumstances. What the Molinist version of middle knowledge lacked—viz., a necessary connection between knowledge of the circumstances within which an agent makes his choice and knowledge of just what choice the agent would make—is here remedied by the replacement of libertarian freedom with compatibilist freedom. So, as a result, middle knowledge is explicable and it "works" when compatibilist freedom is employed, in a way that it does not with libertarian freedom. Now, the question is whether the very notion of middle knowledge is biblical, and how Scripture may indicate its use in understanding more clearly God's control of the world, particularly his control of evil.[10]

Compatibilist Middle Knowledge and God's Relation to Evil. First, we should establish what others have shown also: that Scripture indi-

---

[10] Following the completion of the manuscript for this book, an article was published challenging the coherence and possibility of a Calvinist (or compatibilist) understanding of middle knowledge. See John D. Laing, "The Compatibility of Calvinism and Middle Knowledge," *Journal of the Evangelical Theological Society* 47/3 (September 2004): 455-467. Laing argues that the Calvinist who wishes to incorporate middle knowledge is on the horns of a dilemma: "On the one hand, if she claims that the truth of counterfactuals of compatibilist freedom is grounded in the will of God or in the way God created the creaturely will, then she has denied the prevolitional character of divine knowledge of counterfactuals of creaturely freedom and therefore, her position is not in the middle of anything. On the other hand, if she claims that the truth of counterfactuals of compatibilist freedom are grounded in the character of the creature as he pre-exists in the mind of God, or that the truth of counterfactuals of compatibilistic freedom do not need to be grounded, then her view of freedom is virtually indistinguishable from libertarian freedom" (467).

In all-too-brief response, I suggest that the compatibilist middle knowledge view conceives God as knowing these counterfactuals of creaturely freedom as prevolitional knowledge of the array of actions of what moral agents *would* do were God to actualize a world different than the one that he in fact actualizes and knows with his free knowledge. So, I deny that the advocate of compatibilist middle knowledge succumbs to the first horn of the dilemma.

Further, I suggest that God's middle knowledge (hence, genuine *middle* knowledge) of these counterfactuals is grounded on more than *merely* his knowledge of "the character of the creature as he pre-exists in the mind of God." Rather, this middle knowledge is grounded on four things that God knows prevolitionally: 1) God's perfect knowledge, in his own mind's eye, of the character of the moral individual (or, as Laing puts it, of "the character of the creature as he pre-exists in the mind of God"); 2) God's knowledge of every factor present in any given possible setting in which he envisions this individual making a choice; 3) God's knowledge of just how each unique set of factors, in each unique situation, would work, along with the character of the individual, to produce one strongest inclination within the individual, for each unique situation so envisioned; and 4) God's knowledge of just what choice the individual would in fact make, given the nature of his own character, the relevant factors involved in the particular setting in which he would make this choice, and the strongest inclination that would arise within him given this complete set of factors, giving rise in turn to this one (and only one) choice. And, of course, I would deny that "the truth of counterfactuals of compatibilistic freedom do not need to be grounded," since I've just defended how their truth in fact is grounded. Therefore, I believe that the advocate of compatibilist middle knowledge escapes also the second horn of Laing's dilemma.

cates that God possesses middle knowledge,[11] and that he makes very important use of this middle knowledge. That is, we will demonstrate that Scripture indicates that God knows not only all possibilities and all actualities, but he also knows, contrary to what God decrees *will* happen, what *would have* occurred in any given situation had circumstances been different, and in many cases this knowledge of what "would have been" is put to use by God in some striking and critical ways. Consider a few scriptural examples of God's middle knowledge:

> When Pharaoh let the people go, God did not lead them by the way of the land of the Philistines, although that was near. For God said, "Lest the people change their minds when they see war and return to Egypt" (Ex. 13:17).

> And Saul summoned all the people to war, to go down to Keilah, to besiege David and his men. David knew that Saul was plotting harm against him. And he said to Abiathar the priest, "Bring the ephod here." Then said David, "O LORD, the God of Israel, your servant has surely heard that Saul seeks to come to Keilah, to destroy the city on my account. Will the men of Keilah surrender me into his hand? Will Saul come down, as your servant has heard? O LORD, the God of Israel, please tell your servant." And the LORD said, "He will come down." Then David said, "Will the men of Keilah surrender me and my men into the hand of Saul?" And the LORD said, "They will surrender you." Then David and his men . . . departed from Keilah. . . . And Saul sought him every day, but God did not give him into his hand (1 Sam. 23:8-14).

> "I did not send the prophets, yet they ran; I did not speak to them, yet they prophesied. But if they had stood in my council, then they

---

[11] See, e.g., William Lane Craig, "The Middle-Knowledge View," in James K. Beilby and Paul R. Eddy, eds., *Divine Foreknowledge: Four Views* (Downers Grove, Ill.: InterVarsity Press, 2001), 123-125. Craig comments that the passages he cites clearly support God's knowledge of counterfactuals (i.e., knowledge of states of affairs that are contrary to fact but could have obtained were circumstances different) but whether they are specifically examples of middle knowledge is difficult to know. If one proposes a compatibilist view of freedom, however, it seems clear that all of these are examples from Scripture of divine counterfactual *and* middle knowledge, since these are cases of God's knowledge of what would have been that are different from what his decree established ("free knowledge," in Molina). But presumably his decree took into account what we now see as counterfactual possibilities prior to the decree, or else we cannot understand why he would decree just what has obtained instead of the counterfactual possibility. If God considered these other possible states of affairs prior to the decree, then what God possessed is middle knowledge.

would have proclaimed my words to my people, and they would have turned them from their evil way, and from the evil of their deeds" (Jer. 23:21-22).

"Woe to you, Chorazin! Woe to you, Bethsaida! For if the mighty works done in you had been done in Tyre and Sidon, they would have repented long ago in sackcloth and ashes. But I tell you, it will be more bearable on the day of judgment for Tyre and Sidon than for you. And you, Capernaum, will you be exalted to heaven? You will be brought down to Hades. For if the mighty works done in you had been done in Sodom, it would have remained until this day. But I tell you that it will be more tolerable on the day of judgment for the land of Sodom than for you" (Matt. 11:21-24).

None of the rulers of this age understood this, for if they had, they would not have crucified the Lord of glory (1 Cor. 2:8).

Each of these examples from Scripture is helpful both in establishing that God in fact has middle knowledge (i.e., knowledge of what would have occurred had circumstances been different, contrary to what did in fact occur) and in giving some indication of what use his middle knowledge may be to him in regulating the affairs of the world. Permit me to make a few observations from these texts before proposing more specifically how middle knowledge may assist in our understanding God's relation to evil.

First, notice that middle knowledge is not restricted to God's dealing with evil. For example, Exodus 13:17 indicates that God used his middle knowledge of what Israel would have done had they traveled "by the way of the land of the Philistines" in order to prevent them from returning to Egypt. Similarly, the complicated account cited from 1 Samuel 23 indicates that when God told David that Saul *will* come down and that the men of Keilah *will* surrender him into the hand of Saul, we know that this actually means, "If you stay here, these things *will* happen" (i.e., this was an implicitly conditional divine prediction). We know this because David left, and God spared his life! So, because David left and lived on, we now know from these statements from God that Saul *would have* come down, and the men of Keilah *would have* surrendered him into Saul's hand, had David stayed. It is clear, then, that

God provided David with middle knowledge of what would happen in order to bring about something positive. Therefore, in these cases middle knowledge functions to produce a positive result and doesn't deal with sin or evil, per se. Dealing with evil is a primary application of the use of middle knowledge but not its exclusive one.

Second, God's middle knowledge (i.e., his knowledge of what would have been the case, contrary to what is in fact the case) is so sure and certain that he even invokes it as his basis for determining the varying degrees of punishment that he will mete out in the final judgment. Consider soberly again Matthew 11:21-24. Christ indicates that the judgment upon Chorazin, Bethsaida, and Capernaum will be more severe than (even!) the judgment upon the sinful cities of Tyre, Sidon, and Sodom. Why? What greater offense have Chorazin, Bethsaida, and Capernaum committed? These cities in Jesus' day, hearing his preaching and witnessing his miracles, have not repented. Yet, he says, if the same miracles had been performed in the ancient cities of Tyre, Sidon, and Sodom, they would have repented. So, the relative evaluation of greater offense and greater punishment for these contemporary cities is based upon the reality that would have been true (i.e., contrary to what actually obtained in history) had circumstances been different in these ancient cities. This observation should give anyone pause who thinks that middle knowledge, even if true, is a useless or trivial aspect of God's knowledge. Even more, it should give great consternation to any who would deny flat out that God has middle knowledge. The fact that Jesus indicates that relative weighting both of offense and of final punishment is based upon God's middle knowledge should give all of us an appreciation for the importance, not to mention the usefulness, of God's possession of middle knowledge.

Third and last, Jeremiah 23:21-22, Matthew 11:21-24, and 1 Corinthians 2:8 all indicate God's middle knowledge of what God himself could have provided to others that would have kept them from some evil that they in fact did commit. Yet, God chose not to provide what he could have provided, presumably because he chose that the evil not be precluded or eliminated. Here we come closer to the sort of application we will speak more about shortly, but notice here that while God has middle knowledge, it is clear that he is not obligated to use it to spare others from the evil that will come upon them, or the evil that they will commit. All three of these passages are very sobering, as one contemplates seriously what they indicate. In Jeremiah 23, God could have sent prophets to his disobedient people, and had he done so, the people "would have" turned from their evil. But he did not. In Matthew 11, God could have performed at Tyre, Sidon, and Sodom miracles of the sort Jesus performed at Chorazin, Bethsaida, and Capernaum, and had he done this, they "would have" repented and remained. But he did not. In 1 Corinthians 2, God could have given the rulers of Paul's age an understanding of God's wisdom in Christ, and had he done this, "they would not have crucified the Lord of glory." But he did not do so.

This last example from 1 Corinthians 2 has a particular significance since it relates to the unfolding of God's predestined plan of salvation in Christ. Recall Peter's words in Acts 4, that "there were gathered together against your holy servant Jesus, whom you anointed, both Herod and Pontius Pilate, along with the Gentiles and the peoples of Israel, to do whatever your hand and your plan had predestined to take place" (Acts 4:27-28). When one places 1 Corinthians 2:8 alongside Acts 4:27-28, one realizes that part of the fulfillment of what God's "plan had predestined to take place" involved his middle knowledge of what the "rulers of this age" (which would include, surely, both Herod and Pontius Pilate) should know or not know. God knew what these rulers would do with knowledge of God's wisdom in Christ, and what they would do if they remained ignorant of that knowledge. So, it appears that middle knowledge figured into the fulfillment of what God had "predestined" to occur through these rulers (and others, of course). Here, then, God's middle knowledge assists in the formation of God's predestined decree, by granting him knowledge of what would be true in one situation or in another, so that God is able to select for his decree the particular situation (e.g., the rulers of Paul's age not understanding God's wisdom in Christ) that will advance, not hinder, the fulfillment of God's plan.

Second, we turn now to consider more carefully just what use God's middle knowledge may have particularly in God's regulation of evil, as we've been encouraged to think in this direction from these texts of Scripture themselves. And as we probe this question, we should bear in mind the importance of our previous discussion about the asymmetrical relation of God to good and to evil, respectively. As argued above,

God's relation to good is through his direct-causative agency, since any good that is produced must flow from the only source there is of any and every good, that is, from God's own nature. If, as James 1:17 indicates, *every* good and perfect gift is from the Father of lights, then we must understand God as acting in a direct and causative relationship to all the good manifested in the world. Put differently, all good that is extrinsic to God flows from the intrinsic goodness of God himself. But God's relation to evil must, of necessity, be markedly different. As noted earlier, although God controls both good and evil (Isa. 45:7), God is good and not evil (Ps. 5:4). Therefore, evil cannot flow from God in the way good does, but rather, evil stands diametrically opposed and antithetical to God's nature. God's control of evil, for this reason, cannot be direct or immediately causative as it is with good. Instead, God's relation to evil must be *indirect,* i.e., never in any respect expressive of his nature, yet controlled altogether by his wisdom, authority, and power. And God's relation to evil must be *permissive,* i.e., produced altogether by portions of his sinful creation and never in any respect immediately by him, yet regulated in every instance so to allow or disallow any and every instance of evil that occurs, as his wisdom, authority, and power direct.

How, then, can God's middle knowledge be utilized in his indirect-permissive regulation of evil? Consider this big-picture answer first, before we contemplate some specific cases of its application from Scripture. Before[12] God had created the world, indeed before he had "settled" on the exact plan by which the history of that world would unfold in exacting detail, God was able to envision, by middle knowledge, an array of situations in which his moral creatures (angelic and human) would choose and act as they would. More specifically, God was capable of knowing just what a moral agent would do in one situation, with its particular complex of factors, as opposed to what that agent would do in a slightly different situation, with a slightly different complex of factors.

This information was knowable to God due to four considerations: 1) God could envision exhaustively and exactly the complete sets of fac-

---

[12] Please note that this discussion uses temporal language to describe the deliberations that took place in the mind of God in eternity past, prior to the creation of the world with its time and space. So, while temporal language is used for the sake of our finite and temporally bound understanding, in God such deliberations occur in a non-temporal and logical sequence that is beyond our understanding.

tors that would be true of each and every situation in which moral agents would make choices and perform actions; 2) because the moral creatures he envisioned had a freedom of inclination or compatibilist freedom, he could know the one strongest inclination or highest desire an agent would have in any particular situation he considered, since the agent's own nature would respond to the particular set of factors comprising a specific situation such that those factors would necessarily give rise to that one strongest inclination in the moral agent's mind and heart; 3) because the moral creatures he envisioned had a freedom of inclination or compatibilist freedom, God could know the particular choice an agent would make in each and every situation envisioned, since agents with the freedom of inclination always choose in accordance with their strongest inclinations or highest desires; and 4) God knows all that is knowable, and items 1) through 3) are knowable, and thus are knowable to God.

Among the situations God envisioned were situations in which sinful human beings would act according to their strongest desires and carry out the sinful and evil actions they freely wanted to do. But since these sinful humans all possessed the freedom of inclination, God could also envision slightly changed situations, in which an alteration of factors resulted in those sinful creatures having different highest desires and so carrying out different actions in those particular altered situations. In other words, by controlling the complex of factors prompting the natures of moral agents to develop a strongest inclination within a given situation, God could effectively redirect the choice and action that the agent would carry out. And because there was a necessary correlation between 1) the set of individually necessary and jointly sufficient factors of a given situation and 2) the strongest inclination elicited from those factors in the nature of a moral agent and by which he then would make his choice, God could know with exacting precision just what choices would be made in each and every situation he considered in his mind's eye.

Notice, then, that given his possession of middle knowledge, God would be able to know whether in certain situations he would passively permit an agent to carry out what he was most inclined to do, or whether he would alter the factors of that situation sufficiently to alter the agent's strongest inclination, thus altering also the choice he would make. But in either case, the agent would respond to those factors according to his own nature and hence do what he most wanted to do. As such, he would be free and morally responsible in the choices he makes. And in either case, God has absolute and complete regulation of what the agent does, albeit through either permitting the choice that he could prevent, or by preventing the choice by redirecting the situation such that the agent freely would choose differently.

Middle knowledge is usable to God, as seen in the scriptural passages examined above, both for ensuring some positive outcomes and for regulating the evil that occurs. But this type of indirect-passive divine agency, utilizing middle knowledge, has a special importance for God's regulation of evil. By controlling human sinful choices and actions in this manner, it never is the case that God does evil directly (as he does good directly), nor is it the case that he causes a person to do evil (James 1:13). Some may consider the description above as constituting God's causing the person to do evil, but I wish to argue that this would be a misinterpretation of what actually is taking place. When God envisions various sets of factors within which an agent will develop a strongest inclination to do one thing or another, the strongest inclination that emerges from these factors is not caused by the factors, nor is it caused by God. Rather, in light of the *nature of the person,* when certain factors are present, his nature will respond to those factors and seek to do what he, by nature, wants most to do. In short, the cause of the strongest inclination and the resultant choice is the nature of the person in response to factors presented to him.

By analogy, consider for a moment two persons, one with a serious smoking habit and the other without. Imagine the two walking together outdoors, away from the sight and smell of cigarettes. It may well be the case that in this setting, there would not be anything present at that moment that would give rise in the heart of either person to a strongest inclination to smoke a cigarette. But if the two of them walked past an outdoor café where some people were smoking, just the sight and smell might elicit from the nature of the smoker a strongest inclination to light up a cigarette, whereas that very same sight and smell might elicit from the nature of the nonsmoker a strongest inclination to walk quickly past the café and away from the smoke. In other words, what explains the choices each made is *how their natures respond to the factors presented to them.* Those factors do not cause the choices made, for notice that the factors were identical for the smoker and the nonsmoker, yet the choices made by each were opposite. Nor would controlling the factors cause the choices made, because whether someone had "planted" smokers at that outdoor café or not would not affect the opposite choices of each in response. Rather, the causes of the respective choices were the two (different) natures of the respective individuals. So, the fact is, we act according to our natures, and what various factors in differing situations do is simply and merely to elicit our strongest inclination.

Or consider another analogy. Undercover police often use the mechanism of a "sting operation" for catching criminals in the act of committing a crime. When this is done correctly, the police do not cause or coerce the criminal to commit the crime, but they do intentionally provide a setting in which the criminal, out of his own nature, will have the opportunity to develop a strongest inclination to commit the crime. Undercover policemen may pose, for example, as buyers seeking to purchase illegal drugs, and by so doing they place before the nature of the drug dealer a set of factors that may lead him to want most strongly to sell drugs to the men posing as interested buyers. When the drug dealer hands over the drugs to the buyers and receives payment for them, the crime has been committed and he is arrested and will be held morally (and legally) responsible for his crime. When this operation is done correctly, the criminal is not coerced, nor is he caused to commit the crime. Rather, he is presented with a setting to which his own nature responds the way that it does, wanting most strongly to carry out the illegal activity. The criminal, then, was free; he did what he wanted most to do, and he was not forced or coerced in the process. Yet the situation was "controlled"; factors of a situation were designed and intentionally presented to the criminal so that his nature would be given opportunity to manifest what it truly wanted to do. The cause of the choice was the nature of the criminal; some key factors leading to the choice were provided by others who sought to expose the criminal's nature for what it was. When he made his choice, he showed what truly was in his heart, and in this he was free, and for this he is morally responsible.

Perhaps we should think of God's regulating the factors of a situation, then, as "occasioning" a particular choice to be made, rather than as "causing" a particular choice to be made. Because God knows the natures of each person perfectly, he knows how those natures will respond to particular sets of factors presented to them. Thus, without causing a person to do evil, he nonetheless controls the evil they do. He controls whether evil is done, what evil is done, and in any and every case he could prevent the evil from being done. But in no case does he cause the evil to be done. In this way, God maintains meticulous control over evil while his moral creatures alone are the agents who do evil, and they alone bear moral responsibility for the evil they freely do.

With this big-picture view in mind, please consider now a couple of examples from Scripture where incorporating an understanding of middle knowledge contributes rich explanatory power to what seems to be taking place. First, let me remind the reader of one text already cited above. Recall Exodus 13:17:

> When Pharaoh let the people go, God did not lead them by the way of the land of the Philistines, although that was near. For God said, "Lest the people change their minds when they see war and return to Egypt."

Here we have a clear and indisputable case where God used middle knowledge of what Israel would do under other circumstances in order to regulate what they would in fact choose to do. Judging from what we read here, God knew that the people of Israel would act according to their strongest inclination. And he knew that factors in various different settings would affect both the strongest inclinations they would have, and through these, what choices they would make. God could envision taking them by the way of the land of the Philistines, and he knew, by middle knowledge, that this situation would lead to their natures developing a strongest desire to return to Egypt. Now, of course God could act in this case in a direct-causative manner and simply give them a stronger desire to keep following him despite traveling through the land of the Philistines. But in God's wisdom, he chose instead to adjust the setting and by this to ensure that the strongest inclinations that would develop within the Israelites' hearts would be to continue following him and not to return to Egypt. But one thing is clear from this account: God respects the integrity of their choices, realizing that they truly do carry out what they most want. Therefore, he regulates their choices by presenting them with a situation in which the free choices they make accord with his will for them. God's sovereign control and their free moral agency are compatible, and in this case the compatibility occurs through God's use of middle knowledge.

Consider another biblical account where God's middle knowledge is not mentioned, but I will argue that invoking middle knowledge proves to be enormously fruitful in understanding better what takes place in this text. Consider the Joseph story as recorded in Genesis 37–50. You'll recall that Joseph was, until Benjamin was born, the only son of Jacob through Rachel, and the son of his old age. We are told in Genesis 37:3 that Jacob (Israel) loved Joseph more than any of his other sons, and to show his favor he made Joseph a robe of many colors. Now, immediately after we are told this, we are told of the dreams that God gave to Joseph, dreams that portray him over his brothers and even over his parents. When Joseph tells his brothers and father about the dreams, we read that "his brothers were jealous of him" (Gen. 37:11), and we can understand fully why they were.

It interests me here that at a time when Joseph was already known to be his father's favorite, and the brothers would already have been jealous and bitter for this, it is at this precise time that God adds to the basis for their jealousy by giving Joseph these dreams. Why give him these dreams, especially now?

Perhaps part of the answer comes as we read on in chapter 37. Recall that the brothers were away from home tending their father's flock at a pasture near Dothan. Jacob begins to wonder how they and the flock are faring, and so he sends Joseph to find them and bring word of their condition. As Joseph approaches the brothers, we read that "they saw him from afar, and before he came near to them they conspired against him to kill him" (37:18). And what we read next is fascinating: "They said to one another, 'Here comes this dreamer. Come now, let us kill him and throw him into one of the pits'" (37:19-20). Notice that the first thing the brothers comment on when they see Joseph approaching is the dreams he told them about ("Here comes this dreamer"). Evidently, the dreams that God gave Joseph had a very strong effect on the brothers. No doubt they plotted to kill him precisely because if they did, then these dreams could not come true. Because of the dreams they grew to hate Joseph even more than they had previously.

Yet, even though they plotted to kill Joseph, Reuben, Jacob's oldest son, intervened and refused to let them kill him for fear that their father would despair at Joseph's death. So instead, they threw him into a pit and sat down to eat. A short time later, an Ishmaelite caravan heading for Egypt passed by, and while Reuben was away from the brothers, Judah convinced the rest that if they sold Joseph to the Ishmaelites, not only would they get rid of him, but they would make a profit in addition (37:26-27). When Reuben returned and realized that Joseph was missing and learned that the brothers sold him to the Ishmaelites, he tore his clothes in despair. But the deed had been done and there was nothing to do except make it appear that Joseph had been killed.

Now, move forward all the way to Genesis 45. It is at this point that Joseph reveals his identity to his brothers who had come to Egypt in search of food. Through much affliction, Joseph had been favored by God and had been appointed second in command in all of Egypt. So, when the brothers came to purchase food, they actually appeared before Joseph, yet they did not recognize him. But the time came that Joseph felt compelled to reveal his identity to the brothers. When he does, he says some remarkable things about how he ended up in Egypt. First, he says to them, "I am your brother, Joseph, whom *you sold into Egypt*" (45:4). He repeats the same point in the next verse, but adds to it: "do not be distressed or angry with yourselves because *you sold me here*, for *God sent me* before you to preserve life" (45:5). Amazingly, now in addition to indicating that the brothers sold him into Egypt (which no one would dispute, having read Genesis 37!), he says that God sent him. Notice he does not say that God turned what they did into good. No, God *sent* him, and this is parallel to the action of the brothers, who *sold* him. As we read on, two verses later when Joseph describes how he got to Egypt, of the two answers he has given thus far (the brothers sold him, and God sent him), the only one mentioned is the latter; the brothers' action simply drops out! Joseph says, "And God sent me before you to preserve for you a remnant on earth, and to keep alive for you many survivors" (45:7). The brothers' action no longer is really relevant, since he sees how God has planned and executed the bigger purpose behind his being sent to Egypt. And this is most clearly confirmed by the last statement Joseph makes about this: "So it was not you [the brothers] who sent me here, but God" (45:8). Unlike 45:7, where the brothers simply are not mentioned, here in 45:8 Joseph deliberately says that it was not the brothers' action (ultimately) that accounts for his being in Egypt, "but God" sent him.

Let me underscore that this account does not describe some wicked people doing something that God *later turns into good*. No, such an interpretation fully disregards both the clear language and the intention of the text. Rather, Joseph presents his brothers' action of selling him and God's action of sending him as parallel. Both are past tense, so just as the brothers acted in Genesis 37, so *God acted* in Genesis 37! In fact, in light of 45:7-8, the ultimate and decisive actor of the two (God, and Joseph's brothers) was God: "it was not you who sent me here, *but God*" (45:8, emphasis added).

This raises, then, the important question of how God acted in Genesis 37 to send Joseph into Egypt. Especially since what the brothers did was revengeful, sinful, cruel, and evil, how could God be said to have acted along with the brothers? How could Joseph be correct that ultimately it was God, not the brothers, who sent him to Egypt?

Consider first: Could God be the *direct-causative agent* actually giving the brothers their vengeful motives and jealous disposition, directly willing and causing them to hate Joseph and to make his life miserable by selling him into slavery? Could this be the way God "sent" Joseph to Egypt? The answer is no, for two reasons. First, this is contrary to the very nature of God. God does not do evil and hence he cannot cause (immediately or directly) evil attitudes, motives, or actions (Ps. 5:4; James 1:13). Joseph's sinful brothers are capable of all of those things, but God cannot do evil. Second, Joseph makes clear in Genesis 50:20 that whereas the brothers "meant evil" against him, God "meant it for good." The asymmetrical nature of the respective actions of Joseph's brothers and God is necessary in light of what Genesis 50:20 teaches. God could not have caused, directly and immediately, the evil intentions of the brothers' hearts, since what flowed out of God's heart was a sole intention for good.

Consider, secondly: Could the answer be found in invoking the permissive will of God? That is, could it be that God merely permitted the brothers to do what they wanted to do, and by this Joseph was sent to Egypt? This fulfilled God's will, so we can say that God sent Joseph to Egypt simply through his permitting the brothers to sell him into Egypt.

While this answer is not wrong—in fact it is correct, as far as it goes—it is inadequate in explaining the deliberate and intentional sense whereby Joseph speaks of God acting to "send" Joseph to Egypt. The language of Genesis 45:5-8 and 50:20 requires deliberative action on God's part, action that ensures Joseph is sent to Egypt. But what deliberative action could this be?

Consider next what help we might have in answering this question if God's use of compatibilist middle knowledge is brought into the picture. Several features of the Joseph account lend themselves strongly to the possibility that God used middle knowledge as the major mechanism by which he sent Joseph to Egypt. Here are some of the most fruitful to explore. First, the dreams God gave Joseph clearly played a key role in the actions of the brothers. And surely God would know, by middle knowledge, what sort of disposition the brothers would have toward Joseph had he refrained from giving Joseph the dreams, as opposed to the attitude they did have, owing in part to the dreams. In light of the language of 45:7-8 and 50:20, we have to say that God intended, from the outset, to *send* Joseph to Egypt. But is it not conceivable that God knew that, without the dreams, though the brothers were jealous and bitter toward their brother, their strongest inclination simply would not be to sell him into slavery? So might it well be the case that God deliberately gave Joseph the dreams knowing the effect the dreams would have on the brothers' strongest inclinations? This much we know for sure: God deliberately gave the dreams to Joseph when he didn't have to; these dreams were a source of deep resentment by Joseph's brothers; when Joseph approached the brothers near Dothan, they referred to Joseph as "that dreamer," showing their disdain for him due to these dreams; and their initial plot to kill Joseph was in the context of their desire to prove, by his death, that Joseph's dreams were false. All of this fits best with God's use of these dreams, through his middle knowledge, of providing just what would be needed for the brothers' natures to respond in a way that would seek to get rid of Joseph.

But second, recall that these dreams elicited from the brothers a strongest inclination to *kill* Joseph. Clearly, this is a problem, since God wants Joseph to be sent to Egypt alive. How might God's use of middle knowledge figure in at this point? Consider the presence and absence of Reuben in the account. Notice that when the brothers plot to *kill Joseph*,

Reuben (the oldest son, with authority over his brothers) is *present* and he speaks against the proposal. He suggests instead that they throw Joseph into a pit, all in hopes of later being able to bring Joseph back to his father. But then just a short time later, when the caravan passes by and Judah presents the idea of *selling Joseph* to the Ishmaelites, *Reuben was absent*. Clearly, in light of Reuben's response when he arrived back at camp and found Joseph gone (37:29-30), had Reuben been there, he would have opposed this idea also! He knows how deeply this will grieve their father, and as the eldest son, he knows he's responsible for the youngest brother, their father's favored son. He is horrified at what the brothers have done. Had Reuben been present when Judah spoke up with his idea, Reuben would never have let the brothers go through with it. And don't you know that God knew it! God deliberately had Reuben present when the plot was to kill Joseph, thus sparing his life. But God deliberately had Reuben absent when the plot was to sell Joseph into Egypt, no doubt knowing that if Reuben had been present Joseph would have remained with them while the caravan passed by.

This brings up a third obvious feature of the story that God controlled, knowing how the brothers would respond. This Ishmaelite caravan just "happens" to show up right exactly at the time needed. Recall, Reuben had to be gone! And God had to get Joseph to Egypt. Clearly, the brothers didn't care at all where Joseph might be taken. But God cared. So, in part by God's direct-causative agency, no doubt, and also through his use of middle knowledge in relation to how the brothers would respond to the presence of the caravan—in both of these ways, God acted to ensure that Joseph got sent to Egypt.

By middle knowledge, then—of how the brothers would respond if God gave Joseph the dreams or not, and what actions the brothers would take toward Joseph with Reuben present and with Reuben absent, and how the brothers would respond when seeing the caravan pass by just when they sought some way to get revenge on Joseph—God has acted deliberately and decisively to send Joseph to Egypt, doing so completely by regulating, in highly specific ways, the wicked actions of Joseph's brothers, ensuring that what God planned and designed would surely and certainly take place. Thus, Joseph speaks correctly to his brothers, "it was not you who sent me here, *but God*" (Gen. 45:8, emphasis added).

In summary, although God is good and not evil, clearly he controls both good and evil. Yet this chapter has endeavored to underscore the importance of understanding the manner of God's control of good and evil, respectively, in asymmetrical terms. And we've explored how Calvinist middle knowledge, in particular, can help in comprehending better how God's indirect-permissive agency in regard to evil can be exacting and meticulous in its regulation while preserving God's holiness and goodness in his control over evil. God not only reigns *over* creation, he reigns *through* it. We are free and responsible, yet God regulates our activities so that his purposes are done. We turn next, then, to see more clearly how God's rulership of the world encompasses also his reign *with* creation, in relationship with the created order, and with his people in particular.

5

Ruling With Creation:
Divine-Human Relationality
(Features 6–10)

Thus far we have established that God rules *over* creation with sovereign authority and exhaustive, meticulous governance, regulating the affairs of men by granting them a freedom of inclination by which God's sovereign control and their genuine freedom are rendered fully compatible. And God rules *through* creation, controlling both good and evil, but in asymmetrical ways, often using his compatibilist middle knowledge to steer the course of history, yet never violating the integrity of the free choices of his moral creatures by which they choose and act according to their strongest inclinations. Since God is altogether good and not in any respect evil, yet controls completely both good and evil, we have explored two senses of divine agency and teachings from Scripture that can help us make sense of this complex matter in some limited way.

Now we turn our attention to one of the most astonishing and wondrous of all biblical teachings, that the God who rules over creation, and through creation, also rules *with* creation, in an intimacy of relationship that ought to elicit from within us unending amazement, awe, wonder, and thanksgiving. In order to survey God's relational rulership with creation, we need to consider a number of factors. Several of these factors are enormously complex in and of themselves. Some have occupied the best minds in Christian theology and philosophy over the centuries, and in most cases current discussion and publication rage over these matters. For the purposes of this more global study of God and his relations to the world, we will have to restrict ourselves to brief explorations, offering what I hope will be sufficient discussion to see clearly the place each feature plays in the unfolding of God's purposeful relationship with the world he has made.

In this chapter we will consider five features of God's providential rulership with creation (features 6-10 summarized in the introductory chapter). First, we'll propose an understanding of God's relation to space and time, which is needed to see how God may work *within* the created order while being himself eternally and infinitely *separate from* the created order. Second, we will explore how God's relationship with us requires both that he be forever and unchangeably who he is while also being dynamically and relationally affected in his interaction particularly with his moral creation. Senses of the divine immutability and mutability are both needed to comprehend and appreciate the nature of God's relationship with us. Third, flowing from the previous features, we will need to reconsider how the attributes of God are often understood. Should we label all his attributes as absolute and thereby eliminate any and all contingency from God's own nature and experience? Or does his dynamic mutability not require that we consider God as possessing both contingent as well as eternal and absolute qualities? We'll see here how the first three of these features complement one another, as we reconsider God's relation to time, change, and contingency. Fourth, because God is God, and "God is not man" (Num. 23:19), we should expect that the nature of *real* relationship with him will be unique. We will consider here some of the differences between human relationships and the divine-human relationship. Although the manner of our relating to God will differ from our human relational experience, this divine-human relationship is nonetheless real. Finally, we conclude Part One ("Foundational Theological Bases for Divine Providence") where the Bible both begins and ends, with the uncontested supremacy and unrivaled glory of God alone. We will examine how the end of all of life is the glory of God, and how this alone is the fitting conclusion to the theology of God and of his providential dealings with the world he has made.

APART FROM US AND WITH US: GOD AND SPACE AND TIME

One of the perpetual enigmas of Christian theology has been, and continues to be, God's relation to space and time. Particularly, God's relationship to time has been exceedingly difficult to sort out, and the discussion continues with fervor.[1] Two main views have been represented throughout the history of the church.[2] Most, following the lead of Boethius[3] (c. 480–524) have affirmed a view of *divine timelessness* or *atemporal eternity*. Because God created both space and time, and because God exists as infinitely perfect and independent of all finite, creaturely qualities, God's own essence and existence must be apart from these mediums of created life. God, then, is strictly and only nontemporal and nonspatial, in contrast to the creation, which is both temporal and spatial. God's relation to the world, then, is through a relation of reason, but no real relation is possible. A minority position, now being pursued with much more intensity even among evangelicals,[4] advocates a view of *divine everlastingness* or *temporal eternity*. In this view, time itself is an eternal reality, and God exists in time eternally; thus, there is no beginning or ending (literally) to his existence, but rather he exists in every moment of everlasting time. God has existed, then, in every moment of the infinite past, he does exist in the present, and he will exist in every moment of the infinite future. God alone, then, is infinitely everlasting.

When considering the relative merits of each position, it is worth asking the question whether one must decide between the two. That is, must it be the case that God is either atemporally eternal or temporally eternal, either timeless or everlasting? After all, both positions have strong and valid points to make, and it seems very difficult to side with just one altogether when good reasons remain for the alternate position. Some today are actually seeking some kind of combined understanding

---

[1] See, e.g., Gregory E. Ganssle, ed., *God and Time: Four Views* (Downers Grove, Ill.: InterVarsity Press, 2001). The four views are written, respectively, by Paul Helm (chapter 2, "Divine Timeless Eternity"), Alan G. Padgett (chapter 3, "Eternity as Relative Timelessness"), William Lane Craig (chapter 4, "Timelessness and Omnitemporality"), and Nicholas Wolterstorff (chapter 5, "Unqualified Divine Temporality").

[2] For a helpful discussion of these prominent positions on God and time, see Ronald H. Nash, *The Concept of God* (Grand Rapids, Mich.: Zondervan, 1983), 73-83.

[3] Boethius, *The Consolation of Philosophy*, trans. V. E. Watts (Harmondsworth, U.K.: Penguin, 1969).

[4] See, e.g., John S. Feinberg, *No One Like Him: The Doctrine of God* (Wheaton, Ill.: Crossway, 2001), 375-436, for a very stimulating and innovative proposal, interacting in careful detail with the history of this doctrine, and arguing for a temporalist view of divine eternity.

of these leading positions.[5] Obviously, though, any attempt at synthesis requires a modification of both views! After all, one cannot synthesize the two views that 1) God is both absolutely and only atemporal and 2) God is absolutely and only temporal. But might there be senses of each—a sense of divine atemporality and a sense of divine temporality—that can be rightly joined together?

In what follows, I propose that we seriously consider adopting something of a synthesis of these two positions. In line with the basic framework for the doctrine of God that we discussed in chapter 2, where we considered the strategic importance both of God's transcendent self-existence and of his immanent self-relatedness, perhaps here also we need to inquire whether some kind of duality reductionism has taken place in the doctrine of divine eternity. Must God be viewed exclusively as timeless, or exclusively as temporal? Are there good reasons to consider a model of God's relation to time in which both, in different senses, are true?

My first musings on these questions came some years ago when I was teaching on the attributes of God in a seminary theology course. We were discussing the attributes of the divine eternity and divine omnipresence, and I recall being struck for the first time by the asymmetrical or non-parallel nature of the names of these two doctrines. Many theology texts will list and discuss them just this way—the attribute of God's eternity and the attribute of God's omnipresence—yet these terms reflect quite opposite perspectives on God's relation to time and to space, respectively.

As mentioned above, "eternity," in the classical (and majority) tradition, is the attribute of God's nontemporal existence; God exists necessarily apart from time altogether, so his eternity is "timeless eternity." But consider the difference in what is communicated by the attribute of God's "omnipresence." Here, rather than discussing God as existing necessarily apart from space, or as fully and only nonspatial in his existence, this doctrine regularly has to do with God's "everywhere" presence throughout the entirety of the universe. Psalm 139:7-10 is often cited as a key supporting passage; it begins, "Where shall I go from your Spirit? Or where shall I flee from your presence? If I ascend to heaven, you are there! If I make my bed in Sheol, you are there!" (vv. 7-8). Clearly the thrust is that God is present everywhere that one could imag-

<hr/>

[5] In Ganssle's *God and Time*, at least two of the positions advocated attempt something of a synthesis of these two leading, competing alternative understandings of God and time.

ine, whether the farthest reaches of heaven or the deepest grave. God's omnipresence is most often, then, about the real and universal presence of God throughout the created order.

But of course, we know that God brought the created order into existence, so God's own existence "precedes" or, better, stands apart from the spatial creation he made. In a sense, then, we hold in regard to God's relation to space both 1) that God is nonspatial in himself, apart from the spatial created order that he has made (since at creation he brought into existence the entire universe with its spatial dimension), and 2) that God is everywhere present, in relation to the spatial created order, so that his existence and every quality of his life are present fully at every point of created space. It seems, then, that with regard to God's relation to space, we have given expression to both truths—God is nonspatial in himself (*in se*) apart from creation, and God is everywhere spatially present in relation to creation (*in re*)—and this without conflict or contradiction.

But not so with time. Consider, for example, Louis Berkhof's definitions of God's eternity and God's immensity (i.e., omnipresence), especially in relation to the issues we are discussing. First, eternity:

> His [God's] eternity may be defined as *that perfection of God whereby He is elevated above all temporal limits and all succession of moments, and possesses the whole of His existence in one indivisible present.*[6]

But Berkhof's definition of immensity reads:

> It [divine immensity] may be defined as *that perfection of the Divine Being by which He transcends all spatial limitations, and yet is present in every point of space with His whole Being.*[7]

And he continues with this interesting and helpful comment:

> It [definition of divine immensity] has a negative and a positive side, denying all limitations of space to the Divine Being, and asserting that God is above space and fills every part of it *with His whole Being.*[8]

---

[6] Louis Berkhof, *Systematic Theology* (London: Banner of Truth, 1939, 1958), 60, emphasis in original.

[7] Ibid., emphasis in original.

[8] Ibid., emphasis added.

So Berkhof is very happy to discuss two senses of God's relation to space. God both "transcends all spatial limitations" and "is present in every point of space with His whole Being." That is, God is both non-spatial in himself (*in se*) apart from creation, and everywhere spatially present in relation to creation (*in re*). But interestingly, with regard to time, Berkhof says just one thing: God strictly is "elevated above all temporal limits and all succession of moments." He exists in "one indivisible present" but not in moments of time. Why speak of both aspects in regard to God's relation to space, but not so in regard to time?

I suggest that we follow the same procedure in understanding God's relation to time as Berkhof and most others have of God's relation to space. That is, we should understand God's relation to time as comprising both his atemporal existence in himself (*in se*) apart from creation, and his "omnitemporal" existence in relation to the created order he has made (*in re*). If we do so, both doctrines are made parallel in nature, and what they say is powerful indeed. Put together, they would articulate the dual understandings, first, that "prior" to the creation of the world, God existed in himself, apart from any spatio-temporal reality, in the fullness of his infinite and glorious existence, as transcending both space and time, being essentially (i.e., in his essence or nature) both nonspatial and atemporal. But second, when he created the heavens and earth, he brought into being their two-fold dimensions of spatiality and temporality. Since God chose to become immanent within the creation he had made, he chose, then, to "enter" fully into both the spatial and the temporal dimensions of creation. In so doing, the same God who in himself is intrinsically and eternally both nonspatial and atemporal chose to "fill" all of the space and time he created. Amazingly, then, at creation God became both omnipresent and omnitemporal while remaining, in himself and apart from creation, fully nonspatial and timelessly eternal.

Hence, in becoming omnipresent and omnitemporal, God did not change in any respect who he eternally is apart from creation. He only adds, as it were, the qualities of his being also immanently related to his creation, in all of its points of space and in all of its moments of time. In a manner not dissimilar to the doctrine of the incarnation, where the eternal Son took on (added) to himself the nature of a man while in no respect diminishing his eternal and immutable deity, so too here, the

nonspatial and timelessly eternal God who created a spatial and temporal universe chose to "take on" or inhabit fully its dimensions of space
and time and so become both everywhere present (omnipresent) and
every-time present (omnitemporal).[9] God can be understood, then, as
both transcendent in his eternal nonspatial and atemporal existence
independent of everything created, and immanent in his omnipresent
and omnitemporal inhabiting of everything created. Spatially and temporally, God is apart from us and near us, other than us and with us,
separate from us and close at hand. What glory there is in both sides of
these truths.

What reasons might be advanced for following such a model of
God's parallel relation to both space and time? Consider the following
reasons. First, when God created the world, he created all of what it is,
including both its spatiality and its temporality. Both space and time,
then, are dimensions of the created world, and we ought to treat God's
relation to each of them in the same manner.

Second and related, we should avoid a duality reductionism in our
understanding of God's relation to time (i.e., God is only absolutely
timeless and not in any respect temporal), especially when we have
generally avoided this duality reductionism in our understanding of
God's relation to space (i.e., God is both nonspatial in himself, and he
is everywhere present in relation to creation).

Third, because God is both transcendent and immanent, both apart
from creation and intimately related to what he has made, it seems only
right to speak of God's relation to time, as well as his relation to space,
in ways that give expression to the dual truths of God's otherness and
nearness, his independence from everything created and his devotion
to the world he has made. The dual truths of God's transcendence and
immanence can be "matched" in our understandings of God's relation
to space and to time in ways that fit beautifully and actually assist our
comprehending the meaningfulness of God's transcendence and immanence, respectively.

---

[9] John Frame (*The Doctrine of God* [Phillipsburg, N.J.: Presbyterian & Reformed, 2002], 557-
559) argues for a position very similar to the one advanced here, and Frame uses the language of
spatial omnipresence and temporal omnipresence for the dual sense in which God is "present"
in all of space and in all of time. In relation to the analogy of the incarnation to God's relation
to created space and time, Frame writes, "In Christ, God entered, not a world that is otherwise
strange to him, but a world in which he had been dwelling all along."

Fourth and most important, by doing so, we can account for the dual truths that seem to be taught about God in Scripture. On the one hand, Genesis 1:1 requires that we understand God's existence "prior" to creation as fully independent of what he brought into being. As the creation account of Genesis 1 unfolds, the spatiality of creation is stressed over and again (e.g., the expanse in the midst of the waters, the expanse separating the waters above and below the expanse, the formation of dry land, etc.), but so too its clear temporal succession of moments is emphasized in this text (e.g., the repeated mention of the days of creation, the repeated refrain of "there was evening and there was morning" throughout the chapter, the lights of the expanse to separate day and night, etc.). If spatiality and temporality are intrinsically linked in Genesis 1 to the created order, and God exists "in the beginning" apart from this created order, then we have strong reason to understand God in himself, apart from creation, as both nonspatial and atemporal.

But on the other hand, Scripture also seems to require that we understand God literally in the space and the time of creation, with the difference from creaturely experience being that God (alone) inhabits *all* of space and *all* of time. Recall Psalm 139:7-10 mentioned above. The psalmist here extols God's presence anywhere and everywhere he might imagine going. While we are present in one place at one time only, God is present in his fullness in all points of space in all of the universe. Similarly, the "every-time presence" of God is also extolled by Scripture. Psalm 90:1-2 reads, "Lord, you have been our dwelling place in all generations. Before the mountains were brought forth, or ever you had formed the earth and the world, from everlasting to everlasting you are God." Attempts to read this text as teaching "timeless eternity" fail because of the clear and unmistakable temporal language. The lead thought in verse 1 is that God is our dwelling place *in all generations*. What the psalmist has in mind, then, is God's temporal presence with his people, as far back into the past or forward into the future as one can think. This links with the concept at the end of verse 2, "from everlasting to everlasting you are God." Clearly this text celebrates the temporal longevity of God; he always has existed in the past, and he always will exist in the future. Therefore, Scripture upholds both the "everywhere presence" of God (omnipresence) and the "every-time presence" of God (omnitemporality), though God brought into existence both space and time and so exists apart from both (Genesis 1).

The impact of this conception for understanding the God-human relationship is very significant. We can really embrace the reality that *God is with us* in every place we are, and in every moment of our lives. The real presence and immanent nearness of God is a precious reality that we can rightly hold dear. Yet, God is not limited to space and time as we are. He transcends both as Creator of both. His own existence stands eternally apart from the spatial and temporal confines of creaturely existence; yet he understands and experiences our lives enmeshed, as they are, in space and time.

And the impact for this dual understanding of God in relation to space and time also contributes to a question we will take up shortly, of whether we should think of God as possessing any contingent qualities along with his (timelessly) eternal and immutable essential qualities. From what we have seen here, if God undertakes to "enter" the creaturely dimensions of space and time, and yet he eternally exists apart from those dimensions, it appears that some meaningful sense of "contingent qualities in God" will be required. Far from fearing this as harmful to the doctrine of God, however, we can see here how these contingent qualities of God's omnipresence and omnitemporality are true, precisely because God chooses to enter into relationship with the creation he has made. Shall we begrudge God this desire and plan? Rather, we should celebrate the mercy, grace, kindness, compassion, and favor of the God who, although he needs none of what he has made, chooses to enter into relationship with his creatures. He does this not for what he can receive (for receive, he cannot do!) but for how he can give. And, here, we see his giving expressed through the gift of himself. He enters our space and our time in order to be with us! What joy there is, then, in these truths as they relate both to God in himself, and to God in relation to his creation.

ONTOLOGICALLY/ETHICALLY IMMUTABLE AND RELATIONALLY MUTABLE: GOD AND CHANGE

Another area where we see a tendency in the direction of duality reductionism is in the classic understanding of divine immutability. Early

Christians rightly sought to understand God in ways honoring to his supremacy and transcendence as distinct from the finite realm of creation. But as with the doctrine of divine eternity, where the dominant view historically conceived of God altogether in terms of timeless eternity and complete separation from the temporality of the created order, so here the dominant view through much of the history of the church was to conceive of God as absolutely immutable in every respect. After all, it was often reasoned, if God can change, then this must indicate a change for the better or a change for the worse. But if for the better, then he was not God before; and if for the worse, then he no longer can rightly be conceived of as God.[10] Other arguments for God's absolute immutability appealed to God's simplicity (change requires a compounded nature in which part, not all, is altered), eternity (change requires temporal succession to mark what a thing was before the change compared to what it now is), and immortality (things that change can cease to exist).[11] So, to ensure that God's perfection is secure and that his transcendent excellence is beyond question, God was widely presented as absolutely incapable of any change whatsoever.

I have argued elsewhere for a view that I will only summarize briefly here.[12] As one considers Scripture's teaching on God's relation to change, it is clear that a number of passages indicate the changelessness of God's essential nature (Ps. 102:25-27; Mal. 3:6; James 1:17). That is, fundamental to anything else said on this topic is the conviction that the essential qualities of God's very character—his holiness, goodness, knowledge, wisdom, power—are absolutely changeless. One might refer to this, then, as God's "ontological immutability," since his very being is eternally who he is as God.

Furthermore, Scripture speaks of the immutability not only of the

---

[10] See, e.g., Gregory of Nyssa, *Letter to Eustathia, Ambrosia, and Basilissa,* in *Nicene and Post-Nicene Fathers,* 2nd series, ed. Philip Schaff and Henry Wace (Peabody, Mass.: Hendrickson, 1994), vol. 5, 543, where Gregory writes that God is "incapable of changing to worse or changing to better, because the first is not His nature, the second He does not admit of." Similar statements can be found in Athanasius, Arnobius, Augustine, and others.

[11] More detail on the history of the doctrine of divine immutability can be found in my doctoral dissertation on the subject. See Bruce A. Ware, "An Evangelical Reexamination of the Doctrine of the Immutability of God," Pasadena, Calif.: Fuller Theological Seminary, Ph.D. dissertation, 1984.

[12] Bruce A. Ware, "An Evangelical Reformulation of the Doctrine of the Immutability of God," *Journal of the Evangelical Theological Society* 29/4 (December 1986): 431-446; and Bruce A. Ware, *God's Lesser Glory: The Diminished God of Open Theism* (Wheaton, Ill.: Crossway, 2000), 86-98.

essential nature of God but also of his word and promise. For example, in Malachi 3:6 God's nature and his covenant pledge are linked together in such a way that the changelessness of God's promise is based upon the changelessness of his nature. The prophet writes, "For I the LORD do not change; therefore you, O children of Jacob, are not consumed." Because of the constancy of God's character and nature, his people can be assured that even though God will come as a refiner's fire and destroy all those who persist in their shameful defiance of him (Mal. 3:1-5), nonetheless, since God has pledged his salvation and restoration to his people, they will not be consumed along with the rest. Here, then, we realize how important the surety of God's promise is. God does not go back on his word. He speaks the truth. He is faithful to his pledge. He is a covenant making and covenant keeping God. We might refer to the changelessness of God's word, promise, and pledge, then, as God's "ethical immutability."

Certainly God's ontological immutability is primary, in that God's ethical immutability is grounded in the surety of his nature and could not have the certainty that it does apart from it being an expression of the absolute changelessness of God's character and essential nature. In this sense we could speak of the divine ontological immutability as his first-order changelessness, and of the divine ethical immutability as his second-order changelessness. Also, we should note that God's ontological immutability is both absolute and necessary, in that God's eternal character cannot be other than it is. Yet, his ethical immutability is both derivative and contingent, in that only as God freely grants the word and promise that he does is he then internally obligated to keep the word that he has spoken. In other words, while the essential character qualities of God cannot be other than they are, the promises of God might not have been. After all, God did not have to create a world, nor having created it did he have to pledge to it his promises of saving grace. All of God's promises are freely given by God and contingent on his good pleasure and will. So, while the immutability of God's nature (ontological immutability) is absolute and necessary due to God being the eternal God who always is, the immutability of God's word and promise (ethical immutability), depending as it does on God's having given that word and making that promise, is derivative from God's will and contingent on God's purposes, plans, and good pleasure.

Having said that God is both ontologically and ethically immutable, we have not yet said all that the Bible says about the relation of God to change. Here we must depart from much of the history of this doctrine with its insistence on a strict and absolute sense of God's immutability generally. If we listen attentively to God revealed in Scripture, it is clear that he changes in some very important respects. May I suggest that all of us who have been saved by God's marvelous grace celebrate the fact that while we once faced the severe "wrath of God" revealed from heaven against our "ungodliness and unrighteousness" (Rom. 1:18), yet now in Christ by faith, "we have peace with God through our Lord Jesus Christ" (Rom. 5:1). In our conversion, there is no doubt that God did a work in us so that our dispositions toward him were changed. We who formerly loved the darkness and hated the light were granted sight to see Christ for who he is (2 Cor. 4:6) so as to begin now to love the light that we previously hated (John 3:19-21). But we are not the only ones whose disposition changes. God's disposition toward us in our unforgiven sin is one of judgment, wrath, and condemnation, but in Christ his disposition toward us is one of peace, acceptance, and fatherly love. We once were "children of wrath, like the rest of mankind" (Eph. 2:3), but now by faith we are seated with Christ in the heavenly places "so that in the coming ages he might show the immeasurable riches of his grace in kindness toward us in Christ Jesus" (Eph. 2:7). How can we fail to recognize here that a change has taken place in God's disposition toward us?

This is just an example of what might be called the "relational mutability" of God, a change not of his essential nature, nor of his word or promise, but of his attitude and disposition toward his moral creatures in ways that are commensurate to changes that happen in them. So, when we change, say, from rebellion to repentance, God changes commensurately, as described above. Likewise, when we turn from him in disobedience and rebellion, God's attitude and disposition toward us changes from one of acceptance to one of disappointment and even anger. Recall, for example, God's response to the sin of the children of Israel when Moses lingered longer than they expected with God on Mt. Sinai. As God witnessed Israel construct the golden calf and offer burnt offerings before it, his anger burned against them (Ex. 32:10). Must we not say, then, that God changes in relationship with his creation?

Furthermore, it seems clear that God's relational mutability is in many cases simply an expression of his ethical immutability. That is, because God is faithful to his promise, when the moral situation of his creatures changes, his faithfulness to his own pledge and promise requires that he change in appropriate ways in relation to them. Consider, for example, God's "change of mind" regarding his threatened judgment of Nineveh in the days of Jonah. Following a period of exceeding reluctance, Jonah eventually traveled to Nineveh and proclaimed God's message, "Yet forty days, and Nineveh shall be overthrown!" (Jonah 3:4). When the people of Nineveh repented, believed God, fasted, prayed, and turned from their sin, God "relented of the disaster that he had said he would do to them" (Jonah 3:10). Open theists, of course, endeavor to make much of cases like this, as if God learned something new and so literally changed his mind.[13] In this particular case, if God learned that the Ninevites would repent at the preaching of Jonah, this would be odd, since Jonah seemed already to suspect strongly that this would occur, and hence he refused to obey God's command to preach impending judgment to this people. Rather than presuming Jonah to have more insight than God (!), a far better understanding affords itself in considering the nature of the ethical immutability and the relational mutability of God in this situation. Because God had established from the beginning that those who repent and turn from their sin will be forgiven (e.g., 2 Chron. 7:14; Jer. 18:7-10), he sent Jonah to Nineveh to preach the very message he knew (as Jonah knew) would elicit the repentance that he sought from them. In light of their change of heart, God "relented" from what he had said. I take this simply to mean that because God is ethically immutable, so that when the Ninevites repented at the preaching of Jonah, God honored his long-standing word and so changed in his relationship with them. Rather than bringing them the threatened judgment, he brought them merciful forgiveness. In this, God kept the word of his promise (i.e., if you repent, I will forgive your sin) that required that he change when they changed. Hence, God's ethical immutability formed the basis here for God's relational mutability as expressed in Jonah 3:10.

---

[13] See, e.g., Gregory A. Boyd, *God of the Possible: A Biblical Introduction to the Open View of God* (Grand Rapids, Mich.: Baker, 2000), 55-56; and John Sanders, *The God Who Risks: A Theology of Providence* (Downers Grove, Ill.: InterVarsity Press, 1998), 64-69.

One more very important sense of God's mutability needs to be discussed.[14] Scripture witnesses over and again to various emotions in God. Obviously, for some of the same reasons that the early theologians insisted on the absolute immutability of God, they also tended to argue that the divine emotions spoken of in Scripture either represent a steady and immutable state of God's emotional "bliss"—a perfect and change-less emotional state, as it were—or that they should be understood as anthropomorphic and hence not literally true of God (e.g., as the body parts of God spoken of in Scripture are not literally true of him). For example, Origen writes:

> Now all these passages where God is said to lament, or rejoice, or hate, or be glad, are to be understood as spoken by Scripture in metaphori-cal and human fashion. For the divine nature is remote from all affec-tion of passion, remaining ever unmoved and untroubled in its own summit of bliss.[15]

And Augustine seems to concur that variable emotions can have no place literally in God. He suggests:

> Now when God is said to be angry, we do not attribute to Him such a disturbed feeling as exists in the mind of an angry man; but we call His just displeasure against sin by the name "anger," a word trans-ferred by analogy from human emotions.[16]

In another place, Augustine makes clear that while God may have some-thing like human emotions, he does so with an "impassible nature" such that we (who have passible natures) are unable, ultimately, to compre-hend the emotional experience of God. One thing that is sure, however, is that there can be no variance in the expression of these emotions, as

---

[14] For further discussion, see Ware, "Immutability of God," 444-446.

[15] Origen, *Homily on Numbers*, as quoted in H. Bettenson, ed. and trans., *The Early Christian Fathers* (Oxford: Oxford University Press, 1956), 187.

[16] Augustine, *Enchiridion*, in *Nicene and Post-Nicene Fathers*, 1st series, ed. Philip Schaff (Grand Rapids, Mich.: Eerdmans, 1978), vol. 3, 249. For other representative statements that variable emotions cannot be true of God, see, e.g., Arnobius, *Case Against the Pagans*, in G. E. McCracken, trans., *Arnobius of Sicca: The Case Against the Pagans* (Westminster, Md.: Newman, 1949), I.18, II.26, VI.2; and Stephen Charnock, *The Existence and Attributes of God* (1797; reprint, Minneapolis: Klock & Klock, 1977), 125.

if they could be provoked to change by the created order. Augustine writes,

> Ineffable is therefore that patience, as is His jealousy, as His wrath, and whatever there is like to these. For if we conceive of these as they be in us, in Him are there none. We, namely, can feel none of these without molestation: but be it far from us to surmise that the impassible nature of God is liable to any molestation. But like as He is jealous without any darkening of spirit, wroth without any perturbation, pitiful without any pain, repenteth Him without any wrongness in Him to be set right; so is He patient without aught of passion.[17]

When one looks carefully at the concerns of these theologians over variable emotions in God, their main objections are metaphysical and moral. Metaphysically, if God is simple (noncomposite), timelessly eternal, and immutably perfect, then it would seem that the very nature of God would preclude the possibility of variation of any kind, including variation of emotional states. Morally, they feared that changeable emotions in God would necessarily be conceived of as a form of weakness, or limitation, or inner disturbance (or "molestation," as Augustine put it) that could lead to mishap or poor judgment. After all, emotions in human beings often contribute to excessive actions, ones we often look back at later with regret. Therefore, on metaphysical and moral grounds, they denied of God variable emotions.

But metaphysically, we have already seen good reason to question these traditional conceptions of God that remove him entirely from any possibility of real relationship with the world. Yes, God is timelessly eternal, but he also is omnitemporal, entering fully into the moments of creaturely existence. Yes, God is absolutely immutable in the essential character qualities that are his by virtue of his being God, but this does not require immutability in all respects. While upholding the full transcendence of God in every way that Scripture demands, we should not conceive of God's transcendence so that other clear teachings of Scripture have to be eliminated—as I fear some have done with Scripture's teaching about God's emotions.

Morally, emotions can be highly constructive and beneficial in us,

---

[17] Augustine, *On Patience,* in *Nicene and Post-Nicene Fathers,* 1st series, vol. 3, 527.

just as they can also lead to unwarranted excess. But why can it not be the case in God that his emotions function only in constructive, beneficial ways and never lead God to unwarranted excess? Abraham Heschel is correct on this point, I believe. He writes that "the Bible [does not] share the view that passions are disturbances or weaknesses of the soul, and much less the premise that passion itself is evil, that passion as such in imcompatible [sic] with right thinking or right living."[18] There is no need either metaphysically or morally, then, to deny what is so clearly and often taught in Scripture, that God has and expresses variable emotions.

Consider some of the range of God's emotions. He is said in Scripture to be angry (Num. 12:9; Josh. 7:1; Isa. 42:25), wrathful (2 Kings 22:13; Ps. 110:5; Jer. 10:10), jealous (Ex. 20:5; Josh. 24:19; Zech. 1:14), compassionate and merciful (Ps. 103:8; 145:8; Jer. 3:12), patient and longsuffering (Ex. 34:6; Num. 14:18; 2 Pet. 3:9)—just to name a few. One of the most glorious expressions of God's emotions in all of Scripture is found in Zephaniah 3:17: "The LORD your God is in your midst, a mighty one who will save; he will rejoice over you with gladness; he will quiet you by his love; he will exult over you with loud singing." Just imagine the harm we would do both to this precious truth and to our understanding of God if we were to remove God out of time altogether (what real meaning would be left to "The LORD your God is *in your midst*"?) and in particular, remove from God any real emotions. Unlike in the case of Scripture's references to God's bodily parts, where other Scriptures tell us that God transcends those bodily qualities, understood literally, in the case of emotions we have no Scripture that would lead us to think that God actually transcends the emotions Scripture ascribes to him.[19] Rather, it appears that God is intrinsically emotional, and in all likelihood, the reason that we are emotional beings ourselves is owing to our being made in God's image—the God who himself is emotional. And we should not be surprised here: God is a personal Being, and one of the richest experiences of personal existence is the range of emotions we enjoy. Of course, due to sin, our emotions often are deeply troubling. But remove sin, and we can imagine what this

---

[18] Abraham J. Heschel, *The Prophets*, 2 vols. (New York: Harper, 1962), 2:37-38.

[19] In Ware, "Immutability of God," 442, I offer this definition of an anthropomorphism: "A given ascription to God may rightly be understood as anthropomorphic when Scripture clearly presents God as transcending the very human or finite features it elsewhere attributes to him."

range of emotional life must be like. Scripture indicates clearly, then, the reality of variable emotions in God, and we can embrace this truth knowing how richly expressive this is of God's own life as the personal God he is.

Finally, it may be helpful to consider some of the implications of this understanding of the divine immutability and mutability for the larger doctrines of God and divine providence. First, by ascribing to God not only the omnipresence and omnitemporality described previously but also the senses of his immutability and mutability discussed here, we can understand better the genuineness and dynamism of the God-human relationship that God has designed for us to know. He truly is with us, and there is genuine interaction and interplay in our relationship with him. While his sovereignty assures us that his plans and purposes can never be threatened, his relationality also assures us that he treats us with integrity as persons.

Second, God's relational mutability entails that our lives and choices and actions do have a measured effect on God himself. Care is needed here, to be sure. We must avoid thinking that we can affect God either for the better or for the worse, and in this the older theologians were absolutely correct. But why think that the only change possible would be of this kind? If we consider God more in personal terms along with thinking of him in terms of eternal qualities and perfections, we may understand better the kinds of changes appropriate to God, the perfect personal Being.

Imagine, by way of analogy, the perfect human father. Would the perfect human father, because he is perfect, be absolutely unaffected by anything his children said, or felt, or did? No, not at all. Rather, the perfect human father, both as a person and as perfect, would respond to his children in all the ways appropriate to what is needed and what is best in every different situation. When appropriate, he would laugh with them, and in other cases he would weep, or sympathize, or rejoice, or show his displeasure, or manifest his patience, or give them of his wisdom. The perfect father would relate and respond to his children differently, depending on the situation, but the constant in all of his relationships with them would be his unfaltering desire to bring about what is best for them. Should we not think of God more in these terms, i.e., in terms of God being the perfect personal Being in relationship with other persons whom he has made? If so, clearly we affect him without ever diminishing or enhancing who he is as God. But his care for us, and his design to engender relationship with us, encourages us to relate to God more and more in these terms.

Third, both God's ontological and ethical immutability give us deep confidence that God will never fail in being, and in doing, what is right and good. As wonderful as real relationship with another is, it is not enough by itself, because whether you enjoy and benefit from a relationship depends altogether on what the character of the person is like. God's changelessness of character and the surety of his word are gold. No better foundation could be laid for deep and meaningful relationship than what is found in who God is in himself. And to think that, being who he is, he designs that we enter into relationship with him— this is more wondrous than we can possibly understand, yet we thank God and accept the precious gift.

Fourth and last, as we shall see shortly, the case is mounting for understanding some qualities in God as contingent. As with our understanding of God's omnipresence and omnitemporality, so too here does the picture of God's relation to change indicate that God is affected by the world he has made. Some qualities of God arise and are expressed in ways that simply would not be the case had God not created this world. Some changes in God seem contingent upon his decision to enter into this world as he has. Even some emotional experiences of God would arise out of his nature only in response to the conditions he meets in this created and fallen world. So, as we marvel at God's constancy, stability, and immutability, we should also marvel at his chosen path of variability, relational adaptability, and mutability. What a God, and what an unspeakable privilege to be in relationship with him.

INDEPENDENT OF US AND AFFECTED BY US: GOD AND CONTINGENCY

Drawing from the previous sections where we have already anticipated the issue at hand, it seems clear that part of what it means for God to be immanent with the creation he has made is that he has chosen not only to affect it (the prominent category, to be sure) but he has also chosen to be affected by it (a lesser, but still important, category). Adopting, as we have, categories of God's spatial and temporal presence with us by which he inhabits every point of space and moment of time, and of his relational mutability in which God's disposition changes in response to the changing moral situations of his creatures, it follows that we must speak of some meaningful sense of God being affected by the world he has made along with the stronger and dominant conception of God's effect on the world.

To take this one step further, God, of course, did not have to create the world, and hence, he did not have to embrace the relationship with this world that he has designed. God's eternal nature is infinitely rich and full, with no need of anything he has created (Acts 17:24-25), and hence we can rightly comprehend God apart from the created order, unaffected by anything outside of God, since nothing outside of God exists apart from his creative word. But remarkably, he chose to create; he chose to share the bounty of his infinite fullness with the created vessels he would bring into existence and fill. Clearly, then, the creation is affected by God supremely. For each and every aspect of creation including, most importantly, his moral creation, our very existence, every quality we possess, every resource used for our sustenance and well-being, every ability for contribution outwardly—everything we are and have is graciously granted us by God, and hence his effect upon us is maximal, indeed!

But in these roles in which God relates to us as Provider, Protector, Sustainer, Giver, Commander, Director, Master, Lord, and Lover, he has chosen, in all of these ways of relating, to do so as "with us" in personal relationship. He hears our cries and responds. He understands our weaknesses and sympathizes. He witnesses our defiance and he frowns. He scorns our ultimate treason and he judges. He sees our folly and he grieves. He comprehends our hopelessness and he saves. Therefore, while God's effect on us is maximal, God has so designed that we also affect him. In a manner not unlike what happens if you choose to get to know someone very lonely and needy, the choice to pursue this relationship will mean, inevitably, that he will have an effect on you even though you hope to have a significant positive effect on him. God's choice to relate to creation by establishing lines of personal, even intimate, relationship, requires that we see God as affected by us while supremely he makes the major effect upon us.

Consider now some brief expansion on these ideas, thinking first of how God is necessarily unaffected by us, and then a bit more of what creation's effect on him means in terms of contingency in God. First, as we recall from a portion of our discussion in chapter 2, it should be clear that there are ways in which it is impossible for the creation, in part or in whole, to affect God. Because God is infinitely self-sufficient, we simply cannot add to his glorious fullness. We contribute nothing to God's knowledge, wisdom, power, goodness, holiness, or any other essential quality of God. God possesses each and every quality intrinsically and infinitely, and therefore any effect on God can never be to add to his glorious and infinite fullness. We must never allow the deeply meaningful senses in which God is affected by us somehow to cloud or dissipate our clear apprehension of the truth that God does not need us. He did not have to create. He exists eternally fully satisfied and deeply fulfilled in the tri-personal relationship of Father, Son, and Holy Spirit.[20] Again, here as before, we simply stand in amazement and wonder that the God who needs no relationship apart from his eternal tri-personal relationship nonetheless has deemed it good and wise to design, create, enable, empower, and pursue these external relationships, for his glory and for our good.

Yet, secondly, the existence of creation, by God's choice and design, affects his own life and experience. Consider with me just some of what this involves. First, invoking again the model of the incarnation, we cannot imagine that when God creates the spatio-temporal world and chooses to inhabit all that he made, this has no effect whatsoever on him. Rather, in order for God fully to inhabit the realm of our experience, to live with us as he tells his people over and again through Scripture, surely this "adds" to God what he did not experience apart from the creation of the world. The timelessly eternal God becomes also omnitemporal; his infinite and nonspatial existence now takes on the fullness of the finite spatial world. With no diminution in any respect to his infinite and eternal fullness, he now adds the fullness of creaturely space and time. And this, in order to be the God who insists on being *with* his people.

Second, as alluded to above, certainly some emotions of God found their first experiential expression only in respect to the created world.

---

[20] The eternal tri-personal relations of the Father, Son, and Holy Spirit, along with reflection on their eternal trinitarian roles and the relevance to human life is the subject of my forthcoming book, *Father, Son, and Holy Spirit: Relationships, Roles, and Relevance* (Wheaton, Ill.: Crossway, forthcoming, January 2005).

God's anger, which hits such peak decibels even by Genesis 6 that God destroys the world (save Noah and his family) with a flood, is unthinkable in God apart from both creation and sin. Was God angry within his eternal tri-personal relationship, apart from creation? With no disrespect intended, we need to ask: who was mad at whom? The Father with the Son? The Spirit with the Father? The point is clear, I trust, that to imagine in God himself the same kind of anger he felt and expressed in relation to the created order is absolutely unacceptable. Rather, we must see what now can be thought of as contingent properties in God, e.g., emotions specifically occasioned by the created and fallen order which would not have had expression in God otherwise. Of course, what has been said about God's anger applies to other divine emotions. Pity, for example, has no place in God apart from creation. There simply is nothing pitiful about the Father, the Son, or the Holy Spirit! No, pity is an expression of God's emotional disposition toward what is weak, helpless, destitute, and needy. Again, this emotion can apply only in the context of a finite creation, and only accentuated when that finite creation is also fallen. Hence pity, as a true emotion expressed by God toward creatures, is a contingent property in God. And we could say the same of God's patience, longsuffering, and compassion.

Lest we think, however, that these contingent emotional experiences of God's simply arise *ex nihilo,* it should be clear that while some emotions are "new" when the creation and fall occur, other emotions in God nonetheless "pre-date" the created order. Perhaps it would be best, then, to see the contingent emotions of God as new expressions of what are, in God eternally, fixed emotional properties. For example, the anger of God toward sin and rebellion—a contingent emotional property only rightly expressed in the context of the fallen creation—may be understood as a new expression of God's eternal and necessary emotional property of divine jealousy for his glory. God is eternally passionate for his glory, and now in the context of a fallen creation, when that glory is despised, eternal passionate jealousy gives rise in God to a new and contingent expression of white-hot anger against sin. Similarly, God's eternal and necessary emotional quality of loving tenderness may now, in the context of destitute and despairing sinners, give rise to the new contingent emotional property of pity and compassion. Because God has chosen not only to create but also to relate immanently to his creation, one implication that seems clear is the occasioning, for God, of new and contingent emotional dispositions which give expression to some of God's eternal and necessary emotional properties, but they do so in ways directed toward and appropriate to the finite and (in time) fallen created order.

Third, it is now only a small step to consider also certain attributes of God (often tied to corresponding emotional dispositions) which, likewise, are occasioned by the presence of a created order, and often a created order infested with sin. Just as we spoke of God's anger as an emotion, perhaps we could merely adjust the discussion and think instead about God's attribute of retributive justice (i.e., the quality in God by which God justly punishes sin—e.g., Rom. 2:8-9). Justice, of course, is correctly understood as an attribute of God, but the retributive nature of divine justice necessarily invokes the presence of sinful violation of law requiring punishment. Again, as should be abundantly clear, this situation is simply unthinkable in God apart from the created order. Even creation (alone) without sin precludes the expression of retributive justice. But since Scripture clearly highlights this quality of God (e.g., Rom. 2:2-11; 2 Thess. 1:7-9; Rev. 20:12-13), a quality that cannot be expressed by God except in the context of a fallen creation, then it stands to reason that this divine attribute is a contingent quality in God.

As before, we certainly would want here to insist that the contingent attribute of retributive justice did not simply appear in God *ex nihilo*. Rather, the contingent attribute of retributive justice in God is the expression, in time and space and in ways fully appropriate to the sinful moral setting in which it is expressed, of God's eternal and necessary attributes of holiness and righteousness. Yes indeed, God is eternally holy and eternally righteous, but apart from the creation and fall, God simply would not appropriately be called or thought of as "just" in the retributive sense of justice.

And what is said of retributive justice must, I believe, be said of a number of other attributes of God. Consider, for example, the twin attributes of God's mercy and grace. Surely it must be clear to every reader how utterly horrid it is to imagine that God, in himself and apart from the fallen created order, exhibits mercy or grace within the Godhead! If one thinks carefully here, one should see how it would constitute blasphemy to say that God eternally exhibits mercy within the Trinity, or that grace is shown among the members of the Godhead. To say so is to commit theological treason against God. Why? Simply because both mercy and grace require a context of sin for them meaningfully to be expressed. Mercy is God's favor and compassion shown to those destitute, ruined, helpless and hopeless due to sin (Eph. 2:1-5; Titus 3:3-5). And grace is God's favor and kindness to those fully undeserving of that favor (Rom. 3:23-24; Eph. 2:8-9). So understood, mercy and grace can have *no place in God apart from creation.* So, how shall we think of these attributes of God? The contingent attributes of mercy and grace in God are the expressions, in time and space and in ways fully appropriate to the sinful moral settings to which they are directed, of God's eternal and necessary attributes of goodness and love. Yes indeed, God possesses eternally and necessarily the attributes of goodness and love, but apart from the creation and fall, God simply would not appropriately be called or thought of as "merciful" or "gracious" since neither of these can have any rightful and appropriate expression within the immanent Trinity.[21]

Now, perhaps one might rather think of the attributes of retributive justice, mercy, and grace as eternal and necessary attributes in God (i.e., alongside his eternal and necessary attributes of holiness, righteousness, goodness, and love), but attributes eternally dormant until their first emergence at the presence of sin. But since the creation is not necessary to God, strictly speaking, then I find it problematic to conceive of God as possessing *eternal properties* and *attributes* which have no place in God *in himself* and *apart from creation,* attributes which even have no meaning apart from conceiving of God in relation to a created and fallen order. That is, imagine a God—the very same God as the God who created this world—who chose never to create, ever! Would we say that this

---

[21] As will be explained more below, theologians often distinguish the relations of the Father, Son, and Holy Spirit within the Godhead and *apart from the created order* from the relations of the Father, Son, and Holy Spirit *with the created order* itself. The former is usually referred to as the "immanent Trinity." The latter is usually referred to as the "economic Trinity"—God's trinitarian relationship outwardly expressed as each Person of the Father, Son, and Holy Spirit relates to the world in the "economy" or outworking of this designed relationship. One might think, then, that discussions of the "immanence of God" and of the "immanent Trinity" involve equivocal (i.e., differing) senses of "immanent." In fact, however, what both concepts have in common is the notion of considering God as "near" or "with" another. It's just that the "other" referred to in relation to the immanence of God is we (i.e., God's relation with the created order), whereas the "other" referred to in relation to the immanent Trinity is one or another member of the Trinity (i.e., the Father's relation with the Son, or the Son's relation with the Spirit, etc.).

God, for whom the notion of creation is only hypothetical, possesses the eternal yet dormant attributes of retributive justice, mercy, and grace? Much more natural, it seems to me, is to understand a whole array of changes that take place for God when he creates the world and intentionally chooses to enter into deep and pervasive immanent relationality with this finite, temporal, spatial, and (in time) fallen world. Just as God enters and inhabits the fullness of our space and time, just as he acts and reacts in relationship with us, just as he expresses emotions that would never have been expressed apart from the created world, so too God acquires certain attributes one might think of as creation-specific as he relates to the created order out the fullness of who he eternally and inviolably is. Yet he truly does so with attributes of his being that are only now called forth from him.

Perhaps it would help in this discussion to employ a distinction commonly used in trinitarian discussions and so speak of attributes of the immanent trinitarian God, and attributes of the economic trinitarian God. The *immanent Trinity* refers to the triune persons in relationship with each other apart from the created order, whereas the *economic Trinity* refers to the triune persons each and together in relationship with the created world.[22] While we speak meaningfully in trinitarian discussions about *particular relationships* (i.e., economic relationships) that the Father, Son, and Holy Spirit have with creation that are not true of the relations that they have with one another, apart from creation (i.e., immanent relationships),[23] it seems that we could use similar language to express the *particular attributes* (i.e., economic attributes) which find expression only in relation to the created order and which simply cannot be part of the collection of attributes expressed among the Father, Son, and Holy Spirit, apart from creation (i.e., immanent attributes). And of course we could make the similar analogy to those *particular emotions* (i.e., economic emotions) in God that find their expression

---

[22] For further discussion, see Bruce A. Ware, "How Shall We Think About the Trinity?" in Douglas S. Huffman and Eric L. Johnson, eds., *God Under Fire: Modern Scholarship Reinvents God* (Grand Rapids, Mich.: Zondervan, 2002), 255-257.

[23] That is, the Father, Son, and Holy Spirit each relates to the created order in ways that are unique economically. For example, the Father relates to creation as the Grand Architect of the Plan of creation (Eph. 1:11), including the plan of election by which some would certainly be saved (Eph. 1:3-5). The Son carries out the will of the Father by relating to creation as the Redeemer who pays the penalty for sin and conquers sin and death (Eph. 1:7). And the Spirit is the agent of the Father and the Son to secure the fulfillment in the lives of believers of all that the Father designed and the Son obtained (Eph. 1:13-14).

only in the context of the created order and that could never be a part of those emotions freely expressed within the trinity of persons, apart from creation (i.e., immanent emotions).

This is not to say that the immanent sets of relationships, attributes, and emotions cannot have appropriate expression also economically, as God deems best. But the attempt here is to understand better how certain qualities and expressions of God's own nature arise only when he creates and relates to the finite and (in time) fallen world. We tend to give less thought than we should, it seems to me, to what "God's relationship with the world" means for God. It means everything for us! But for God, it requires entering into a new realm of his life and experience, one which in no respect diminishes his eternal and infinite glory, but one that does require of him the acceptance of change. Contingency as well as necessity, then, are categories needed to understand the true meaning of God's immanence and transcendence, respectively. In order to do justice to both God's transcendent self-existence and his immanent self-relatedness, while maintaining the priority of his transcendence and freedom to become immanent in the ways he chooses, these expressions of self-chosen contingency in God's relationships, emotions, and attributes are needed.

ALIKE AND DIFFERENT: GOD AND HUMANS IN UNIQUE RELATIONSHIP

Our relationship with God is both like our human relationships and different. I think it is safe to say, though, that our tendency (a natural one, no doubt) is to try to understand our relationship with God in ways as much like human relationships as possible. After all, if our relationship with God is like those we have with others, it feels more "real" to us. But in light of our previous discussion, should we not anticipate significant differences to mark the divine-human relationship? Is it possible that this relationship, though genuinely real, may not seem real when compared to what we normally experience at the human level? Let's consider, then, some of the characteristics of the divine-human relationship that flow from our previous inquiry.

Understanding rightly our relationship with God *must* begin with the supremacy, the superiority, the sovereignty, and the self-sufficiency of God. Our urge to have a relationship with God just like we do with a good friend falters right here! Like it or not (and, by the way, by God's grace we should and shall like it if we do not now), this is not a relationship among equals, nor is it even a relationship with one older and wiser than myself. Rather, this relationship is radically unlike any human relationship, and one for which no explanation exists on the human level. Why would the divine partner in this relationship care to be in relationship with another?

For in this relationship, one Member of the relationship knows absolutely everything (and this is not a hyperbolic expression, in this case), and the other knows far less than he thinks. One Member has perfect foresight and knows every detail of what the future holds, and the other has difficulty knowing where to lay hands on his keys before he heads to the car. One Member has such perfect wisdom, insight, and discernment that there never has been a time in his entire history (a long one at that!) that his plans have proved misguided or his judgment has been askew—while the other member of the relationship thought himself wise once when he figured out a clever shortcut to take, until he ended up on a long dead-end road! One Member possesses every quality or perfection in his being both infinitely and intrinsically—while the other possesses only a miniscule amount and only then because any and all of it has graciously been given to him by the One who has it all! One Member cannot make a rock bigger than he can lift, because his power to do anything he chooses simply cannot be limited—while the other has difficulty most mornings making it out of bed, much less getting in his coffee and devotions and morning run. One Member is absolutely honest, completely trustworthy, never breaks a promise, always keeps his word, is always on (his) time, and always does his work exactly right, every time—while the other . . . well, let's just say that the other doesn't fare well here.

What is it like to be in relationship with one who is infinitely wise, powerful, holy, truthful, and good? Perhaps from God's side of the picture, this relationship is summed up with the words, "he knows our frame; he remembers that we are dust" (Ps. 103:14). The disparity between us and God is impossible really to imagine. Analogies fail, because the disparity here is between what is infinite and what is finite and, at present, fallen. Why should we think that this relationship would be like any of our other relationships?

Our only rightful place before the true God, in relationship to him, is to be in the position of humble dependence and single-minded devotion. Our place is to seek him with all of our hearts, for in him alone are the riches of life. Our place is to thank him constantly for the bounty of his favor and the forgiveness of our despicable sin. Our place is to fear his just judgment against all that opposes him, and to trust him without hesitation or reservation in every way that he commands, or corrects, or instructs, or directs. Our place is to love him supremely, with heart, soul, mind, and strength.

In short, much of what characterizes the God-human relationship is its asymmetry. The provision and the protection and the favor and the truth and the grace run one way, from God to us. And from us toward him should flow dependence, obedience, longing, thanksgiving, trust, hope, and love. God is the Giver, we are the receivers. God is rich, we are needy and empty. God is our all in all, and we are nothing without him.

Oh, how much we should long for our relationship with God to be so *unlike* any other. In this sense, we ought to long for it to seem and feel very "unreal." The asymmetry of this relationship ought to strike us constantly. The infinite disparity between God and us should never leave our consciousness, even for a moment. His call upon our lives for absolute obedience should ring in our ears. His demand for our purity and holiness, integrity and faithfulness, compassion and kindness should be impressed on our minds and hearts with indelible seriousness. In our approach to God, we should resist the urge to come to him as to a mere friend, but instead we should seek him, fear him, respect him, adore him, love him, and honor him. We should come desperate to listen, to learn, to heed, to grow, to follow. Yes, a real relationship with God—the true and living God—will be quite unreal, by comparison to any merely human relationship.

But not fully.

And here is where even more astonishment impresses us. For we realize that the awesome and independent God who needs none of us *seeks relationship with us!* Some of the most startling words in all the Bible come from the lips of Jesus to a Samaritan woman—a cultural nobody, by most people's estimate. But to this woman he relays the glorious news, "But the hour is coming, and is now here, when the true worshipers will worship the Father in spirit and truth, *for the Father is*

seeking such people to worship him" (John 4:23, emphasis added).
Imagine that. The Father seeks worshipers. And when we understand
the nature of worship, we marvel yet again.

For worship requires that we see God as high and exalted, supreme
and glorious, holy and pure, mighty and loving. And this view of God is
not from an indifferent distance, as it were; a purely objective, ice-cold,
merely factual "seeing" of God will not elicit worship. Rather, worship
happens only when we are granted eyes to behold God's magnificence,
and splendor, and glory, and majesty. This is a seeing with deep and
abiding longing, a seeing that savors, eliciting a savoring that satisfies.
In this seeing, God invades our lives, and we experience the truths about
him that we have beheld. Truth about him becomes existential within
our own minds, hearts, hopes, fears, plans, dreams, values, and desires.
We marvel at his character, we embrace his will and his ways as we savor
the richness and bounty of all that he is. And as this happens—as we are
deeply satisfied in God—we worship. So, God seeks worshipers because
he seeks to fill us with himself, that we in turn may give to him the honor,
thanks, and praise due only to him.[24]

And what does God do to make this a reality? The God who doesn't
need us comes to us. He enters our space and time. He speaks our language. He meets us where we live. He chooses to be affected by us as
part of the Grand Plan to bring about the most incredible effect upon
us. He accepts ridicule and rejection, when he deserves nothing but laud
and honor. He makes pledges and promises of merciful salvation, when
he could abandon and condemn. He accepts what it means to be in
relationship with us, even though he demonstrated from the very beginning how much he hated our defiance. Biblical accounts of the flood,
and God's judgment on Sodom and Gomorrah, and the incident of the
golden calf, and Korah's rebellion—these and so many more picture for
us how detestable our sin and rebellion is to this glorious God. But his
love endures forever, and so he perseveres in this relationship. The God
who exists in glorious independence apart from us is determined, and

---

[24] Many readers will notice here my dependence on language for these truths that is often
expressed by John Piper. I gratefully acknowledge this dependence and commend readers unfa-
miliar with his work especially to read John Piper, *The Pleasures of God: Meditations on God's
Delight in Being God,* rev. and expanded (Sisters, Ore.: Multnomah, 2000). I've written a brief
review of this excellent and profound work, and it appears in the *Journal of the Evangelical
Theological Society* 44/4 (December 2001): 754-756.

he will not fail, to bring about the truest of all relationships for us human creatures, and this with a formerly rebellious people, but a people of his choosing. In this relationship, God enters our world, comes to us, seeks us out, accommodates himself to our level, accepts how we affect him, and experiences all that is needed to seek and make and remake those who will be forever worshipers of him. As seen most fully in his Son on the cross, God demonstrates a determination unparalleled in seeking and saving that which was lost, yet seeking, to be sure, that which he does not need.

In the end, relationship with God is as diffcrent as infinite is from finite. And yet, by God's grace and condescension, it is at the same time the epitome of what intimate and joyful relationship with another should be. And indeed, it is a relationship in which so much of the joy and the fulfillment is found precisely in remembering always the infinite disparity that exists between God and us. We must call to mind always Who is glorious and why. Only then will we cast aside our sinful pretense and bow, receive, delight, and worship in a joyous intimacy unrivaled by any human relationship. Here, then, is true relationship with the transcendent-immanent God, a relationship that is remarkably unreal in the fullness of its reality.

GLORY, HONOR, AND PRAISE: GOD AND GOD ALONE

We conclude this survey of foundational theological bases for understanding God and divine providence by focusing attention on the end toward which every other feature points. From the first verse of inspired Scripture to the last chapter of Revelation, God makes clear in ten thousand ways that the greatest value in the universe, and the final end of all of life, is the uncontested supremacy and unrivaled glory of God alone. As we contemplate the God-human relationship, surely it must be clear to us that the great purpose for human life is *not* human self-directedness, human self-attainment, human self-actualization, or human self-esteem. In fact, each of these represents an expression of the idolatry of sinful human existence. Rather, the end of life is God—God's worth and glory extolled as needy and humble creatures live in full and happy dependence upon him, to the glory of his name. Our good *is* his glory, and to see this is to enter into the *raison d'être* of God's glorious and gracious design for human life.

Oh how much we make of ourselves in the culture in which we now live, and yet how little do we know either of ourselves or, surely far, far less, of God. What should be hitting us with the force of a sledge hammer by this point in our study is how the doctrine of God and his providence, at every turn, extols God's magnificence and glory and supremacy, and yet how the very human extolling of these truths—or better, of the God of whom they are true—results not in our diminished worth or weakened happiness, but in just the opposite. Our pretense of self-esteem is replaced with the infinitely full treasure store of God's worth, accessed through God-esteem. Our dead-end routes of self-directedness are replaced with unsurpassable wisdom and knowledge that leads unfailingly to life and goodness and peace and joy. So, when we turn from the deceptive emptiness of self-satisfaction and self-attainment to the fullness of God-given satisfaction and God-empowered attainment, we realize that by acknowledging our bankruptcy and God's endless riches, we now trade in our poverty for never-ending wealth. Yes, indeed, God's glory *is* our good. We praise and honor him who alone is worthy, for granting us the unspeakable privilege of this relationship with him. We do so with deep and sincere gratitude, respect, love, awe, and wonder. How great is our God, and how wondrous it is to be in relationship with him.

PART TWO

Practical Christian Relevance of Divine Providence

6

Living Behind God:
Veiled to the Purpose of God in Suffering

LIVING WITH SUFFERING BEHIND THE VEIL

I'm so grateful that the book of Job is in the Bible. Clearer here than anywhere else in Scripture is the revelation of God-intended conceal-ment, the unveiling of purposeful veiling. That is, we are told what Job was not told. We are allowed to listen in behind the scenes, as it were, backstage, to hear the Director of the play discuss and disagree with one of the play's less visible yet prominent actors about just how the script is unfolding. As we listen in, we realize that although the disgruntled actor seems to have persuaded the Director to move the script in a decidedly different direction, yet if we have listened carefully, we will have heard the nearly inaudible voice of the Director insisting, "Indeed, do as you wish, but within boundaries I establish, and for purposes I have long ago ordained, fulfilling what will only rightly be understood as My work."

How much of life, our life, is like this: we simply don't know. In our experiences of suffering and affliction, we are often in the position Job was in, where we don't even know *that* we don't know, and certainly we don't know *what* the bigger picture is that would explain and make sense of our confusion and bewilderment. Behind the scenes, backstage, discussions are brewing and the Director is carefully regulating intrica-cies and details that relate to our lives, all the while whispering to those who have ears to hear, "Don't be afraid. Place your trust and confidence in Me. For these evil forces may do as they wish, but . . . My child, do you remember Job? They will only act within boundaries I establish, and for purposes I have long ago ordained, fulfilling what will only rightly be understood as My work. Be assured of this, My child, and hope!"

In what follows I wish to reflect on the implications and applications of our previous study of God and his providential dealings with his human creation, particularly here in relation to suffering. We will discuss several biblical and theological principles that Christian people should know and take to heart, principles that can be a source of deep comfort and strong encouragement during times of affliction. It is sometimes said that our views of God are exposed for what they are at the onset of suffering. How true. And how important for us to know God rightly and to understand what he has revealed about his purposes and will and ways for his children in order, in part, to face with strength and joy whatever God brings into our lives, for his glory and our good. So then, here at the existential level of facing suffering, we hope to propose biblical and theological truths that will strengthen our hope and confidence in God.

UNDERSTANDING SUFFERING BIBLICALLY AND THEOLOGICALLY[1]

Because Scripture is the only final and ultimately authoritative source for Christian faith and practice, committed Christians will want to explore what principles the Bible itself teaches for helping believers face and deal with affliction that they or others experience. We propose, then, to consider some of Scripture's most precious principles and truths regarding suffering that can give strength and confidence to all who know and trust the Lord. At the outset, though, we should be clear that this is not a checklist of all of the possible "reasons" for why any one of God's children experiences suffering. We cannot go down through the numbers of the following points necessarily and stop at one and say, "Ah, here it is, here's the reason for my suffering," and have all our questions answered. Rather, most of what we consider here are *principles* from Scripture, not *reasons* with a one-to-one correspondence to your suffering or mine. And this is true even though we do consider, in the process, a number of reasons from Scripture for why suffering happens. The difficulty is "matching" one particular reason with one particular circumstance of suffering in a one-to-one way. And further, what

---

[1] The following section is an expansion and revision of material published previously in Bruce A. Ware, *Their God Is Too Small: Open Theism and the Undermining of Confidence in God* (Wheaton, Ill.: Crossway, 2003), 68-76.

we'll discover after all the principles are read and understood is that exactly *why* suffering in many cases occurs is not made known to us. "The secret things belong to the LORD our God" (Deut. 29:29a), Moses wisely told the people of Israel. And surely some of those secret things involve for us, as they did for Job, just what God's reasons are for our suffering.

However, even though we are often veiled to God's purposes, be assured: God is fulfilling his purposes in and through our suffering, because God's hands are extended into our affliction rather than being tied behind his back rendering him unable to exert any control over this supposedly pointless suffering. No, the God who veils from us his reasons for our suffering does so just so that we will keep our eyes fixed on him, trusting that his wisdom and power are every bit as much active now as they are when the sun shines and the flowers bud. I invite you, then, to consider these precious and faith-building biblical principles, and my prayer is that they will fuel your longing to put your confidence ever more in our glorious and wholly good God.

1. *Suffering is not, in itself, an* essential *good.* Perhaps the single most important biblical truth to establish at the beginning of this examination of principles related to suffering is one we have underscored several times already: Scripture is absolutely clear that God is good, and *only* good, and in *no respect* is he evil! Psalm 5:4 affirms, "For you are not a God who delights in wickedness; evil may not dwell with you" (cf. Ps. 11:5-7; 92:15); Psalm 107:1 exhorts, "Oh give thanks to the LORD, for he is good, for his steadfast love endures forever!" (cf. Ps. 100:5; 106:1; 136:1); and 1 John 1:5 declares that "God is light, and in him is no darkness at all." And Scripture is equally clear that the creation that God made was, like God, good and *only* good. "And God saw everything that he had made, and behold, it was very good. And there was evening and there was morning, the sixth day" (Gen. 1:31). Further still, it is also clear that in the future re-creation of God we call heaven, all evil, suffering, and pain will be done away with entirely. Revelation 21:3-4 states, "And I heard a loud voice from the throne saying, 'Behold, the dwelling place of God is with man. He will dwell with them, and they will be his people, and God himself will be with them as their God. He will wipe away every tear from their eyes, and death shall be no

more, neither shall there be mourning nor crying nor pain anymore, for the former things have passed away" (cf. Rev. 22:1-5). We must affirm, and we gladly affirm, then, that evil can have no place either in the very nature of God or in the created order as God created it, or in the heaven God will re-create. Suffering, then, is not essential to the nature of God or of creation as made by God.

Therefore when believers experience suffering, they are not wrong to feel deeply that what is happening to them simply is not at all right. When a loved one who knows the Lord dies, we accept the glorious truth that he or she is now "away from the body and at home with the Lord" (2 Cor. 5:8) while we also want to look death in the face and scream. No, suffering is not right, and evil is not good. Even when suffering is used for good, this does not *make* it good in itself. Suffering, affliction, pain, grief, and death are enemies that Christ came to defeat; they are not "goods" that make up the kingdom of righteousness. Christians should never be led to think that, if they were really spiritual, they should "feel good" about suffering and evil. Absolutely not. But notice: it is quite a different thing, as we shall see, to feel good about *God* in the midst of suffering. By way of analogy, couldn't a cancer patient feel good—really and genuinely good—about the surgeon that the Lord led her to, a doctor with enormous experience and background and a nationwide reputation for his capacities of analysis, treatment, and surgical skill, while at the same time despising the wickedness of the intruding cancerous tumor that has violated her body and her person? Yes, it is one thing to trust and love and adore and lean on God during suffering, but it is another thing altogether to think that our suffering is itself a "good." Suffering is not good; God does not think so, nor should we.

So let's be clear: evil is evil, suffering is suffering, and death is death. No amount of good that may be brought about through them can change what they are in their essence. And more than anyone, God—who is eternally and infinitely good—knows this! Hence, Christ has come, sin has been vanquished, the resurrection is a future certainty, and in the age to come "death shall be no more, neither shall there be mourning nor crying nor pain anymore, for the former things have passed away" (Rev. 21:4). Indeed, suffering is definitely *not* an essential good.

2. *But suffering is ordained by God, and often[2] it is intentionally used by God as an* instrumental *good.* That is, although suffering is not good in itself, it can and often does serve good purposes, as an instrument in God's hand. These good purposes, then, often stand behind suffering as part of God's wise and good design for people. And for Christians, this principle is the difference between despair and hope, between giving up and hanging on. Scripture is clear, and Christians have held over the centuries, that in his unsurpassable knowledge and wisdom, and by his unassailable holiness and goodness, God intentionally designs at least some suffering for the express purpose of bringing about some good through it. Consider some examples from Scripture where we see God employing pain and affliction as his instruments to do his good and perfect will.

First, suffering can sometimes be God's designed and appointed means of divine judgment over those who are opposed to him, even bringing them to death if their hardness of heart continues (e.g., Num. 16:31-35, 41-50; Isa. 10:5-19). In such cases, the suffering that divine judgment brings may function to bring some of those judged to repentance even if the judgment results in death for others. Also, much good often is intended by God for others who witness or learn of this judgment of God for sin and so turn from their own sin to follow God in obedience. So, while some of the suffering from divine judgment is punitive altogether (e.g., some of those judged are brought to death precisely by the judgment itself), in many cases this divine judgment may serve good purposes in others of those judged who repent and live, and surely in the lives of many others (e.g., us today, who read these biblical accounts of God's judgment on others) who learn from the sin and judgment so as themselves to live obediently before the Lord.

Second, similarly, God designs some pain and suffering to function as his tool of discipline to call wayward children back to him (e.g., Prov. 3:12; Heb. 12:9-11). As C. S. Lewis has said, pain is God's "megaphone" calling to rebellious hearts.[3] I have observed a tendency in

---

[2] As discussed at length in chapter 4, all evil and suffering is ordained by God, since he "works all things according to the counsel of his will" (Eph. 1:11). But not all suffering is ordained *as an instrumental good* for the one suffering. Some suffering is strictly punitive in nature. The clearest example is eternal hell, in which people will suffer forever such that their suffering cannot ultimately serve some good purpose for them. So, all suffering is ordained by God, but much (not all) is ordained to function as an instrumental good.

[3] C. S. Lewis, *The Problem of Pain* (New York: Macmillan, 1959), 81.

Christian circles today to dismiss quickly the idea that some suffering may have come into a believer's life due to sin. It is as though we have "overlearned" what the book of Job helpfully teaches us. In Job, one of the main lessons is that suffering is not necessarily due to sin; sometimes suffering happens to godly, faithful, obedient, caring, loving, gracious believers. So very true. However, the point of the book of Job simply cannot be that suffering is *never* due to sin! Rather, Christian people need to take to heart what Hebrews 12:9-11 tells us. Because God loves us so much, because he is our Father and he wants what is best for his children, he manifests his fatherly care on occasions by bringing discipline (i.e., suffering) into our lives in order that it will then yield "the peaceful fruit of righteousness to those who have been trained by it" (12:11). Yes, sometimes believers are called back to God, and sometimes they are preserved from further harm, through the gracious instrument of divinely-initiated suffering.

Third, affliction can be appointed by God for the growth and strengthening of believers' faith (e.g., Rom. 5:3-5; James 1:2-4). The difference between the previous point and this one is simply that, here, suffering is not linked with past sin, strictly speaking. Here, suffering does not function as God's rod of discipline for wayward children. Rather, God often designs affliction and pain and suffering to strengthen our faith even when we are being faithful, to cause us to trust him in even greater ways when we already have hearts of trust, to love and honor him now in the midst of great difficulty as we have loved and adored him during days of pleasure, bounty, and relative ease (Phil. 4:11-12). Yes, God intends our growth, and sometimes his wisdom ordains that suffering assist us in making the progress God knows is best.

One of the greatest illustrations of this divine purpose for suffering, I believe, is seen in Jesus' own life. Hebrews 5:8 tells us concerning Christ, "Although he was a son, he *learned obedience* through *what he suffered*" (emphasis added). What could it mean that he "learned obedience," and how would "suffering" contribute to this? Well, clearly it cannot be the case that Christ "learned obedience" by moving, in his own life, from disobedience into obedience! Christ never disobeyed— not once, ever! And the writer to the Hebrews is very aware of this, for just a few verses earlier he said of Christ that in every respect he "has been tempted as we are, *yet without sin*" (Heb. 4:15b, emphasis added).

Could it not be, instead, that Christ learned obedience by being given ever greater challenges to his obedience? That is, the Father designed that he would face, over the years, ever increasingly difficult demands that he would obey, leading to the ultimate demand of the Father upon his life: "My Son, go to the cross." Christ's own agony in the garden of Gethsemane (Matt. 26:36-46), crying out three times, "My Father, if it be possible, let this cup pass from me" (Matt. 26:39), surely is evidence that accepting the Father's will at this point was extraordinarily difficult. We dare not trivialize the agony of Christ here by thinking that somehow, because he was God, this obedience was easy or automatic. It was no such thing. Rather, as a man, Jesus obeyed the Father, in the power of the Spirit, and as such he had to "learn obedience" by being tested in harder and harder ways, leading up to the supreme test of the cross.[4] So then, suffering played a key role in Jesus' own life of trust and obedience before his Father. As such, do we think we should escape such important lessons? No, for us as well, God has designed that some of our growth will happen only as we are called into valleys of suffering. Yes indeed, God often appoints suffering and affliction for the growth and strengthening of believers' faith.

Fourth, affliction can reveal human weakness so that the surpassing strength and glory of God may be more evident (e.g., 2 Cor. 4:8-12; 12:8-10). Although momentarily we will consider more fully Paul's own experience of suffering the "thorn in the flesh," here we should observe the principle that the purpose Paul saw in the suffering he endured had to do ultimately with manifesting the surpassing greatness and glory of God in the midst of his suffering. As he says, "I will boast all the more gladly of my weaknesses, so that the power of Christ may rest upon me" (2 Cor. 12:9). What a godly man the apostle Paul was. I am constantly amazed at his Scripture-saturated mind, his gospel-proclaiming zeal, and his God-honoring heart. And what we see here is Paul's willingness to accept some great difficulty in his life, because through this difficulty it would be evident both to him and to others that it is God's strength, not his own, that enables him to minister as he does. That Christ's power be made known in a way that required his own weakness through suffering was enough for him. God some-

---

[4] See Gerald F. Hawthorne, *The Presence and the Power: The Significance of the Holy Spirit in the Life and Ministry of Jesus* (Dallas: Word, 1991), 179-184.

times ordains affliction, then, precisely for his glory, power, and grace to be more fully and clearly manifested.

Fifth, affliction can be given by God so that believers will be better able to minister to others who, likewise, experience pain and suffering in their lives (e.g., 2 Cor. 1:3-7). Over the years I have met and spoken with many people whose testimonies have been very similar in nature. They go something like this: I went through a very difficult time in my life and I thought that it would never end. I was deeply distressed and overwhelmed with the pain and agony of the situation. But God in his grace brought me through in ways I never would have anticipated. Since then, God has brought many people into my life with similar difficulties and he has used my past experiences both of suffering and of God's grace to encourage and strengthen the faith of others.

As Paul indicates in 2 Corinthians 1, God does intend that the comfort we receive from him be passed on. His grace is to be received, yes, but it is to be shared also. Suffering, then, is sometimes designed by God as the instrument of sharing and ministering his grace.

Sixth, suffering is simply a necessary and expected part of one's discipleship to Christ, in that following the path Christ walked will bring with it suffering to prove and test our allegiance to, and hope in, him alone (e.g., John 15:18-20; Phil. 3:10; 2 Tim. 3:12). Most of us have lived through a period of recent history in North America in which there has been little persecution, and when it has come, in most cases it has been relatively mild. Surely this has not been the experience of Christian people in many other ages of church history, nor is it the experience of many today in other parts of the world.[5] And of course, it may well be that those of us who live in Western cultures will find the growing antagonism and hostility to the exclusivity of Christ and the truth of the gospel to result in more overt and harsh forms of persecution. We must come to terms with Christ's call on our lives, that "If they persecuted me, they will also persecute you" (John 15:20). But may we also never lose sight of the hope that Jesus extends to those who suffer for him and the gospel:

---

[5] John Foxe, *Foxe's Christian Martyrs of the World,* revised ed. (Chicago, Ill.: Moody, n.d.); and for information regarding the state of Christian persecution throughout the world, see http://www.persecutedchurch.org.

"Blessed are those who are persecuted for righteousness' sake, for theirs is the kingdom of heaven. Blessed are you when others revile you and persecute you and utter all kinds of evil against you falsely on my account. Rejoice and be glad, for your reward is great in heaven, for so they persecuted the prophets who were before you" (Matt. 5:10-12).

We must prepare our minds, hearts, and wills not merely to accept but even to embrace whatever God has in store for us, as those who follow Christ as Savior and Lord. With Paul, we must affirm with passion, zeal, and hope, "to live is Christ, and to die is gain" (Phil. 1:21). If we have a wrongful and idolatrous grip on this world, we must let go of it. If we fear the possible pain and torture of suffering, we must look beyond the suffering to Jesus, "the founder and perfecter of our faith, who for the joy that was set before him endured the cross, despising the shame, and is seated at the right hand of the throne of God" (Heb. 12:2). If we waver in our confession of faith, unsure of whether Christ's death and resurrection alone is the exclusive hope for sinners, or whether the unsaved must know and believe the gospel of Christ to be saved, or whether there really is a hell—if we lack strong and firm convictions on these matters, we must gain them! The pressures to renounce the exclusivity of the truths regarding Christ and the gospel are so strong and growing that wavering here is fatal. May God grant grace and strength to Christian people to be faithful to the end, facing with joy and anticipation even the persecution and attending reward that come with being a follower of Christ.

3. *In particular, God has promised his children that nothing befalls their lives that is not ordered and used by him for their ultimate good.* Romans 8:28 offers to Christians a promise so precious, so comforting, it is unimaginable that one could deny this and still affirm the "same" Christian faith. For here we read, "And we know that for those who love God all things work together for good, for those who are called according to his purpose." This glorious hope for Christians stands diametrically opposed to the despair that is unavoidably conveyed in open theism, with its God who neither knows future suffering that will befall us nor is working any good purpose in and through it. So, when John Sanders says, "God does not have a specific purpose in mind for these

[tragic] occurrences,"[6] and when Greg Boyd asserts regarding the betrayal by her husband that the woman named "Suzanne" experienced, "She didn't have to abandon all confidence in her ability to hear God and didn't have to accept that somehow God intended this ordeal 'for her own good,'"[7] this counsel by open theists strips from Christians the very hope and confidence in God that Scripture intends them to have. Over and over, throughout the pages of Scripture, whether through the story of Job, or Joseph, or David, or Daniel, or Jesus, or Paul, or Peter, or so many, many more—throughout the Bible, the message is clear: God orchestrates and uses suffering in the lives of his children for the purpose of bringing to them some ultimate (and at times, some immediate) good. God *does* intend good purposes through suffering, and Christians are robbed of this precious confidence by open theism's denial of this precious truth.[8]

Recently I spoke at a conference in which we thought at some length together about how Christians should understand and face suffering. During the Q&A time, one sincere Christian woman asked, "I know that we are supposed to give thanks *in* everything that comes our way, but we're not expected to give thanks *for* everything, are we?" Well, the truth is, we are. Scripture commands both—thanks *in* and thanks *for* all that comes into our lives (see 1 Thess. 5:18 and Eph. 5:20, respectively). And, of course, this only makes sense. If the suffering that comes into our lives is pointless, if God has no good intent for it, and if all that it does is cause harm, then there is no reason to give thanks *in* the suffering, and certainly not *for* the suffering. You cannot genuinely give thanks in the suffering if you think at the time, there is simply nothing about this painful experience that will necessarily prove good; in fact, I should accept the fact that it probably is entirely pointless. For if that is the case, then it cannot possibly be a basis for giving thanks! God is not in it (in fact, he feels badly about it and wishes it weren't happening), Satan is chuckling over this, knowing that it serves no good purpose and will

---

[6] John Sanders, *The God Who Risks: A Theology of Providence* (Downers Grove, Ill.: InterVarsity Press, 1998), 262.

[7] Gregory A. Boyd, *God of the Possible: A Biblical Introduction to the Open View of God* (Grand Rapids, Mich.: Baker, 2000), 106.

[8] For lengthier discussions of problems with open theism, see chapter 10 of this book, and see also two books I've written critiquing its deeply troubling theology: in Bruce A. Ware, *God's Lesser Glory: The Diminished God of Open Theism* (Wheaton, Ill.: Crossway, 2000); and Ware, *Their God Is Too Small.*

only bring harm, and there is no assurance that the suffering will end any differently than it began—pointless, meaningless, and void of any and all possible good purpose. If that is how we think of suffering, we can only (rightly) despair *in* it and *for* it!

But if the promises of God are sure, and they are (!); if God has promised believers that he will ensure that *all things* will work together for their good (Rom. 8:28); if God has promised that "those who seek the LORD lack no good thing" (Ps. 34:10; cf. Ps. 84:11); and if God wishes us to embrace his loving commitment to us as demonstrated when he says, "He who did not spare his own Son but gave him up for us all, how will he not also with him graciously give us all things?" (Rom. 8:32); then we have good reason to give God thanks both *in* and *for* all that occurs. God will not fail! He reigns over the suffering of our lives, and he purposes our good through everything that happens, ensuring that all the good he intends for us to have, we will have. What hope, what confidence, what peace, what joy, and what strength, all in the midst of suffering, God wants his people to have.

4. *God is more concerned with our character than with our comfort, with our transformation than with the trials necessary to get us where he wants us to be.* Two passages sing this truth with echoes like the Hallelujah Chorus. James has the audacity (or so it would seem) to command suffering and persecuted Christians to, "Count it all joy, my brothers, when you meet trials of various kinds, for you know that the testing of your faith produces steadfastness. And let steadfastness have its full effect, that you may be perfect and complete, lacking in nothing" (James 1:2-4). *All joy.* What an incredible expectation and command. The only way that any person could find trials and afflic-tion "all joy" is to know that they have been designed for great gain and *ultimate joy.* Clearly the joy does not reside in the experience of affliction taken by itself. James is not living in denial. He is not trivial-izing the agony of affliction or the pain often endured in trials. But he encourages all believers to look past the pain to the purpose, i.e., to see what God intends to accomplish through it. We dare not fix our eyes so much on the affliction that we miss its God-designed outcome. And what outcome is that? Hear these words: ". . . *for you know* that the testing of your faith produces steadfastness . . . that you may be

perfect and complete, lacking in nothing." So now we see how a believer can have "all joy" in the midst of affliction. The believer with all joy knows with confidence and certainty that God's good purposes of his or her growth and maturity are being accomplished through the suffering. Because God cares most about our character transformation, and because this is what we should long for above all else for our own personal lives, the trials that God ordains for us can be received with *all joy.*

So, with Christians through the centuries who have understood exactly why James instructs them to "count it all joy" when suffering and trials come, we affirm the sovereign control of God over our suffering. God's good hand is not absent but present and active in and through the suffering, so that we can believe and hold on to our confidence that the suffering that God has designed for us to endure, he will use for the strengthening of our faith. Far from viewing trials as the purposeless by-products of living in a world in which forces of nature are run amuck, or in which wicked free creatures have their way in attempting to ruin our lives, rather we are instructed to see the powerful, wise, and good hand of God in all the trials of life, and so we have hope.

Similarly, Paul enjoins us believers to "rejoice in our sufferings, knowing that suffering produces endurance, and endurance produces character, and character produces hope, and hope does not put us to shame, because God's love has been poured into our hearts through the Holy Spirit who has been given to us" (Rom. 5:3-5). As with James, the only possible way that believers can rejoice and not despair in the face of suffering is if the good hand of God is in those very sufferings. Take away the providential hand of God, take away the good purpose served by the suffering, take away the character formation, hope, and holiness that stand behind the suffering, and you take away all reason to rejoice. Only because God intends good through suffering can Christians live their lives as Scripture commands, and as countless numbers of Christians have lived over the centuries. Because God cares most deeply about our conformity to the very character of Christ as his holy people (see Eph. 1:4 and Rom. 8:29), and because God has deemed it wise and good to enlist suffering as one of his tools to bring about this good and perfect goal, we too can rejoice in our sufferings—not that the sufferings in themselves are good, but that they have a built-in purpose that is good. Apart from this good purpose, there is no hope, but with this purpose well in mind and deeply rooted in our hearts, we truly can "count it all joy" and "rejoice."

5. *Accepting the divine purpose for suffering does not require a passive acquiescence to suffering.* Christians who believe that God's good purposes are fulfilled through suffering also realize that suffering *in itself* is not a good (as discussed above), and so deliverance from it may rightly be sought. Yet, while rightly seeking deliverance from suffering, Christians must also be ready to accept and embrace the possibility that God's best for us may include our continuing experience of the very suffering from which we correctly and passionately pray to be delivered. Paul's own experience here is instructive. Recall Paul's description of his struggle with affliction as he recounts it to us in 2 Corinthians 12:7-10:

> So to keep me from being too elated by the surpassing greatness of the revelations [described in 12:1-6], a thorn was given me in the flesh, a messenger of Satan to harass me, to keep me from being too elated. Three times I pleaded with the Lord about this, that it should leave me. But he said to me, "My grace is sufficient for you, for my power is made perfect in weakness." Therefore I will boast all the more gladly of my weaknesses, so that the power of Christ may rest upon me. For the sake of Christ, then, I am content with weaknesses, insults, hardships, persecutions, and calamities. For when I am weak, then I am strong.

The same Paul who admonished believers to "rejoice in our sufferings" (Rom. 5:3) here, in the midst of what must have been agonizing affliction, seeks God fervently to be released from the suffering he's undergoing. Is this an inconsistency? Not at all. For Paul knows that suffering is not a good thing in itself; its only "good" comes in what we learn through it, or how we grow because of it. So Paul pleads to the Lord in prayer three times that God would take the affliction from him. But when it becomes clear to him that this thorn in the flesh, sent by Satan, was actually God's ordained tool to accomplish in Paul the work that this alone could do, Paul was able (then and only then) to accept the suffering as part of God's good purpose in his life.

Notice, too, the instructive tension presented in this passage between Paul seeing this affliction as a messenger from *Satan* while praying to the *Lord* to remove it. This helps enormously in understanding Paul's mindset as he considered the nature of the suffering he currently underwent. In the midst of his suffering, Paul did not look to God merely to comfort him during this time of supposedly unwanted and purposeless affliction that had been brought to him exclusively from Satan. On the contrary, Paul prayed to God to *remove* the affliction, believing that God had full power and authority over this affliction and could remove it if he wished. So then, while this affliction came directly from Satan to harm Paul, indirectly and ultimately this affliction was permitted by the intentional agency and sovereign ordination of God, who could allow it to be given at all, could remove it when and if he wished, and would ordain that Paul experience it only if it served the good purposes that he (God), not Satan, designed it to bring.

It is only in light of Paul's confidence that God's hand, ultimately, is behind his present affliction that he can generalize the application of what he has here experienced: "Therefore I will boast all the more gladly of my weaknesses, so that the power of Christ may rest upon me. For the sake of Christ, then, I am content with weaknesses, insults, hardships, persecutions, and calamities. For when I am weak, then I am strong" (2 Cor. 12:9b-10). His movement from this "thorn" of affliction (singular), now to say that he will boast gladly of his weaknesses (plural), and be content with weaknesses, insults, hardships, persecutions, and calamities (all plural), indicates his view that all such experiences for believers are, similarly, under the oversight and providential guidance of God. Believers may have hope that when they seek God earnestly and humbly, and when God says no to their prayers for deliverance, he does so for their good. Such confidence alone can account for the boasting and contentment in weaknesses that Paul urges. "Never doubt," he would say to us, "that God is actively at work in and through the affliction, that God is for us, and that his good and sovereign purposes are accomplished through what he has designed us to experience."

Another instructive feature of this account deserves our attention.

Notice that Paul prayed *three times* for deliverance from this affliction. Not that 'three' is magical; that's not the point. But rather, consider the following principles we can derive from this account.

1) Paul's praying three times, instead of only once or not at all, indicates *persistence in prayer*. He might have looked at the seriousness of the situation, the extensiveness of the affliction, and concluded that it was just "not realistic" to keep praying about this (on this point, see also Rom. 4:18-22 for a most amazing example of persistent faith when it was not "realistic" to keep believing). Or he might simply have succumbed to discouragement in which he never seriously considered praying or, having begun, ceased immediately praying altogether. So, "three times" helps us see Paul's persevering faith in continuing to bring to God the deep desire and burden of his heart.

2) But praying three times, instead of endless prayers for deliverance, indicates *Paul's willingness to accept no as God's answer* to his fervent, heart-felt pleading. In other words, Paul prayed with persistence and perseverance, demonstrating his deep and real longing for God to grant what he sought, but then Paul assessed the stubborn truthfulness of his ongoing affliction and came to see that God would not deliver him as he wanted so badly. At this point, Paul's whole disposition toward that unwelcome trial changed. Previously, it was unwanted and hurtful only. Now, seeing the good hand of God in ordaining that he have it, it became something of a gift from God's love and longing for him and for his best. He stopped praying, not out of disbelief but out of even greater faith. He now came to see that God intended him to continue experiencing these afflictions because of the wise and good purposes that God had designed through—and only through—them.

Clearly, then, Paul's prayers to *escape* the suffering (i.e., he prayed three times for this) had now changed to a longing to *embrace* God's purpose in that very suffering (i.e., he then ceased praying for this). And mind you, this was no mere acceptance of the inevitability of this affliction. Rather, the "boasting" and "contentment" in this and other afflictions indicate that Paul now saw his weakness more for the good that it would accomplish than for the hardship that it continued to bring him. Such is the wonder of knowing that God's good hand stands behind, and not apart from, our suffering.

Given these divinely ordained reasons for any and all suffering that comes into our lives as believers, it is no wonder that James can so boldly proclaim, "Count it all joy, my brothers, when you meet trials of various kinds" (James 1:2). Graham Kendrick has captured something of the wonder of God's purposes in suffering in the lyrics to "Consider It Joy." May God enable us to see more clearly his good and wise hand in the trials of life he ordains for us.

Though trials will come
Don't fear, don't run
Lift up your eyes
Hold fast, be strong
Have faith, keep on believing
Lift up your eyes
For God is at work in us
Moulding and shaping us
Out of his love for us
Making us more like Jesus

Consider it joy, pure joy
When troubles come
Many trials will make you strong
Consider it joy, pure joy
And stand your ground
Then at last you'll wear a crown

Though trials will come
Won't fear, won't run
We'll lift up our eyes
Hold fast, be strong
Have faith, keep on believing
We'll lift up our eyes
For God is at work in us
Moulding and shaping us
Out of his love for us
Making us more like Jesus

Joy, pure joy
Consider it joy, pure joy

Joy, pure joy
Consider it joy, pure joy

Patiently trusting him
Ready for anything
'Til we're complete in him
In everything more like Jesus

Consider it joy, pure joy
When troubles come
Many trials will make you strong
Consider it joy, pure joy
And stand your ground
Then at last you'll wear a crown
Then at last you'll wear a crown
Then at last you'll wear a crown[9]

BEHIND THE VEIL, BUT NOT BLIND

While God often chooses not to reveal to us exact reasons for why particular instances of suffering occur, yet he has not left us blind altogether on this matter. Rather, in his grace, he has made clear his ultimate and glorious purposes for suffering, and most importantly, he has made clear that suffering and affliction are tools in his hands, employed by him in the manner he specifies, serving the exact reasons that he has designed, and always directed for the good of his children and the glory of his name. So, just as Paul was concerned for those whose loved ones had passed away, that they "may not grieve as others do who have no hope" (1 Thess. 4:13b), so too here, our longing and prayer is that as God designs and orchestrates the suffering in our lives, we will not suffer as others do who have no hope. Rather, may we trust the heart of God, and place confidence in the wisdom of God, and believe the power of God, so that our hope truly may be stayed on him.

And let us remember Job. Behind the scenes, backstage, the Director oversees every movement and action that occurs, ensuring that as the plot unfolds and the story develops, the results are what he has designed

---

[9] Graham Kendrick, "Consider It Joy," ©2001 Make Way Music, P.O. Box 263, Croydon CR9 5AP, UK. International copyright secured. All rights reserved. Used by permission.

and according to what he intends. May we be among those who have ears to hear the sometimes nearly inaudible voice of the Director, reminding us who are caught up in the fray of the story's unfolding drama, "Don't be afraid. Place your trust and confidence in Me. For these evil forces may do as they wish, but remember, and never, never forget, that they will act only within boundaries I establish, and for purposes I have long ago ordained, fulfilling what will only rightly be understood as My work. Be assured of this, my child, and hope!"

Yes, by God's grace, we will remember Job.

7

Living Before God:
Trusting the Character of God in Prayer

LIVING HUMAN LIFE CORAM DEO

If at times we are called to live *behind* God, veiled to his reasons for the suffering we endure, we are called in all of life to live *before* God (*coram Deo*) with trust, faith, obedience, loyalty, and love. That is, our lives are to represent what is true of both God and us by nature, respectively. We are to relate to God in ways fitting to the nature and reality that is true of him, and from the nature and reality that is true of us. We can live before God with integrity only as we truly are, recognizing and responding appropriately to the way he truly is. We have already developed at length some of the important truths on both sides of this relationship—truths of God's nature and of ours—but for the sake of now considering more fully life lived before God, we need to be reminded of the essentials of our respective natures.

God, by nature, is completely satisfied in the fullness of his infinite worth as the fully self-sufficient and tri-personal God that he is. He is glorious and mighty, infinitely wise and powerful, ruling the heavens and the earth as the uncontested sovereign King over all. In short, God is both self-sufficient and sovereign. He possesses all and he rules all. He has no intrinsic needs or lacks, and the power and authority of his sovereign hand is never stayed. Both of these truths are essential to a biblical understanding of God, and as we will see here, both are essential to a biblical understanding of prayer. But first, let us review a bit more thoroughly the nature of God's self-sufficiency and his sovereignty, and then of our natures in light of what we understand about God.

God exists eternally independent of creation, possessing within himself, intrinsically and infinitely, every quality and perfection. All goodness is God's goodness, and he possesses it in infinite measure. All beauty is God's beauty, and he possesses it in infinite measure. All power and wisdom and every perfection or quality that exists, exists in God, who possesses each and every one infinitely and intrinsically. Therefore, God needs none of what he has made, and nothing external to God can contribute anything to him, for in principle nothing can be added to this One who possesses already every quality without measure. Instead, everything that exists external to God does so only because God has granted it existence and has filled it with any and every quality it possesses (Acts 17:24-25).

And not only is God eternally and infinitely self-sufficient, he likewise is universally and incontestably sovereign over the world he has made. As the chastened and corrected King Nebuchadnezzar of Babylon exclaimed, "he [God] does according to his will among the host of heaven and among the inhabitants of the earth; and none can stay his hand or say to him, 'What have you done?'" (Dan. 4:35b). God elects and predestines what he wills, and he does so according to his purpose "who works all things according to the counsel of his will" (Eph. 1:11b). And in his ruling of the universe, and his commanding of kings, princes, and nations, God neither receives counsel (Isa. 40:13-14) nor is he, in any respect, thwarted by the collective power and will of humankind (Dan. 4:35a). This God, the true and living God, is both fully self-sufficient and hence independent of any intrinsic need for the world, and fully sovereign and hence creation's ultimate governing wisdom and power, ruling all the affairs and events of the world in precise fulfillment of his designed purposes.

By contrast, we human creations of God have no existence apart from God's gracious and creative word by which he spoke into existence *ex nihilo* what formerly had no life or any quality apart from his will to create (Heb. 11:3; Rev. 4:11). By our created natures, then, we are needy, helpless, and dependent, receiving from God everything that is required for our lives. And when sin is added to the picture, our natures, now as fallen, become warped and twisted, so that our minds, affections, wills, and bodies all suffer the effects of sin. Though we once knew truth (given to us) and had whole bodies, minds, and emotions (given to us), yet now, due to sin, we become misguided, foolish, and deceived, and our bodies show constantly the marks of our fall to death.

The contrast could not be greater. While God possesses his infinite fullness intrinsically, we possess the pittance we have derivatively. While God needs nothing that he has made, we need him and what he provides for us every moment of our lives. While God's hand cannot be stayed and his will cannot ultimately be defeated, we have hands too frail and wills too weak to affect anything in his creation save what he purposely permits. He is, in a word, independent; we are, in a word, dependent. And if we are ever tempted to doubt this, all we need do is to bring to mind what would happen to us should God suddenly remove from our immediate environment the oxygen we now depend on for our next breath.

Clearly one of the most staggering, humbling, and profound teachings in all of Scripture is that God simply does not need the world that he has made and that he rules, and included in this, he does not need any of us, his human creation (Acts 17:24-25). Whereas our need for him is absolute, his need for us is nonexistent. Living *coram Deo* cannot get off the ground unless we start here.

THE CHRISTIAN'S LIFE OF PRAYER LIVED OUT CORAM DEO

Given this context in which human life is to be lived out before God, recognizing the true natures of God and of us, respectively, one wonders seriously, then, why God chose to make prayer—petitionary prayer specifically—a part of the experience of his people with himself. Given who God is, and who we are, why did God institute the practice of prayer?

After all, think about it. When we bring our requests before God in prayer, can we ever inform God of anything? The answer clearly is no. By prayer we never can tell God anything that he doesn't already know. His knowledge is boundless, as the psalmist proclaims (Ps. 147:5), and it includes everything that can be known about everything, whether past, present, or future. God challenges the pretender deities of Isaiah's day to state what is going to happen in the future so that we may know that they are gods (Isa. 41:23). But of course they cannot, because they are not. Therefore, God mocks and ridicules both them and anyone who would bow down and worship these so-called deities (Isa. 41:24, 29).[1]

In addition, God's knowledge of us is perfect, even far beyond what we can know about ourselves. As David declares, God searches us and knows us intimately, knowing our every move, our thoughts, and knowing even the words we say before they come off our tongues (Ps. 139:1-5). And with David we affirm, "Such knowledge is too wonderful for me; it is high; I cannot attain it" (Ps. 139:6). But perhaps, we might wonder, what about the deepest desires and felt needs of our hearts? Perhaps here we can inform God. But again, we are instructed by Scripture that this simply cannot be. 1 Chronicles 28:9 tells us, ". . . for the Lord searches all hearts and understands every plan and thought"; and 1 Samuel 16:7 says, "For the Lord sees not as man sees: man looks on the outward appearance, but the Lord looks on the heart." And recall Jesus' admonition to his followers not to worry about their lives, even for the food or clothing that they need to live. After drawing some analogies of God's care from the realm of nature, he then directs his next words of instruction to the root of the anxiety of their hearts, and says, "Therefore, do not be anxious, saying, 'What shall we eat?' or 'What shall we drink?' or 'What shall we wear?' For the Gentiles seek after all these things, and your heavenly Father knows that you need them all. But seek first the kingdom of God and his righteousness, and all these things will be added to you" (Matt. 6:31-33). Amazingly, after just having taught his disciples to pray, ". . . Give us this day our daily bread" (Matt. 6:11), he then tells them that their heavenly Father already knows their needs for food, drink, and clothing. Surely in prayer, then, when they ask the Father to provide for their needs, they never can be informing God of what they long for. He knows it already.

Is it possible, though, that we might have some insight or perspective that would assist God as he considers some of the issues we bring to him in our prayers? Can he at least benefit from *our* point of view as he considers what is best to do? Again, in view of God's supremacy, the idea becomes silly. Recall the rhetorical questions God asks through the prophet Isaiah: "Whom did he [God] consult, and who made him under-

---

[1] For discussion of God's supremacy and exclusive deity when compared to the idols chided in Isaiah 41–48, see Bruce A. Ware, *God's Lesser Glory: The Diminished God of Open Theism* (Wheaton, Ill.: Crossway, 2000), 100-121.

stand? Who taught him the path of justice, and taught him knowledge, and showed him the way of understanding?" (Isa. 40:14). God seeks no counsel because he needs none. It strictly is impossible for anything we might think, or perspectives we might have, or proposed plans we might wish to suggest, or deep longings of our hearts—it is absolutely impossible for these or any other sort of personal information shared from us to God *ever* to instruct God, inform God, counsel God, teach God, or enlighten God. Simply put, he knows it all—period.

So, why prayer? What is the point, if anything and everything we bring to God in prayer he already knows more fully and accurately than we? Why does he want us to bring our burdens to him? Why does he command us to pray without ceasing? What is the point, when everything we tell him or ask him is already fully known by him? Or, think again about Jesus' instruction to his disciples not to be anxious about their need for food or clothing. Remember Jesus had just instructed them to pray, "Give us this day our daily bread" (Matt. 6:11), when he then encourages them not to be anxious about the food and clothing they need, because "your heavenly Father knows that you need them all" (Matt. 6:32). Now, we might imagine reading instead, "Since your heavenly Father knows that you need these things already, there is no need to pray about them. Really, prayer is pointless, because anything you pray for, well, the fact is that the Father has already known about it from before the world began. Any desire, any fear, any need, any request—he already knows. So, don't bother praying. Since the Father already knows whatever you might say or ask of him, prayer simply is a waste of time."

But of course, Jesus does not talk this way, and the fact is, he does instruct his disciples to pray for the very things that he says the Father already knows. Clearly, Jesus doesn't see a conflict between 1) our complete and total inability to inform God of anything, and 2) our prayers being meaningful, significant, and necessary. But how can this be? Why did God institute and command the practice of prayer, and what is prayer intended to accomplish? Allow me to suggest just two broad and glorious purposes that are fulfilled in prayer, purposes that get at the very heart of what it means to live life *coram Deo*. The first of these purposes of prayer is rooted in the *self-sufficiency* of God, i.e., his infinite and intrinsic possession of every quality and perfection within his very being; and the second purpose of prayer extends from the *sovereignty* of God, i.e., God's absolute authority, wisdom, and power to plan and carry out his perfect will, over heaven and earth, without failure or defeat of any detail or of its overall purposes. So, what is prayer? And why has God designed that his people pray? And how is prayer linked to these characteristics of God's nature?

1. *God has devised prayer as a means to draw us into close and intimate relationship with him, the self-sufficient God who possesses all.* Marvel at the fact that although God already knows our needs, and already knows every request we could ever make, nonetheless he commands us to bring these very needs and requests before him. Why? Certainly not so that he can learn what these are from us. Rather, the God who does not need us is nevertheless passionate about relationship with us. Although he cannot gain or benefit from what we bring to him, he deeply desires us to come before him with all of our concerns. Admonitions like "casting all your anxieties on him, because he cares for you" (1 Pet. 5:7), and "do not be anxious about anything, but in everything by prayer and supplication with thanksgiving let your requests be made known to God. And the peace of God, which surpasses all understanding, will guard your hearts and your minds in Christ Jesus" (Phil. 4:6-7), show us how much God wants us to come before him with all our needs. He longs for us to demonstrate our dependence upon him and our absolute trust in his character by coming to him in petitionary prayer.

Clearly, God does not need us to bring our concerns to him for him to know what we need or to know how best to act. He is God! He knows perfectly our backgrounds, our families, our friends, our circumstances, our jobs, our relationships, our struggles, our difficulties, our needs, our desires, our fears, our dreams, our longings, our strengths, our weaknesses, our successes, our failures, our sins. He doesn't need us to pray. He doesn't learn anything when we do. He isn't helped in knowing better what course of action to take. The fact is, nothing that we are or have or give can benefit God in any respect whatsoever, and our prayers are no exception. Therefore, God's purpose in instituting prayer, and in longing for us to pray, simply cannot have to do with some supposed help to God that prayer is to him.

Rather, to a large degree, prayer has to do with one simple thing:

relationship—relationship *coram Deo,* that is. One great and glorious reason why God devised prayer was as a mechanism to draw us to himself, to help us see how much we need him, to face us constantly with the realization that he is everything that we are not. We are weak, but he is strong; we are foolish, but he is wise; we are untrustworthy, but he is faithful; we are ignorant, but he knows everything; we are poor and empty, but he is rich and full. Imagine this: although God does not need any of what we bring to him in prayer, he longs for us to bring all that we do and so much more! He wants us to pray without ceasing (1 Thess. 5:17) in part because our need for him never ceases. Prayer is not instituted, then, as a means of helping God out. Just the opposite, it is for our sake, and for ours alone. In God's commands to pray, we are compelled by the force of divine authority to come and drink of the living water, to receive bread from heaven, and to realize afresh moment by moment by moment that all that we long for, and everything that is good, is found in one and only one place: in God.

This is like no human relationship on earth, to be sure. In no human relationship is one of the parties self-sufficient! No husband or wife or friend alive is "needless." But God is. Remember Romans 11:36: "from him and through him and to him are" . . . all things! And Acts 17:25: God is not "served by human hands, as though he needed anything, since he himself gives to all mankind life and breath and everything." And James 1:17: "Every good gift and every perfect gift is from above, coming down from the Father of lights with whom there is no variation or shadow due to change." Indeed, in this relationship *coram Deo* one of the parties has it all (literally), and the other is desperately needy. God knows this better than we do, given our propensity to pretension (otherwise known as sinful pride), and so he calls us, summons us, commands us, woos us, entices us, admonishes us, and in every way longs for us . . . to pray.

What he wants for us so much in our praying is simply to see him for who he is, and in light of that glorious vision, to see ourselves for who we are. Remember the prophet Isaiah, who was granted a vision of the Lord sitting on his throne lofty and exalted, with the train of his robe filling the temple, and seraphim hovering with eyes and feet covered, exclaiming, "Holy, holy, holy is the LORD of hosts; the whole earth is full of his glory!" Having beheld God in his splendor and majesty,

Isaiah fell before this glorious and holy God and confessed, "Woe is me! For I am lost; for I am a man of unclean lips and I dwell in the midst of a people of unclean lips; for my eyes have seen the King, the LORD of hosts!" (Isa. 6:1-5). God longs for us to know the incomparable wisdom and wealth, the glory and goodness, the majesty and mercy, the sufficiency and supremacy, the compassion and kindness that are exclusively and infinitely his. And with this, he longs for us to know and embrace, within the very depths of our own souls, the immensity of our total dependency upon him.

But that's not all. Amazingly, God longs for us to know yet one more thing, and it is this: God loves to share the bounty. He loves being the Giver. He loves granting to his humble and dependent children what is best for them. He takes great pleasure in being the source of "every good gift and every perfect gift," and he is lavish and generous and gracious and compassionate so that "no good thing does he withhold from those who walk uprightly" (Ps. 84:11). Therefore, he summons his people . . . to pray.

Listen afresh to the heart of God from the teaching of our Savior:

> "Ask, and it will be given to you; seek, and you will find; knock, and it will be opened to you. For everyone who asks receives, and the one who seeks finds, and to the one who knocks it will be opened. Or which one of you, if his son asks him for bread, will give him a stone? Or if he asks for a fish, will give him a serpent? If you then, who are evil, know how to give good gifts to your children, how much more will your Father who is in heaven give good things to those who ask him!" (Matt. 7:7-11).

This is much of what prayer is about. To know the riches of God and the poverty of our human lives is one of the key foundation pillars for prayer. As we pray in humble dependence, God grants from the store-house of his treasury. And as we are enriched by God, we then give to him our heartfelt thanksgiving and honor and worship. It is the heart of God to give, so he calls his people to ask.

Relationship *coram Deo*, then, is what God longs to further through prayer. Prayer is not an end in itself but a God-ordained, God-designed means by which God extends mercy and grace to our lives. Through prayer, God gives himself to us and we are drawn into his presence and his fullness. We do ourselves no favor, then, when we hold on to pretenses of self-ability and self-attainment, for in any and every way that we refuse to humble ourselves before God, we lose. But God, in his grace, wants us to gain! And therefore, God in his grace wants us to want him! "Come to me" is heard not only on Jesus' lips as he speaks to Jerusalem (Matt. 11:28); it echoes throughout the Scriptures. As we close this section with one more entreaty from God, may our response be to hear, and to heed, and to come, and . . . to pray:

> Come, everyone who thirsts, come to the waters;
>   and he who has no money, come, buy and eat!
> Come, buy wine and milk
>   without money and without price.
> Why do you spend your money for that which is not bread,
>   and your labor for that which does not satisfy?
> Listen diligently to me, and eat what is good,
>   and delight yourselves in rich food.
> Incline your ear, and come to me;
>   hear, that your soul may live (Isa. 55:1-3a).

2. *God has devised prayer as a means of enlisting us as participants in the work he has ordained, as part of the outworking of his sovereign rulership over all.* Marvel at the fact that although God possesses absolute authority, wisdom, and power by which he devises exactly the plan of his choosing for all of his creation for all of its history, and by which he carries out that plan in meticulous detail, without failure or defeat, nonetheless, he commands his people to pray *because* whether they pray or not makes a difference! But surely some would have us believe that prayer cannot really make a difference, and that prayer must actually be an exercise in futility, in a universe over which God exercises absolute sovereign control. If God "does according to his will among the host of heaven and among the inhabitants of the earth; and none can stay his hand or say to him, 'What have you done?'" (Dan. 4:35b), then why pray?

And there is something very important about this question that we should note. The premise of the question, that God has absolute sovereignty, is absolutely true! After all, this is exactly what the Scripture text just quoted plainly says, as do scores of other passages. So we won't solve this problem by denying what Scripture clearly teaches, and by stripping away from God the self-proclaimed qualities of his deity and majesty. How dare we diminish what God has said about himself? How dare we think that we know better the way God should be than the way God has told us himself? How dare we make God more acceptable to the culture in which we live while making God unacceptable to God himself! If we love and fear God—the true and living God of the Bible—and if our passion is to know and believe the truth, then we will stand faithful with Scripture no matter how many persons, Christian or non-Christian, object. Let us live with less-than-fully-resolved tensions, if necessary, but let us live faithful to God and his word.

Since we accept the premise of the question, then what is the purpose and significance of prayer in a universe over which God exercises absolute sovereign control? As with our previous discussion on the relation between God's self-sufficiency and prayer, here, too, the answer leads us into a green and lush meadow of delights with rugged mountainous splendor surrounding us in every direction. In a word, the relation of divine sovereignty and prayer is *participation*.

Being the sovereign God that he is, God simply is in no need of our participation with him in accomplishing his work. Sometimes we think so, because we mistakenly confuse the *call* of God to work for him with a *need* in God for us so to work. Let's take the call of God to missions as an example. *Does* God call some of his children to serve him by crossing cultural boundaries in order to bring the gospel of Jesus Christ to those who have never heard? Absolutely yes! From Matthew 28:18-20, to Acts 1:8, to Paul's own conversion and calling in Acts 9:1-19, to the spread of the gospel through much of the known world by the end of the book of Acts, yes, God calls some of his children to serve in the missionary enterprise. But, *must* God call some to serve as missionaries in order for others to hear the gospel and be saved?

We must be very careful in how we think about this question. It is not a simple one. The answer, it seems, must be yes and no simultaneously, but in different senses. In light of God's design that the lost hear the gospel as missionaries go and preach, *yes,* God must call some as missionaries for this work to be done; but in the sense that God could have chosen a different mechanism to get the gospel to lost people, *no,* it is not necessary in an absolute sense for God to call missionaries for people to be saved. After all, he is sovereign, and he could accomplish this task in a multitude of ways. He could write it in the sky, or proclaim it from a heavenly loudspeaker, or send the message by way of angels, or speak directly into the minds and hearts of individuals. But God has designed not to do it in these ways. Rather, he has designed for the gospel to be spread through his call on the hearts of some to go and preach, so that others might hear, and believe, and call upon the name of the Lord, and be saved (Rom. 10:13-15).

Because God is sovereign, he can rule the world unilaterally, if you will, with no participation from anyone at all. His infinite wisdom and power, along with his uncontested authority, give him all he needs to accomplish everything he wants to do without your help or mine. His sovereignty, then, renders prayer unnecessary—in principle.

But here is where the wonder and amazement enter again; here is where we approach that meadow and get our first glimpse of its delicate wildflowers and mountainous backdrop. Although God is fully capable of "doing it on his own," nonetheless, he enlists his people to join him in the work that is his, and his alone ultimately. And one chief means that he employs for our participation with him in this work is prayer. How does prayer function, then, as a tool designed by God to enlist our participation in his work? Consider the following.

First, and central to what follows, God has designed not only that prayer come to be, but that prayer sometimes be a *necessary means* for accomplishing the ends he has ordained. In other words, God purposely designed how things would work so that some of what he accomplishes can only be accomplished as people pray. All of the commands and admonitions in Scripture to pray certainly indicate that this is the case. Consider, for example, James 5:14-15: "Is anyone among you sick? Let him call for the elders of the church, and let them pray over him, anointing him with oil in the name of the Lord. And the prayer of faith will save the one who is sick, and the Lord will raise him up." Surely this implies that prayer (of the elders, in this case) is part of the God-ordained means by which God's healing of the sick would occur. If prayer were not linked with the outcome (i.e., healing), then why admonish the sick to call for the elders to pray? But notice another important point: since God is sovereign, he could just heal this sick person as he wills, fully apart from whether anyone prays or not. God's power to heal is not subject to or hindered by lack of prayer, in the absolute sense. Yet here it is clear that God has chosen that the fulfillment of his work is tied to prayer. Some of God's work, then, is designed by God to be fulfilled only as people pray.

Second, prayer functions as a tool designed by God to enlist our participation in his work as we are led, by the Spirit, to have our minds and wills reshaped to the mind and will of God. Recall that in our Lord's prayer, he told us to pray, "Your kingdom come, *your will be done,* on earth as it is in heaven" (Matt. 6:10, emphasis added). This indicates that the perfect will of God precedes my praying and yours. We are not told to pray, "your will be *formed*," but "your will be *done*." As should be abundantly clear from our preceding discussion on God's self-sufficiency and prayer, God doesn't need to be informed by us about the state of affairs of some situation, nor does he need (or want!) advice regarding what is best to do.

If anyone thinks that somehow, in a literal sense, our prayers can change God's mind such that he will now do what he never before intended because of some new information we have brought to him, I would like to ask that person, Who do you think you are! What could you (or I) know that has escaped God's attention? What perspective do you (or I) have that he lacks? When we consider the extremely limited knowledge we have, our lack of foresight compared to God's perfect foreknowledge, or our record of poor decisions and bad judgment in far more cases than we'd like to remember, not to mention our morally twisted natures and as-of-yet unreformed affections and values, do we really want God to listen to our advice? I could not act more foolishly than to come to God in prayer suggesting that he see things my way and do as I want. No, "your will be done" means that Another's will precedes mine, and thankfully, this will has been formed out of an omniscient (all-knowing) and omnisapient (all-wise) mind and heart. In prayer, we seek to pray "according to the will" of God, and "in the name" of Jesus, indicating our longing to have our minds, desires, affections, and wills reshaped to be more like God's.

Third, prayer is God's tool to enlist our participation in his work as we pray on behalf of others and so minister God's grace to them. Ministers of grace! What a privilege and precious calling this is. Bear in mind, here, the first point above. It is only because prayer functions necessarily as a God-ordained means for the fulfillment of some of God's work that this ministry of prayer on behalf of others can take place. But by God's grace, he has chosen to minister some of his grace to others through our prayers. When you hear someone say something like, "Well, all I could do is pray," remember that while this statement makes it sound as though nothing *really* useful is being done when a person prays, from God's vantage point one of his most important and strategic means of accomplishing his work is being employed. To use a warfare analogy, praying for another is not like rolling bandages back at the base; rather, prayer constitutes the General's orders to bring out the big guns and take them to the front lines. Why is prayer this important since clearly God did not need to do it this way? The answer, as we have seen, is captured in one word: participation. God has willed to enlist our participation in his work, and prayer is one of the ways he gets us to the front lines.

Fourth, prayer enlists our participation in God's work as we are made more fully aware of what he is doing and, as a result, praise him when it is accomplished. What if God did his work unilaterally, without using prayer? If he did this, so much of what he accomplished would take place with little if any *notice* by his people, and little if any *praise* to God for the great work he had done. But by designing prayer, he allows us the privileged position of being "insiders" to kingdom strategy and kingdom operations. We are drawn into the unfolding of his plans, we sense the great stakes that are faced, and we realize how important it is for God to act and work and reign. And when prayers are answered and God's work is done, we will be able to praise and worship him for the things we have seen accomplished, having anticipated the need for the answer, and having been attuned to the marvelous work that God has now done. Great joy is ours both in being enlisted to pray, and in seeing the results of prayer. This joy of God is ours since he has graciously granted us the privilege of being involved in his work by prayer.

Last, prayer is a tool designed by God to enlist our participation in his work as we persist in prayer, sometimes for long periods and through agonizing trials. Through these times of persevering prayer, God ministers his grace, comfort, peace, and hope to us, even when his answer to our deep longings, ultimately, is no. As we observed in the previous chapter, Paul prayed earnestly three times for the thorn in the flesh to be removed, and when God said no to Paul, he had grown much as a result

(2 Cor. 12:7-10). Prayer, then, is as much a tool of our sanctification, by God's grace, as it is a tool of ministering God's grace to others.

THE SATISFACTION OF LIFE LIVED CORAM DEO

Both God's self-sufficiency and his sovereignty have wondrous implications for the Christian's life of prayer. Even though prayer is not necessary to God, and even though his work could fully have been accomplished without the use of prayer, yet God has chosen the instrument of prayer to be a great and gracious gift to his children. By prayer, we are drawn into *relationship* with the One from whom all blessings flow; and by prayer, we are called into *participation* in the work of the One from whom all sovereign rulership is made known. Because God is *self-sufficient*, we come in prayer with joyous anticipation, knowing that in God's grace he offers of his fullness for our emptiness and of his wisdom for our folly. We believe the word announced, that God "rewards those who seek him" (Heb. 11:6b), and so we come and seek God in prayer, and we find in him our comfort, our strength, our direction, our forgiveness, our joy, indeed our life. And because God is *sovereign*, we come in prayer believing that God has ordained this instrument as his gracious tool by which he enlists us into participation in his glorious work. We are not mere bystanders, though many of God's works simply unfold before us as we are granted eyes to see and to rejoice. Rather, we are involved participants through prayer in the very work of God himself, as prayer is made a necessary means for accomplishing much of God's ordained work.

What satisfaction there is, then, to live life before the face of *this God*. Although he is both self-sufficient and fully sovereign, in his grace and love he calls us into rich and wondrous relationship, and he beckons us into meaningful and fruitful participation with him in the work he wills to accomplish. Even though prayer could be rendered pointless in light of God's character, it is his very character itself that summons both our relationship and our participation with him. It is all of grace, then. All of God's love. All out of his longing that we, his people, enter into the fullness of who he is and what he does. Yes indeed, the life of truest satisfaction is the one lived *coram Deo*.

8

Living Under God:
Seeing the Generosity of God
in Our Service to Him

SERVICE AS GENEROUS OR ONEROUS?

If at times we are called to live *behind* God, veiled to the reasons for the suffering he designs for us to endure, and if in all of life we are called to live *before* God (*coram Deo*) in prayerful relationships and participation with the fully self-sufficient and sovereign God, we also are called, as his servants, to live *under* God, receiving from him the commands and orders we are to carry out as well as the empowerment and grace to do what God so ordains. Under his authority and dependent on his provision—this, too, marks our lives as lived out in relationship with the true and living God.

But why, you might ask, does this chapter title suggest that our service to God is somehow an expression of *his* generosity? Certainly God's service to us is generous of him. But just as surely (or so it would seem) it cannot be that God is generous in allowing *us* to serve *him*—and this for two reasons. First, it sounds a bit like the cunning father with a child not yet old enough to catch the "trick" when he says, "Say, how about let's have some fun together and get out there and pull up some weeds." As we all know, this works only for a short time, and soon even slightly older children catch on. "Ah," they come to reason, "this isn't fun, it's work!" So, are you claiming that God is treating us like little children, calling us to "have some fun" when really, what he has for us is plain old hard work? Second, given the kind of work God often calls his people to, the sacrifices and hardships involved simply make it impossible to see "serving God" as generous. Generous of us, perhaps, but work like this, quite frankly, is onerous, not generous.

Since much of this chapter will address this question, I'll offer just a brief reply at this point—perhaps enough to whet your appetite for more that is unfolded shortly. Service as an expression of generosity by God (i.e., God's generosity shown in calling us and permitting us to serve him) makes sense when you understand two grand truths in particular about God. First, as the *sovereign Ruler* over all, he calls us to serve on the side that wins, with orders and commands that advance kingdom purposes and that also result in our greater well-being. In other words, it's a win-win-win situation: we're called onto the winning team, commanded to do a winning work in kingdom advance, performing a winning service for our own well-being, both now and for the age to come. Second, since the God who calls us to serve is himself the fully *self-sufficient Giver,* everything needed for the completion of our work— yes, everything!—is provided by him. His empowerment for our service means that a calling and commandment that otherwise would have been impossible for us to do is now not only possible but cannot, in the end, fail. How gracious and kind and caring, and yes, generous of God to call us into this glorious service.

In what follows, we will consider more carefully the lavish generosity of God in calling us, commanding us, equipping us, empowering us, and rewarding us in relation to the work that is his alone to do. We are granted the privilege of being sharers in God's glorious gospel and kingdom work, and since this is for a lifetime of service, we should understand better what this particular work is all about. First, we will consider something of what this service is not. A common view of Christian service will be put to the test and found wanting. Second, we'll consider service under the sovereignty of God, as we submit to his authority and carry out his command. And third, we'll examine service fueled by the self-sufficiency of God, and we'll be led to revel in the generosity of God both to command what he will, and to will what he commands, as Augustine put it. That God is both absolutely sovereign and fully self-sufficient forms the basis, again here, for the expression of his tender-hearted generosity in commanding his children to "serve the Lord."

WHEN SERVICE PRETENDS TO BE OVER GOD, NOT UNDER GOD

In his classic treatment of the attributes of God, *The Knowledge of the Holy*, A. W. Tozer comments that calls to Christian service are often insults to the might, majesty, and magnificence of God.[1] In far too numerous cases, Christians are appealed to in a way such as this: "God wants to do this wonderful and glorious work, but he needs you to step up and volunteer. If you don't do it, how will it get done? God needs laborers to be willing to go into the harvest, and if you refuse to heed the call of God on your life, to go and to serve, God's work will remain unfinished." I grew up in a Christian home with godly parents and was raised in a Baptist church. From my earliest years I remember vividly calls to missionary service and full-time Christian service that were variations of the one just sketched. These "calls" to service were often made by visiting preachers, or at special missions conferences, but each time another such call was delivered, I felt that it was my personal obligation and responsibility to help God out. "Poor God," I recall thinking as a boy. "All this work to do and just not enough people willing to help." Even from a young age, I felt the pangs of guilt and sensed that the fate of lost tribes in Africa was resting on my shoulders—was I willing to serve God?

It was not until my freshman year in college that my whole understanding of God and his relation to the world first became unraveled, and then slowly re-stitched. The main source that the Lord used in my life at this point was Tozer's book. I read this book at a point of deep spiritual searching at the recommendation of my brother-in-law, Wayne Pickens. Wayne, for many years now a very fine pastor, was at that time a seminary student, and he thought this book would help with what I most wanted—what really is the true and living God like? I had been fasting previously, asking God to make himself known to me, and for

---

[1] A. W. Tozer, *The Knowledge of the Holy* (New York: Harper & Row, 1961), 41, writes, "Probably the hardest thought of all for our natural egotism to entertain is that God does not need our help. We commonly represent Him as a busy, eager, somewhat frustrated Father hurrying about seeking help to carry out His benevolent plan to bring peace and salvation to the world. . . . Too many missionary appeals are based upon this fancied frustration of Almighty God. An effective speaker can easily excite pity in his hearers, not only for the heathen but for the God who has tried so hard and so long to save them and has failed for want of support. I fear that thousands of young persons enter Christian service from no higher motive than to help deliver God from the embarrassing situation His love has gotten Him into and His limited abilities seem unable to get Him out of."

days my prayers seemed to hit a ceiling. In desperation, I borrowed this book from Wayne, went home, and read it in one long sitting. Little did I know when I opened that book that God was about to begin the revolutionary process of opening my eyes to see who the God of the Bible really is; and by his grace, this has been my main pursuit ever since.

I have come to see that those calls to service were horribly belittling to God and falsely exalting of us. Notice who is the needy one, and notice again who comes to the other's rescue. God is portrayed with a big heart, but he simply is unable to accomplish his work unless we cooperate. Our free choice,[2] in this understanding, is so prominent that God himself is subject to whether we "volunteer" to help him or not. His hands are tied, but ours are free. His feet can't go, and only ours can get the job done. His eyes can see the needs, but only our work can meet them. God, then, is the needy one, and we come and provide what God lacks in order to help out "poor God." "No wonder we get rewards," I thought as a boy. "We deserve them!"

This God-belittling, self-promoting view of Christian service is an abomination before the true and living God. Consider Psalm 50, for example, where God chastises the people of Israel for thinking of him in the way their pagan neighbors thought about their gods. Among the religions surrounding Israel, it was common to believe that the gods were quite needy. For example, they would get hungry, so the people would offer animal sacrifices to fill the gods' bellies. Now full and content, the gods would then send rain and other blessings. In Israel, evidently, the people of God had adopted this theology of sacrifice, believing that Yahweh (the God of Israel) needed the sacrifices the people brought and that he actually ate the animals offered. With obvious affront and offense, God puts Israel on trial (see Ps. 50:6-7) and instructs her, "I will not accept a bull from your house or goats from your folds. For every beast of the forest is mine, the cattle on a thousand hills. I know all the birds of the hills, and all that moves in the field is mine" (Ps. 50:9-11). Notice the emphasis on God's prior ownership of all. He does not want a bull from their houses or goats from their folds for one simple reason: he wishes to disabuse them of the false idea that they actually possess something that God lacks, something that they give to

---

[2] Clearly, libertarian freedom is required by this model.

God and make him better off than he was before! No, the Lord says. God already owns all the beasts of the forests, the cattle on a thousand hills, and everything that moves in the fields. He owns it all, and therefore the Israelites cannot give him anything.

He continues, "If I were hungry, I would not tell you, for the world and its fullness are mine. Do I eat the flesh of bulls or drink the blood of goats? Offer to God a sacrifice of thanksgiving, and perform your vows to the Most High, and call upon me in the day of trouble; I will deliver you, and you shall glorify me" (Ps. 50:12-15). So the people of Israel are dead wrong in thinking that Yahweh needs what they bring him. Instead, the mindset they need to adopt is this: call on God in the day of your trouble, and God will deliver you! The point is simple: God is the Giver, they are the receivers; God is the Protector, they are the vulnerable ones in need of deliverance; God is Lord and Owner of all, and they have nothing that is not already his. It is only right, then, that they offer to him a sacrifice of *thanksgiving* (Ps. 50:14), for when you thank someone, you acknowledge that he did something for you, and you are indebted to him. And out of their thanksgiving to God, they then shall glorify him (Ps. 50:23). The apostle Paul's summary statement in Acts 17 is quite appropriate here: the true God is not "served by human hands, as though he needed anything, since he himself gives to all mankind life and breath and everything" (Acts 17:25).

This false, pretentious, arrogant, self-deceived, self-promoting, God-demoting, God-belittling, Bible-disregarding view of God and Christian service needs to go—period! Service done out of motives driven by this model of God cannot help but be of the flesh. Since God cannot do anything without my help, then my effort is what makes the difference. And if I did the work, I should get the credit. But the God of the Bible will have none of this. "My glory I give to no other" (Isa. 42:8), he declares. And Paul states that all that God does is done in such a way that "no human being might boast in the presence of God" (1 Cor. 1:29). Service *over* God, then, may appear pious, but if it involves one of us supposedly helping God out or contributing where he lacks, then it is pious idolatry, for the real god of such service is the human being himself. But service *under* God—well, that is another thing. Let's consider now these aspects of service under the God who is the sovereign Ruler over all and self-sufficient Giver of all.

GOD'S GENEROUS COMMAND TO SERVE UNDER HIS SOVEREIGN AUTHORITY

We are commanded to serve God! It is not a mere option, or a matter of preference or individual desire or career calling. Every believer is commanded to serve the Lord. For example, in Deuteronomy 10:12-13, Moses summarized Israel's obligations before Yahweh, the Lord: "And now, Israel, what does the LORD your God require of you, but to fear the LORD your God, to walk in all his ways, to love him, to serve the LORD your God with all your heart and with all your soul, and to keep the commandments and statutes of the LORD, which I am commanding you today for your good?" Psalm 2:11 commands, "Serve the LORD with fear, and rejoice with trembling." And Psalm 100:2 declares, "Serve the LORD with gladness! Come into his presence with singing!"

Perhaps we should give a moment's thought to what may appear to be a conflict in biblical teaching. As we just read, Psalm 100:2 says, "serve the LORD with gladness," but as we have seen earlier, in Acts 17:25 Paul says that God is not "served by human hands, as though he needed anything." Is this a conflict? No, it is not, because the two passages represent two different kinds of "serving God," one that is right, and the other . . . well, we've seen it recently, and it fails! The majority of texts that command us to serve the Lord (as Psalm 100:2 does) simply indicate that since God is both Lord and God of us, we are duty-bound to make it our delight (i.e., "serve the LORD with *gladness*") to obey, fear, follow, love, heed, and in all of these ways to serve the Lord. But in Acts 17, Paul clearly has a different idea in mind, as is apparent from the context. Notice that immediately after he says that God is not "served by human hands" he follows this with the phrase, "as though he needed anything." So, the kind of service that Paul denies can be rendered to God is the kind that thinks God needs what the human "servant" has to offer him. Not only does God not need what any human would bring him, he doesn't need "anything"! So, rightful service acknowledges the Godness of God, and our duty to serve God with delight. Wrongful service seeks to serve God by giving to him what we think he lacks. No such service of this second kind is possible, while all of us owe to God the kind of service commanded in Psalm 100.

Given that we are commanded to serve the Lord, how is this command an expression of God's generosity to us? Several responses are appropriate. First, the generosity of God is shown in giving us good, right, and holy commands. As indicated above, God's commands were *for Israel's good!* (Deut. 10:12-13). That our culture despises authority does not change the fact that *good* commands are *good for us*. Even amid today's relativism, some commands are viewed this way. "Don't use drugs" or "Eat more vegetables" are examples of current commands that, even in our relativistic culture, are widely viewed as "good" for us to follow. How much more the commands of God. Recall in Romans 7, where Paul raised the issue of whether sin reigned in death because of the law: absolutely not, he would argue, for the "law is holy, and the commandment is holy and righteous and good" (Rom. 7:12). God's generosity is shown by granting us what might be called commandments of life. He commands and leads and directs in ways that are good for his people, and this is true even when following those commands results in persecution or death (Matt. 5:10-12).

Second, in commanding us to serve the Lord unreservedly, God is calling us to live like Jesus. If we think that anyone who follows someone else's orders just isn't free, then we'd have to conclude that not only was *Jesus* not free—he lived behind twenty-foot-high prison walls with no door and no windows! For Jesus made clear over and again that he lived the entirety of his life *always* and *only* obeying the will of his Father. In John 8:28, Jesus says, "I do nothing on my own authority, but speak just as the Father taught me," and verse 29 follows with, "I always do the things that are pleasing to him." The words "nothing" and "always" in these two verses are both startling and sobering. Jesus *never* did something just because he wanted to do it; he *never* spoke just what he, on his own, felt like saying. He *always* did what he knew the Father wanted him to do; he *always* sought to do what was pleasing to the Father. And of course, this has to be the case, for Jesus never sinned (2 Cor. 5:21; Heb. 4:15), which means he always did the will of the Father.

But even more amazing is this: Jesus *loved* obeying the Father! After his conversation with the Samaritan woman, having had nothing to eat for quite some time, the disciples brought him some food, but he refused it, saying, "My food is to do the will of him who sent me and to accomplish his work." Incredible! And in John 14:31 he said, "I do as the Father has commanded me, so that the world may know that I love the Father." And again, in John 15:10-11, Jesus said, "If you keep my commandments, you will abide in my love, just as I have kept my Father's commandments and abide in his love. These things I have spoken to you, that my joy may be in you, and that your joy may be full." So, Jesus' joy was found in keeping the commandments of his Father, and our joy, likewise, is found as we keep Christ's commandments. The sovereign Lord of all generously calls us to obey his commandments, just as Jesus obeyed all the commandments of his Father; and as we obey, we experience the joy that Jesus knew. What grace, to be commanded to live like Jesus and know true joy.

Third, the sovereign Lord is generous in commanding us to obey him, for the path that he calls us to is one that advances the kingdom and brings him glory. As wonderful as it is to know that the commandments of God are good and that they bring true joy, also deeply meaningful is that these commands lead us to service that matters, service in kingdom work, service that bears fruit for eternity. No work or service can be meaningful, long term, that means little or nothing. We've all heard stories about one work crew digging a bunch of holes one day only to see them filled in by tomorrow's crew. What is the point? But praise be to God, the service he calls us to is fruitful forever in its advancement of his kingdom. Essentially, the service God calls all of us to involves both the spread of the gospel so that sinners may be saved (Acts 1:8), and then the use of our gifts in the church so that saved sinners may grow in Christ (Eph. 4:11-13). Becoming like Christ is God's goal for all believers, the goal he established before the creation of the world when he predestined us "to be conformed to the image of his Son" (Rom. 8:29). There is no greater purpose for service than to participate in the work of the conversion and transformation of sinners into the likeness of Christ. What a privilege to be called to this service.

And, because the service to which we are called involves bringing sinners to faith and building up believers in the body of Christ, we know that this work cannot fail. Jesus Christ declared to his disciples that he *will* build his church and that "the gates of hell *shall not* prevail against it" (Matt. 16:18, emphasis added). The ultimate victory and success of the service God graciously grants us is so very strengthening and encouraging. We dare not read our newspapers and be led to doubt what Jesus declared. Remember, the same Jesus who declared that he would build his church now sits at the right hand of his Father, "far above all rule and authority and power and dominion, and above every name that is named, not only in this age but also in the one to come. And he [God the Father] put all things under his feet and gave him as head over all things to the church, which is his body, the fullness of him who fills all in all" (Eph. 1:21-23). In this work, the victory is secured because the victory has already been won. What joy and confidence we gain from knowing that we are called to a work that cannot fail.

Last, as mentioned in the previous chapter in relation to prayer, God's call to service is so gracious and generous because it is a call to participate in the work that is *his own*. Since God is fully sovereign, he could carry out everything he wanted without enlisting our participation. Unlike the missionary calls of my youth, God doesn't need me or anyone to respond for his work to be done. Recall the rebuke that John the Baptist gave to the Pharisees, who prided themselves on their Jewish lineage. He said to the crowd and to them, "do not begin to say to yourselves, 'We have Abraham as our father.' For I tell you, God is able from these stones to raise up children for Abraham" (Luke 3:8).

But, while it is true that God doesn't need our service, it is nonetheless astonishing that he wants and commands and enlists and uses our service, in participation with him, in the work that is his alone. I am amazed at the generosity of God to share the doing of his work with people like you and me. My own temperament borders on being somewhat perfectionistic, and so I tend to care about how my work is done. If others help me, whether I say so or not, I care whether they do it "my way" (which translates, in my mind, to "the right way"). On things that matter to me, I would often rather do it myself. Astonishingly, God is not so stingy. Rather, considering that the work is his alone, and that he cares about it so very much, how incredibly generous it is for him to invite our participation. He could have set things up so that all we did was watch from afar, but instead he devised a plan involving our participation. How grateful we should be for the service God calls us to, and for the lavish generosity of God's heart that shares so bountifully with us.

GOD'S GENEROUS ENABLEMENT TO SERVE UNDER HIS SELF-SUFFICIENT PROVISION

Not only does God express his generous nature by calling us to serve in such meaningful work, and with such privileged participation, but his generosity extends beyond his call even to providing all that we need in fulfilling the demands of our service. That is, not only does he call, by his grace; he also, by his grace, empowers the fulfillment of the call. Let's consider some of what it means to serve under the God who is fully self-sufficient and lavishly generous.

A very helpful and illuminating passage is Philippians 2:12-13. Here Paul writes, "Therefore, my beloved, as you have always obeyed, so now, not only as in my presence but much more in my absence, work out your own salvation with fear and trembling, for it is God who works in you, both to will and to work for his good pleasure." One of the most important features of this text is also one that involves something of a mystery: salvation involves our sincere and serious effort, and yet it is an effort that ultimately comes, in its entirety, from God's work in us and through us.

Notice the first of these two truths. We are commanded to "work out" our salvation with "fear and trembling," indicating the sincerity of mind, heart, and will with which we are to undertake growing in Christlikeness (look back to Phil. 2:5, where Paul commends Christ's example for us). That is, Philippians 2:12 gives the clear indication that we are responsible for our growth, and it is a responsibility we should take with the utmost seriousness. But add the second truth, and things need to be rethought completely.

In Philippians 2:13, Paul adds, "for it is God who works in you, both to will and to work for his good pleasure." In other words, God has not given us the responsibility for becoming Christlike in such a way that he leaves with us alone the obligation for its full implementation. Rather, the very same God who commands us to work out our salvation with fear and trembling is the God who also works within us so that what he has commanded is accomplished. He commands what he wills, but then he wills to provide for what he commands.

Notice also the extent of God's work in us. God works "both to *will* and to *work* for his good pleasure." It seems that Paul is purposely indicating that God works in all that we do for our sanctification to progress. His work in our *will* is an internal work, shaping the very will that forms within us that seeks to do the things necessary to grow in Christ. And his work in our *work* is his empowerment to take what we have willed and put it into practice, or to apply what the will has determined should be done. The whole of our responsibility for our growth in Christlikeness is empowered by God's work both to shape our will and to strengthen our work, as God is pleased so to do.

There is such hope, then, in the service God calls us to. He never calls us only then to abandon us. He never commands his children to do what he does without equipping them also to carry it out. His generosity doesn't stop with the kindness of granting us the favor of participation in kingdom work. The generosity and grace continue now to empower the fulfillment of this kingdom work.

And what difference does it make to know that the God who graciously calls us to service, and now graciously empowers us to accomplish this service, is the Creator God who alone is fully self-sufficient? What difference does it make to know that this God possesses intrinsically every quality and perfection in infinite measure? What an encouragement and strengthening of our faith arises from this truth! Every resource we will need, and all the power, wisdom, knowledge, patience, and skill that the fulfillment of our service requires—all is available and provided by the God of infinite resource. How incredible to know that not only is our eternal joy fueled by God's self-sufficiency, but the eternal fruitfulness of our ministry likewise is empowered by the infinite resources possessed fully and exclusively by God. How great is God's generosity to call us to service and empower us for service, both to the glory of his name and the growth and well-being of God's redeemed.

One last comment is needed here on the relation of God's ultimate glory in this work and his generous enablement of us to serve under the resource of his self-sufficient fullness. Only when we become convinced of these truths are we freed to minister in such a way that we can resist our sinful urge to take the credit for the good accomplished through our ministries. Oh, how our sinful flesh rears its ugly head immediately after some opportunity for meaningful ministry! In our minds and hearts, but very likely never mentioned to others, we feel the impulse to take to ourselves the honor and praise for the good accomplished. But if we truly understand the comprehensive nature of God's work in and through us for any and all good works we do, we will immediately and regularly remind ourselves that all that is done of eternal value was done entirely by God's gracious work, even though God may have given you or me the privilege to be the conduits through which that grace flowed to others. Yes, we are privileged participants in what is exclusively God's kingdom work; but as participants, while we are invited to enter fully in the joy of the work, we are simply not permitted to share in its glory.

Understanding this truth has made sense for me of an otherwise puzzling statement by Jesus. In Matthew 5:16, Jesus commands, "let your light shine before others, so that they may see *your good works* and give *glory to your Father* who is in heaven" (emphasis added). A natural question would be, if they are "your" good works, then why should the glory for these good works go to "your Father" in heaven instead of to you? Surely the only answer is the one suggested by our present subject, namely, that God gets the credit for good works done through us, since all the "willing" and "working" of these good works was accomplished by God, in and through us. This understanding of Matthew 5:16 is supported, I believe, by the fact that this statement follows right on the heels of the beatitudes, in which those who are blessed in nearly every case are the humble, who recognize fully their need for God to work on their behalf. Those who are "poor in spirit" and "meek" and "merciful" and "pure in heart" are humble, dependent people. A deep sense of God-bred humility must be joined, then, with a strong dependence on God-empowered sufficiency for us to see that any and all kingdom work done, by any child of God in any capacity of service or ministry, is accomplished ultimately by the power and agency of God alone, and therefore all glory for it must be directed to God alone. So, fellow servants of Christ, let us revel and take joy in our privileged roles as invited, called, and empowered participants in the service of God, but let us guard carefully that God alone be glorified for the work he alone has designed, directed, enabled, and accomplished.

Conclusion

9

On Narrowing the
"Distance from Majesty":
Longing to Behold God More as He Is

As we draw this study to a close, I am reminded of a drive some weeks ago through the Mt. Hood National Forest in the state of Oregon. I left on an early spring morning, and the day simply could not have been more beautiful for the drive I was about to take. From Portland east on Highway 26, the road skirted just south of the mountain. From time to time startling views seemed to emerge out of nowhere as the road wound through thick forests and then broke into clearings where the mountain could be seen in all her majesty. So pure she stood, with her thick winter coating of nearly blinding radiant white still covering her fully. Black, upright jagged peaks topped the scene, with pristine and cloudless deep blue crowning the mountain all around till it met the towering firs and led back to the ground.

I prayed and worshiped and sang and watched with eagerness for yet another good look as the highway continued its route, now more southward. Eventually the road left the mountain in the distance, directly behind so I could continue my sightings for a number of miles whenever the road's curves cooperated. But after a short while, what was once so immense and overwhelming had now become nearly trivial in its overall appearance. With the landscape to either side now broad and wide, the mountain was rendered virtually undetectable. It is curious, I thought, how something so imposing and grand could so soon appear hardly even noticeable. Distance from majesty, it occurred to me, will trivialize and minimize in our sight the nature of true grandeur.

Distance from majesty, indeed. If that doesn't describe the state of the knowledge of God in our day, I don't know what does. The road that many even in the church have chosen to travel is leaving behind in the far distance the imposing majesty and splendor of God's true nature. Only a vague remembrance of glory remains, and even this dim memory of Greatness is being pushed out by more "relevant" and "acceptable" ideas "appropriate" for deity. What now is thought of as God is so pale, and placid, and tolerant, and trite, that no luster remains, much less any startling and frightening brilliance. "Ichabod" of old has been written again over much of the church in our age. The glory has departed, the majesty is no more, and God appears on the horizon in the rearview mirror as a mere relic of a former Greatness.

The true and living God of Scripture cannot be pleased with this picture. God will not abide indefinitely being trivialized and demeaned. The imposing and awesome Creator and Sustainer of all that is *will* be glorified; that we know with certainty. In some manner, God will vindicate the holiness of his name, and he will do so among all the nations in all the world. Our worry should not be that God may be unable to set the record straight on who the true God is. Not to worry; he can, and he will. In this sense, we need not concern ourselves about God! He can take care of himself. And there is no doubt that the world will one day know, with clarity, forcefulness, conviction, and certainty, that the one true and living God . . . is God!

But here is the rub for us. As we have had opportunity in this study to examine something of the nature of God and his providential oversight of this world, we surely have been made aware that the immense and glorious picture God gives of himself in Scripture stands utterly contrary to "the gods of our age." Even the views of God in our churches are often partial understandings of the true God, at best, or increasingly demeaning, even blasphemous representations at worst. Some simply mock the name "God." Common to these misrepresentations of God abounding in our culture, and flourishing even in many of our churches, is this: in their various ways, each is a contemporary expression of the "distance from majesty" that results when a more "acceptable" vision of deity compels its worshipers further away from true but offensive Greatness. These alternate and progressive visions continue widening the distance until finally, the nature of true Greatness, Grandeur, and

Majesty appears, on the faraway landscape, essentially unnoticeable and unknown.

This situation is unacceptable for worshipers and lovers of true yet despised Majesty. What has been forsaken by this distancing is of such great magnitude that responses calling for "tolerance" and recognition of "diversity" are spoken, wittingly or not, in the spirit of Beelzebul. Neither apathy nor tacit acceptance is acceptable. True worshipers of the true God must yearn and labor for a narrowing of the distance from Majesty. They must long, for themselves and for others, to behold yet more nearly and more clearly the true and living God . . . as He *is*.

This course of action is not optional for those granted the unspeakable privilege of possessing and passing on the Grand Deposit of the Faith once for all given to the saints (1 Tim. 6:20; 2 Tim. 1:14; Jude 3). We cannot hide behind the facade of "fair and objective presentation of various views" if the one view that alone is true and glorifying to Majesty is not rendered before others as fully and exclusively majestic. Those of us who take our places behind pulpits and lecterns are not given the option in this case of noncombatant status. Our positions have given us marching orders from on high. And unless we yearn and seek to bring about a narrowing of the distance from Majesty, we will have Majesty to contend with. If the fear of men—or better, for many of us, the fear of the Academy—renders passive or passé the fear of God, the fear of men will be granted, and "Ichabod" will in time be written atop sermon manuscripts and scholarly works.

We who possess this Grand Deposit and who have remained near to glorious Majesty are, as Paul expresses it, "stewards of the mysteries of God" (1 Cor. 4:1). And our orders from on high are here made known and clear: "Moreover, it is required of stewards that they be found trustworthy" (4:2). There we have it in one word. Who could imagine that this single term "trustworthy" could convey so wondrous and weighty a calling and with stakes so high? The one criterion that matters most in the job description of "steward" of the mysteries of God might be put like this: "a steward must be worthy of being entrusted with the Grand Deposit of Truth of the transcendent majesty and immanent mercy of the one True and Glorious God."

Paul's description of himself and others as stewards of the mysteries of God must produce within our souls a simultaneous sense of enormous privilege and an equally weighty resolve. On the one hand, the reality of being entrusted with unspeakably precious truth should overwhelm us with wonder and with joy. We must relish the opportunities to teach and preach and tell of the glory, greatness, and goodness of almighty God. We must rejoice over these truths, evidencing first and foremost that we embrace them deeply and that they shape the contours of our lives. We must love the truth we know lest someday we know it no more. And we must bow before Deity and render heartfelt thanksgiving for the privilege of trafficking in Glory.

At the same time we must feel deeply the weight of responsibility attaching to our privileged calling and inquire whether we are indeed worthy of being entrusted with such a treasure. We must preach and teach this weighty Truth with a proportionate weightiness of confidence and conviction. We must teach and preach with care, accuracy, passion, and authority. With the apostle, we must have as our highest ambition to be pleasing to the Lord (2 Cor. 5:9), and we must contemplate often standing before the judgment seat of Christ to give an account of what we have spoken and whether we have been faithful (2 Cor. 5:10). And faithful we must be to the end, or we have failed.

In closing, if we are to call back those now distant from Majesty to the nearness of true joy and fear in the presence of the God Who Is, we must proclaim his excellencies and fear not the displeasure of the culture. The pleasure or displeasure of God will be all that matters. Each steward, in each setting, with trustworthy proclamation, in pulpit and classroom and meeting hall, can make a difference for some in each place who are drawn toward the distance. We can put forth a vision of Goodness and Greatness and Grandeur that will compel those granted sight to move nearer. The big picture of which direction our culture will travel in the years to come is in God's sovereign watch care. Our stewardship and calling relates to the small pictures each of us is given. May God grant us hearts that long supremely to know and love true Glory and true Deity. "Trustworthy stewards of the Grand Deposit" shall be our motto and aspiration, that nearness to Majesty may be claimed and reclaimed. For the greater glory of God, and the everlasting good of his people. Amen.

Appendix

Defining Evangelicalism's Boundaries Theologically: Is Open Theism Evangelical?[1]

INTRODUCTION

Clark Pinnock is exactly right. After noting (correctly) in his *Most Moved Mover* that Arminians and Augustinians have coexisted throughout much of the church's history, and further that a number of evangelical theologians today (and not just open theists) are working toward refinements in an evangelical doctrine of God, "Why," he asks, "draw the line at foreknowledge?"[2] A few pages later, he returns to this question: "In raising the issue of the divine foreknowledge, we have not transgressed some rule of theological discourse and placed ourselves outside the pale of orthodoxy. Why can an evangelical not propose a different view of this matter? What church council has declared it to be impossible? Since when has this become the criterion of being orthodox or unorthodox, evangelical or not evangelical?"[3]

What does Pinnock mean when he says that open theists have raised the issue of divine foreknowledge? Simply this: Open theism affirms God's exhaustive knowledge of the past and present, but it denies exhaustive divine foreknowledge, in that it denies that God knows—or can

---

[1] Paper delivered at the 53rd Annual Meetings of the Evangelical Theological Society, Colorado Springs, November 15, 2001; and published in the *Journal of the Evangelical Theological Society* 45/2 (June 2002): 193-212. Reprinted with permission.
[2] Clark H. Pinnock, *Most Moved Mover: A Theology of God's Openness* (Grand Rapids, Mich.: Baker, 2001), 106.
[3] Ibid., 110.

know—the future free decisions and actions of his moral creatures, even while it affirms that God knows all future possibilities and all divinely determined and logically necessary future actualities. As William Hasker explains, "Since the future is genuinely open, since it is possible for a free agent to act in any of several different ways, it follows that it is not possible for God to have complete and exhaustive knowledge of the entire future."[4] So, the specific denial of exhaustive divine foreknowledge is embraced in open theism as central and essential to its own identity.

And essential it is. For to open theists, the very notion of the future's "openness" is viable only if future free choices and actions are both fully unknown and fully unknowable to God. Were God to know some future choice, say, of what you will have for dinner this evening, since God's knowledge is infallible, it must be the case that you will have for dinner what God knows you will, in which case, you are not free to choose otherwise. As central and essential as libertarian freedom is to open theism, so equally central and essential is its denial of exhaustive divine foreknowledge.

Now, why is Pinnock right to raise this question about the openness understanding of divine foreknowledge in particular? Two answers are needed. First, it is precisely here, in open theism's denial of exhaustive divine foreknowledge, that the open view has separated itself from classical Arminianism specifically and from all versions of classical theism generally. Let's be clear about this: some of open theism's most basic and fundamental theological commitments are held in common with the entirety of the classical tradition.[5] For example, openness proponents could not be clearer in rejecting the process model of a co-eternal and interdependent God-world relationship in favor of a strong commitment to the classical doctrines of God's aseity, the divine self-sufficiency, and *creatio ex nihilo*.[6] And some other of open theism's most basic and fun-

---

[4] William Hasker, "An Adequate God," in John B. Cobb, Jr., and Clark H. Pinnock, eds., *Searching for an Adequate God: A Dialogue Between Process and Free Will Theists* (Grand Rapids, Mich.: Eerdmans, 2000), 218.

[5] So Pinnock is justified to say, "The open view is also a 'traditional' view and it belongs to a family of theologies that witness to the dynamic nature of God" (*Most Moved Mover*, 105).

[6] See, e.g., Clark Pinnock, Richard Rice, John Sanders, William Hasker, and David Basinger, *The Openness of God: A Biblical Challenge to the Traditional Understanding of God* (Downers Grove, Ill.: InterVarsity Press, 1994), 108-112, 138-141; John Sanders, *The God Who Risks: A Theology of Providence* (Downers Grove, Ill.: InterVarsity Press, 1998), 30, 41; and Cobb and Pinnock, eds., *Searching for an Adequate God*, x-xi, 185.

damental theological commitments are shared with large segments of the broader evangelical and orthodox heritage. For example, open theism shares with classical Arminianism their common commitment to the centrality of the love of God and the necessity of libertarian freedom for moral experience, worship, love, and genuine relationship.[7] *None of these openness commitments shared in common with classical theism generally or with Arminianism specifically raises the question of its rightful place within the boundaries of evangelicalism.* Rather, it is the *specific and distinctive openness denial of exhaustive divine foreknowledge* that *separates it* from its otherwise endearing relationship to Arminianism and its significant connection to much of the classical heritage, and it is *this denial,* defended only in open theism and in no other branch of orthodoxy or evangelicalism, *that raises the boundary question.*[8]

The second reason Pinnock is right to raise the foreknowledge question is this: open theism has, by this denial, entertained and promoted a reformulated understanding of God and God's relationship to the world in ways that are massive in its implications both theologically and practically. Perhaps when Pinnock asked, "Why draw the line at foreknowledge?" he meant us to take it rhetorically, implying that no good reason could be given. But with Pinnock's concluding chapter, I agree that "it is time now to ponder the implications"[9] of the openness proposal. And so, I propose in the body of this paper to take the question "why draw the line at foreknowledge?" seriously. Has sufficient careful consideration been given to what implications follow from this specific denial? It seems to me that before we can think responsibly about whether open theism should rightly be conceived as within or without the bounds of evangelicalism, we must ponder as carefully and fully as

---

[7] Pinnock, *Most Moved Mover* (p. 45), writes, "Had God not granted us significant freedom, including the freedom to disappoint him, we would not be creatures capable of entering into loving relationships with him. Love, not freedom, is the central issue. Freedom was given to make loving relations possible. . . . The biblical story presupposes what we call libertarian freedom. This is plain in the ways God invites us to love him and in the ways in which he holds us responsible for what we decide."

[8] While in my book (Bruce A. Ware, *God's Lesser Glory: The Diminished God of Open Theism* [Wheaton, Ill.: Crossway, 2000]), I offer a more holistic critique of open theism including, of necessity, some discussion of the openness (and more general Arminian) commitment to libertarian freedom, here in this paper, since the question is specifically whether open theism is in the boundaries of evangelicalism, I restrict my critique strictly to what distinguishes open theism from Arminianism and all other branches of evangelicalism and orthodoxy, viz, its distinctive denial of exhaustive divine foreknowledge.

[9] Ibid., 179.

we can just what open theism's distinctive doctrine (i.e., its denial of exhaustive divine foreknowledge) leaves us with theologically and practically. After all, open theism is nothing without this doctrine. So, if it turns out that this specific doctrinal departure has innocuous or acceptable theological and practical implications, then open theism as a model cannot be discredited on the grounds of this, its distinctive doctrinal tenet. However, if it is demonstrable that the openness denial of exhaustive divine foreknowledge has seriously unacceptable theological and practical implications, then open theism as a model must likewise be deemed unacceptable.

In what follows, then, we shall consider at some length implications that follow from open theism's distinctive tenet, viz., that God cannot know the future free choices and actions of moral creatures, and hence, God does not have exhaustive foreknowledge. We will examine these implications within four broad headings, both theological and practical. Following this examination, the paper will conclude with an assessment of open theism on the boundary question.

IMPLICATIONS OF THE OPENNESS DENIAL OF EXHAUSTIVE DIVINE FOREKNOWLEDGE

No doubt there are more. But I have given long and hard consideration to the question of what implications follow, both for our theology and for the life of faith, when one affirms that God does not know the future free choices and actions of moral creatures. I believe that the implications are both numerous and weighty. Consider with me implications under four broad headings: 1) God—his character, purposes, and work; 2) revelation and Scripture—their accuracy and surety; 3) the gospel of salvation—its design and truthfulness; and 4) the Christian life—its faith and hope in God.

Bear two things in mind as I present these implications: 1) Clearly, while some are weightier than others, all are important, and my endeavor is to be truthful and honest with each. So, consider the validity of each point, the importance of each (some greater than others), but also bear in mind both the interconnectedness of many of these points and their overall cumulative force. 2) For many points made, thoroughness would require engaging possible openness responses, followed by counter-responses. I can seldom afford to do this due to time constraints. On some of the most crucial points, I will. But if I don't, please don't assume that I am unaware either of what openness proponents might say or of what answers might be given. So now, to our question: What theological and practical implications follow from the openness denial of exhaustive divine foreknowledge?

God—His Character, Purposes, and Work

1. Open theism's denial of exhaustive divine foreknowledge entails God's ignorance not only of the entirety of future creaturely free decisions and actions themselves but also of the *incalculably great multitude of entailments* flowing causally from *whether* particular free choices and actions obtain or not, and from *which specific* free choices and actions in fact do obtain.

Think from the beginning of human history: What if Adam, in his anger at Eve shortly after their sin, had killed Eve as Cain later killed Abel? What of the proto-evangel in Genesis 3:15 that the seed of *the woman* would crush the serpent's head? No woman, no seed, no human race, no Savior, no crushing. And in Genesis 3, could God have known what Adam would or would not do? Moving ahead a bit, what if Noah, upon being the recipient of the jeering and mocking of his friends, had decided he would not endure such ignominy by continuing to build this ridiculous ark? And what if Noah—the only righteous man, you recall— had now joined his neighbors in their wickedness? Implausible, you say? Well, we all know that the implausible can occur in the open view. But what then of God's already stated purpose to destroy the whole earth and all the wicked by a flood? And we could go on, and on, and on! Just *what specific actions with their accompanying entailments* Adam or Eve, Cain or Abel, Noah or Abraham—and on through history—might choose were altogether unknown to God. Imagine the multitude of entailments that flow into human history from the various choices that free creatures make every moment of every day. On openness grounds, God can know neither *whether particular choices* will be made, nor just

what specific choices in fact will be made, nor *all of the entailments* arising from whatever choices in fact obtain.

2.   Open theism's denial of exhaustive divine foreknowledge pre-
     cludes the possibility of God's knowing from eternity past *just
     what persons would actually be conceived and born,* at any
     and every point, throughout the history of humankind. That is,
     exactly who, how many, and obviously, anything about any of
     them, would be completely and fully unknown to God.

Consider your own existence. Could God have known from eternity past that *you* would exist? On openness grounds, absolutely not!
Consider the contingencies. Your parents decide to marry—yes, that
particular man and woman, not another pair. And they decide whether
to have children, whether to use birth control or not, how many children
to have, and in all this the genetic combinations vary for each possible
conception. None of this God can know ahead of time. What is true of
you is, of course, true also for each of your parents, and their parents,
and so on all the way back to the garden. The fact is, God can no more
know *now* who will be born a year from right now than you or I can.

3.   Open theism's denial of exhaustive divine foreknowledge
     severely implicates the complete and perfect *belief structure
     within the knowledge of God* (even on openness standards of
     omniscience) since God must, at any and every moment, pos-
     sess innumerable false beliefs about what will happen in the
     future.[10]

For example, John Sanders proposes that God *believed* that the
man and woman in a perfect garden and apart from sin would continue
in obedience, but, alas, that belief was tragically wrong.[11] The fact that
God knew as a possibility that they could sin does not change the fact
that he genuinely believed they would not—otherwise the first sin could

---

[10] Sanders, *God Who Risks,* 205, writes, "Is it possible for God to have mistaken beliefs about
the future? The traditional theological answer is that God cannot, but there are several biblical
texts that seem to affirm that what God thought would happen did not come about (for example,
Jer. 3:7, 19-20)."
[11] Ibid., 45-49.

not have been implausible to God as Sanders claims. Now, please don't dismiss this as a problem just in Sanders's particular presentation of open theism. Whether other open theists follow Sanders on that specific interpretation of Genesis 3 or not, the problem is inherent to the openness model. To see this, consider, for example, the openness understanding of Jeremiah 3:7 (God says, "I thought, 'After she has done all these things she will return to Me'; but she did not return" [NASB]). God genuinely believed one thing would happen but, sadly and deeply disappointing to God, its opposite came to pass instead. Concerning this passage, Greg Boyd writes, "We need to ask ourselves seriously, how could the Lord honestly say he *thought* Israel would turn to him if he was always certain that they would never do so?"[12] I cannot here engage Boyd's specific interpretation of this text, except to note that in Deuteronomy 31 God declares that Israel *will turn away* from him, and here in Jeremiah 3, a few verses later, God announces that Israel *will return,* demonstrating that God knows full well what Israel will do. But the point here is that, for Boyd and open theists generally, it is literally true that in this case God *thought wrongly* about what would transpire in the future. So, while all versions of classical theism have affirmed that all of God's beliefs are true because they accord with what truly is or what truly will be, open theism envisions God as having both true and false beliefs. And when one considers the first point above, just how much of the future God is ignorant of, one begins to realize how expansive, then, must be this category of false beliefs in God's mind.

4. Open theism's denial of exhaustive divine foreknowledge severely implicates the complete and perfect *wisdom of God,* who sometimes looks back at his own past decisions and now, in retrospect, determines that what he previously decided may not in fact have been the best decision. Just how often this occurs, we could never fully know, but given his *expansive ignorance* and innumerable *mistaken beliefs* about the future, we might expect that there are likewise many *misguided decisions* that are simply, and sadly, unavoidable for God.

---

[12] Gregory A. Boyd, *God of the Possible: A Biblical Introduction to the Open View of God* (Grand Rapids, Mich.: Baker, 2000), 60, emphasis in original.

Since the quality of our decisions is affected centrally by the quantity and quality of the information relevant to those decisions, and since many of God's decisions relate to what he or others should do in the future, it is clear that God's ignorance of the vast majority of the future of human affairs cannot help but to give God less than perfect judgment and lead him to make faulty decisions. Hear David Basinger's words: "[S]ince God does not necessarily know exactly what will happen in the future, it is always possible that even that which God in his unparalleled wisdom believes to be the best course of action at any given time may not produce the anticipated results in the long run."[13] The now-well-known Suzanne story told by Greg Boyd in *God of the Possible* also comes to mind here. Had God only known that this prospective husband would prove to be so hurtful, his leading, one would presume, would have been different.

Now, is the God of open theism absolved here because in formulating his wise plans he does in fact make use of all available and logically possible knowledge, so that it would be unfair to discredit the perfect wisdom of his decisions just because he did not take into consideration knowledge of the future, which knowledge is logically impossible to have? No, to the contrary, what it exposes is that *a God lacking exhaustive foreknowledge is intrinsically and unavoidably fallible and faulty in making his future plans.* He may have *unparalleled* wisdom, as Basinger states, but if God himself evaluates his decisions in retrospect and says, "things didn't work as I had hoped; this is not what I intended and I don't like what happened; knowing what I now know, I would have done differently," then in no real sense could misguided plans, whether unintentional or not, whether unavoidable or not, be said to arise from One with *perfect* wisdom.

5. [A parallel point:] Open theism's denial of exhaustive divine foreknowledge severely implicates the complete and perfect *rightness of God's actions,* since God may do things that he later realizes, in retrospect, were not best.

God not only makes misguided decisions, but he then implements them in action. And rather than finding this a troubling notion, open the-

---

[13] David Basinger, "Practical Implications," in *Openness of God,* 165.

ists seem to make use of God's mistaken decisions and actions as part of their explanation of why God sometimes changes his mind about things he has said or done. As one notable example, recall how Sanders suggests we might understand God's promise never again to flood the earth: "It may be the case that although human evil caused God great pain, the destruction of what he had made caused him even greater suffering. Although his judgment was righteous, God decides to try different courses of action in the future."[14] In other words, God reasons, 'although just, this may not have been best. Certainly, I won't do this again.' How often may God so evaluate his own actions as less than best? We have no way to know, but given his expansive ignorance and mistaken beliefs about the future, we may someday be surprised to learn how many times, and in how many ways, God regretted doing what *he did,* thinking after it occurred, 'I wish I had acted differently.'

6. Open theism's denial of exhaustive divine foreknowledge encourages in its followers adherence to a view of God which is strikingly and centrally similar to the biblical idolatry denounced in Isaiah 40–48. What is true both of the God of open theism and of these idols is this: neither can declare what specific future events will unfold, events that involve innumerable future free choices and actions of human beings.

But the true God can! For example, the expansiveness and comprehensiveness of God's foreknowledge claim in Isaiah 46:10 ("Declaring the end from the beginning, and from ancient times things which have not been done" [NASB]) is then expressed in concrete form in 46:11 ("calling a bird of prey from the east, the man of my purpose from a far country" [NASB]) as he predicts the coming of a man, Cyrus no doubt, who he knows will accomplish his purposes. That is, God knows specific future events, people, free choices and actions, and their effects. But which of the idols can do this, asks the Lord! Furthermore, God says of the *worshipers* of those idols which do not know and cannot declare such future actions of free creatures, "he who chooses you is an *abomination*" (Isa. 41:24, NASB), and of the *idols* themselves,

---

[14] Sanders, *God Who Risks,* 50.

"Behold, all of them are *false;* their works are *worthless,* their molten images are *wind and emptiness*" (Isa. 41:29, NASB). By its denying of God's foreknowledge of free creaturely choices and actions, open theism is vulnerable to the charge of commending as God one whom the true God himself declares is false and worthless.

7. Open theism's denial of exhaustive divine foreknowledge dishonors and belittles both the true and living God and the divine Son of the Father, by denying of both, one of their self-chosen bases for asserting the uniqueness of their deity, viz., that God alone, *as God,* knows and declares what the future will be.

In Isaiah 41:23, God challenges the idols, "Declare the things that are going to come afterward, that we may know that you are gods." They cannot; but God, *because he is God,* declares the future. And what God declares, over and over again, involves countless future choices and actions of his free creatures (e.g., Isa. 41:21-29; 42:8-9; 43:8-13; 44:6-8; 45:1-7, 18-25; 46:8-11; 48:3-8). Jesus likewise is here dishonored, for just like God in Isaiah, so too Jesus asserts his claim to deity as resting in part on his ability to declare the future. In John 13:19 (NASB), Jesus says, "From now on I am telling you before it comes to pass, so that when it does occur, you may believe that I am He." Is it mere coincidence that just a few verses later we hear Jesus declare unequivocally to Peter, "Truly, truly, I say to you [not: 'Probably, probably, I tell you my well-informed prognostication], a rooster will not crow until you deny Me three times"? How dare we deny of God what God himself has chosen as a basis for asserting his own unique deity!

8. Open theism's denial of exhaustive divine foreknowledge advances a hermeneutic that could reasonably (i.e., on general openness hermeneutical criteria) be used to advocate yet greater divine deficiencies than merely God's lack of exhaustive foreknowledge with its attending drawbacks.

For example, one can easily imagine the openness hermeneutic proposing, from a literal, straightforward reading of texts, God's lack of exhaustive present knowledge, God's lack of exhaustive past knowl-

edge, God's specific spatial locatedness, God's poor memory and
unavoidable forgetfulness, God's sometimes uncontrolled temper,
God's increase in wisdom and insight through the counsel he receives
from others, and more. I can hear the next generation of open theists
now: "If God wanted us to understand that he needed help remembering things, how could he have made it any more plain than he did in
Genesis 9:13-16? For here, God says, 'When the bow is in the cloud,
then I will look upon it, to remember the everlasting covenant' (9:16,
NASB). How could it be clearer! When God sees the rainbow, then (and
only then) does he remember!" Given openness hermeneutical theory,
what would prevent this extension of their beliefs? All one needs to do
is explain how some biblical statements that teach God's perfect knowledge (e.g., Ps. 147:5) are actually restrictive (i.e., perfect in restricted
senses), to accommodate God's limited knowledge of the past and present as evident in other texts. And by openness standards, wouldn't this
make God even more glorious? Because, after all, which is easier: run-
ning the world when it is your nature to remember everything, or doing
so when you have to work hard at remembering (and you just might
forget), and yet you succeed in steering the world to its desired outcome? The openness hermeneutic is driven by its commitment to deny
of God knowledge of future free creaturely choices and actions. If this
hermeneutic is allowed legitimacy, use may be made of it to propose
even greater dishonor to God.

Revelation and Scripture—Their Accuracy and Surety

1.   Open theism's denial of exhaustive divine foreknowledge is de-
     rived from what can arguably be called, in light of the entirety
     of orthodox and evangelical interpretive histories, a pervasive
     misinterpretation of Scripture.[15]

Open theism misunderstands both the so-called restricted future
determination texts (e.g., Isa. 46:8-11), and the so-called future openness texts (e.g., Gen. 22:12). Concerning Isa. 46:8-11—the broad and

---

[15] A major burden of *God's Lesser Glory* is to defend this claim. See particularly chapter 4,
"Assessing Open Theism's Denial of Exhaustive Divine Foreknowledge," and chapter 5,
"Scriptural Affirmation of Exhaustive Divine Foreknowledge." My present, brief discussion of
this claim is a mere sampling and sketch of the relevant evidence.

sweeping claim to know the end from the beginning is unjustifiably narrowed in open theism, while the specific implicit reference to the calling of Cyrus shows God's knowledge of what open theists deny God can have, viz., of innumerable future free actions associated with the birth, naming, rearing, rise to power, reign, and successes of this future king. Concerning Gen. 22:12—to say that God learns that Abraham fears God only when he raises the knife over the bound body of Isaac contradicts 1) God's intimate and perfect knowledge of our hearts (1 Chron. 28:9; 1 Sam. 16:7); 2) God's knowledge of Abraham's faith and hope in God as celebrated in Romans 4 and Hebrews 11; and 3) Abraham's own belief, while traveling to Mt. Moriah, that God would raise his slain son, Isaac, from the dead (Gen. 22:5; Heb. 11:19).

2. Open theism's denial of exhaustive divine foreknowledge renders unintelligible and ultimately *ad hoc* the overall course and development of biblical redemptive history, with its intentional, built-in, forward-directed, and anticipatory type and anti-type, prophecy and fulfillment, structure.

If God's dealing with free human persons is likened to a "choose your own adventure" book,[16] then it is impossible to build in at the outset clearly defined and specifically designed typological and prophetic features that require exactly certain outcomes and no others for their later fulfillment. So, the question is this: does the story line of the Bible read more like a "choose your own adventure" book or, say, like a carefully crafted and intricately navigated mystery novel?

3. Open theism's denial of exhaustive divine foreknowledge distorts and denies the reality of many specific and inviolable divine predictions that involve future free human decisions and actions.

Deuteronomy18:22 (NASB) states, "When a prophet speaks in the name of the LORD, if the thing does not come about or come true, that is the thing which the LORD has not spoken." Admittedly, this is a com-

---

[16] See Boyd, *God of the Possible*, 42-43, 150-151.

plicated area, for God also says in Jeremiah 18:7-10 that he may say one thing, and then, if his people change, he also will change what he had said. I don't believe Jeremiah 18 cancels out Deuteronomy 18. Rather, in Jeremiah, God is announcing again his standing purpose to extend mercy to those who repent and discipline to those who turn from him. But not all of God's declarations are in this kind of context. So many, many prophecies in Scripture announce simply what others *will* certainly do, or what *will* certainly happen. And as we know, often when these are fulfilled just as God prophesied, the Scripture writer will note that this happened just as the Lord said—e.g., 1 Kings 21:17-24 concerning Jezebel is fulfilled in 2 Kings 9:30-37, and the author writes, "This is the word of the LORD, which He spoke by His servant Elijah" (9:36, NASB). Steve Roy conducted a comprehensive survey of Scripture on this question, and counted, among other findings, that there are 1,893 texts that state predictively that God will do something or other in or through human beings, and 1,474 texts that state predictively what human beings will do, apart from God directly acting in or through them.[17]

Regarding predictions that are fulfilled through the future actions of free agents, will it do to account for these predictions by any one of the three categories advanced by openness proponents?—i.e., 1) predictions of God's unilateral determination that require for their fulfillment no future free human choices, 2) predictions based on probabilities of what most likely, but not certainly, will occur, or 3) predictions containing explicit or implicit conditions by which God may in fact act differently than he states in the prediction. The answer is no, but the main problem here is not with these three categories, per se, but in what they omit. Open theists leave out one major category of predictive prophecy, viz., specific and inviolable divine predictions whose fulfillment involves, in some direct or indirect fashion, future free creaturely choices and actions. Perhaps no better example can be given than Daniel 11. Consider just the first four verses:

> "In the first year of Darius the Mede, I arose to be an encouragement and a protection for him. And now I will tell you the truth. Behold, three more kings are going to arise in Persia. Then a fourth will gain

---

[17] See the full tabulation of Roy's findings, as listed in Ware, *God's Lesser Glory*, 100, f.n. 2.

far more riches than all of them; as soon as he becomes strong through his riches, he will arouse the whole empire against the realm of Greece. And a mighty king will arise, and he will rule with great authority and do as he pleases. But as soon as he has arisen, his kingdom will be broken up and parceled out toward the four points of the compass, though not to his own descendants, nor according to his authority which he wielded, for his sovereignty will be uprooted and given to others besides them" (NASB).

The number of future free choices and actions predicted—either explicitly or implicitly—in just these four verses boggles the mind! Now, don't misconstrue the point. My argument is by no means dependent on Daniel 11; this chapter is merely illustrative of hundreds of such passages. Give Daniel to the critical scholars!—well, don't, but you could—and you still have the rest of your Bible filled with specific, inviolable divine predictions involving future choices and actions of free creatures.

4. Open theism's denial of exhaustive divine foreknowledge makes it impossible to affirm Scripture's inerrancy unequivocally prior to the fulfillment of any and all of its specific and inviolable divine predictions that involve future free human decisions and actions; that is, insofar as there are such predictions, whether they are fulfilled or not depends on future free choices and actions of which God can have no advance knowledge and over which he has no ultimate control.

It seems, then, one faces a dilemma: either 1) one denies the reality of the many specific and inviolable divine predictions that involve future free human decisions and actions, or 2) one accepts these predictions and acknowledges that the truth value of them is in question due to their relationship to future free agents who may or may not do what was predicted. In the first instance, one has the formidable task of accounting for hundreds of texts the church has interpreted for two millennia as literally predictive of future human actions (e.g., 70 year captivity, 15 years extended life, destruction of Jeroboam's altar, naming and activities of

Josiah, naming and activities of Cyrus, birth in Bethlehem, divided clothing, unbroken bones, rich man's tomb, three denials); in the second, one
can no longer in principle affirm the inerrancy of Scripture's predictive
teachings, when those predictions are of future actions and events that
might go contrary to what was predicted.

Clark Pinnock seems to vacillate between these options, holding one
and then the other. Apparently in line with the first approach, he writes,
"the fulfillment of a prophecy may differ from what the prophet had in
mind,"[18] indicating, I take it, that prophecies are conditional or have a
level of imprecision that allows for unexpected kinds of fulfillment. But
then in an explanatory footnote to the same discussion, he continues
apparently in line with the second approach, saying, "We may not want
to admit it but prophecies often go unfulfilled," and as examples he
offers, "despite the Baptist, Jesus did not cast the wicked into the fire;
contrary to Paul, the second coming was not just around the corner . . . ;
despite Jesus, in the destruction of the temple, some stones were left one
on the other."[19] This would seem to suggest that what was prophesied
was simply mistaken. So, in the first instance where "God is free in the
manner of fulfilling prophecy," one can maintain inerrancy only at the
price of denying specific, inviolable predictions involving free creatures;
yet in the second instance, where "prophecies often go unfulfilled,"[20] it
seems here difficult to see how inerrancy is not abandoned when admit-
ting that predictions simply failed.

5. Open theism's denial of exhaustive divine foreknowledge
    severely implicates the complete and perfect *accuracy of God's
    word,* since God may state something that he believes to be
    true but later realizes, in retrospect, he was mistaken and in
    error.

To put it bluntly, God unavoidably lies, but he never means to. For
example, in Jeremiah 3:19-20, God states that Israel would prosper and
would follow him, but in fact they forgot the Lord their God. For open
theists, what God states in 3:19 is shown to be wrong in light of what

[18] Pinnock, *Most Moved Mover,* 51.
[19] Ibid., 51, f.n. 66.
[20] Both statements are found in the same footnote, ibid.

Israel does in 3:20.[21] Because of God's massive ignorance regarding the future of human affairs, it is entirely possible for God to say things about that future which prove wrong. Although formally, he means always to speak the truth, materially, what he says may in fact be mistaken and in error.

THE GOSPEL OF SALVATION—ITS DESIGN AND TRUTHFULNESS

1.   Open theism's denial of exhaustive divine foreknowledge precludes the possibility of God's knowing from eternity past whether sin would enter his created world.

Pinnock says that when God created free creatures, he "accepted a degree of risk with the possibility, not certainty, of sin and evil occurring."[22] For Sanders, sin was not only not foreknown, its occurrence in the garden was, to God, "implausible."[23] However, if God did not know that sin would occur, he could not predetermine to save, prior to the creation of humans and the actual sinful action they commit. At best, God could have a contingency plan in the event that sin occurred. But consider 1 Peter 1:19-20 (NASB): we were redeemed "with precious blood, as of a lamb unblemished and spotless, the blood of Christ. For *He was foreknown before the foundation of the world,* but has appeared in these last times for the sake of you." And however Revelation 13:8 is translated (either the saints' names are written from the foundation of the world, or Christ was slain from the foundation of the world), God's eternal purpose has been to save sinners. Surely the gospel is not God's *ad hoc* plan B, but if sin is a mere possibility, perhaps even an implausibility before Genesis 3, then no set plan would already be in place. The gospel, however, announces God's eternal and set purpose to save, which means he knows the sin that will occur and he has already planned for our rescue before he even creates.

---

[21] See Sanders, *God Who Risks,* 132, 205; and Boyd, *God of the Possible,* 60. Ironically, Boyd charges the classical view with entailing the view that God lies, if God has said one thing *knowing* it not to be true as he said it. Clearly, what God's intention was as he made such a claim has to be carefully considered. For discussion on this issue, see my *God's Lesser Glory,* 92-98.

[22] Pinnock, *Most Moved Mover,* 41-42.

[23] Sanders, *God Who Risks,* 45-46.

2. Open theism's denial of exhaustive divine foreknowledge renders it impossible for God to have foreknown and chosen those who would be saved in Christ—in either the Calvinist or Arminian understandings of these doctrines—before the foundation of the world.

This is so, in part, because God could not have known then even *who would exist.* The specific individuals who will populate human history along with any and all of their future choices and actions cannot be known by God in advance of their very lives. He cannot have known "you" until you came into existence. But notice in Romans 8:29 that Paul uses a relative pronoun "whom" to indicate what God foreknew: *"whom* he foreknew, these he predestined . . . , and *whom* he predestined, he called . . ." And Ephesians 1:4 says that God chose *us* in Christ before the foundation of the world. Whether this is corporate or individual, it refers to a specific group comprised of those who will be saved. God knows who we will be before he creates, and he knows whether we will be among those saved.

3. Open theism's denial of exhaustive divine foreknowledge jeopardizes the substitutionary nature of Christ's death for our sin.

Because God cannot know in advance just who will be living at any and every point of human history, therefore, when Christ died on the cross, he simply could not, in any real sense, have substituted in his death and payment of sin for "you" or for "me." While his death could have been quite literally in the place of, or as a substitute for, those living up to the point of his death, this could not be the case with those to be conceived and born yet in the future. While advocates of limited and unlimited atonement differ over those for whom Christ died, all agree that when he died, he died in the place of sinners, i.e., actual sinful people whose deaths and payments for sin he took upon himself. Hence, the substitutionary nature of the atonement can obtain only if God knows not only those prior to Christ's death, but also those yet future, for whom Christ died.

4. Open theism's denial of exhaustive divine foreknowledge
    jeopardizes Christ's actually bearing "our sins in his body on
    the cross" (1 Pet. 2:24).

At the point in human history when Christ was crucified, not only
would it be impossible for God to know whether and who would come
to exist in the future (so he could not actually substitute for them in his
death), in addition, God would also be clueless regarding what sin(s)
would be committed in the future. Therefore, there could be no actual
imputation of our sin to Christ (à la Isa. 53:4-6, "the LORD has caused
the *iniquity of us all to fall on Him*"; 1 Cor. 15:3, "Christ died for *our
sins*"; 2 Cor. 5:21, God made Christ "who knew no sin *to be sin . . .*";
1 Pet. 2:24, "He Himself *bore our sins in His body* on the cross") (all
NASB). Since no future sin yet existed, on openness grounds, God could
not know any of that future sin for which Christ's atonement was meant
to pay. The effect of this and the previous point is to see the crucifixion,
as it relates to people conceived after Christ's death, as an impersonal
and abstract sort of substitution and payment. He cannot really have
died personally in *their* place nor for *their* very own sin. In fact, Christ
would have had reason to wonder, as he hung on that cross, whether
for any, or for how many, and for what sins, he was now giving his life.
The sin paid for could only be sin in principle, and not sin by imputation,
and the people died for was a blurry, impersonal, faceless, nameless, and
numberless potential grouping.

5. Open theism's denial of exhaustive divine foreknowledge
    renders unsure God's own covenant promise to bring blessing
    and salvation to the nations through the seed of Abraham.

Open theists take the test of Abraham in Genesis 22 as a *real test*,
presumably one Abraham could fail thus disqualifying him from being
the covenant partner through whom God would bring blessing to the
world.[24] Concerning this test, Sanders writes, "God needs to know if
Abraham is the sort of person on whom God can count for collabora-
tion toward the fulfillment of the divine project. Will he be faithful? Or

---

[24] Ibid., 52-53; and Boyd, *God of the Possible*, 64.

must God find someone else through whom to achieve his purpose?"[25] But if so, how shall we understand God's promise to Abraham in Genesis 12:2-3 (NASB): "I will make *you* a great nation, and I will bless *you,* and make *your name* great; and so *you* shall be a blessing, . . . and in *you* all the families of the earth will be blessed"? If *this* covenant could be fulfilled through another, then what does God's word mean? Furthermore, if Abraham fails this test, what assurances can we have that another, and then another, and then another, might not also fail?

6. Open theism's denial of exhaustive divine foreknowledge renders uncertain the execution of God's plan of salvation through the delivering up of his Son by crucifixion on the cross; or, if God foreknows and predestines the death of Christ, then, by openness standards of freedom and morality, it renders Christ's obedience and offering himself up to be crucified the determined, constrained, and morally vacuous actions of a divinely engineered robot. We'll consider each possibility in order.

First, while it is harmful enough to the surety of God's covenant commitment to say, as Sanders has, that had Abraham not obeyed, God might seek another through whom to fulfill his covenant promise to bless the nations, it is altogether more devastating to the truthfulness of God's long salvific covenant pledge to suggest that Christ, as a free agent, might not have chosen to go to the cross. Sanders writes, "Although Scripture attests that the incarnation was planned from the creation of the world, this is not so with the cross. The path of the cross comes about only through God's interaction with humans in history. Until this moment in history other routes were, perhaps, open."[26] Though startling, does not the open view require this possibility? If Christ is a moral agent and if his actions are free, it follows that Christ could choose to be given over or not, and then it follows that God cannot have known, prior to his choice, just what Christ would do. In light of Psalm 22; Isaiah 52:13-53:12; Acts 2:23; 4:27-28; 1 Peter 1:20, this implication of the open view contradicts precious biblical teaching

---

[25] Sanders, *God Who Risks,* 45-46, emphasis added.
[26] Ibid., 100.

while it undercuts the certainty and surety of God's eternal saving promise and purpose.

But second, some may be aware that Greg Boyd asserts a different position from Sanders on this point, claiming that "Scripture portrays the crucifixion as a predestined event" even if "it was not certain from eternity that Pilot [*sic*], Herod, or Caiaphas would play the roles they played in the crucifixion."[27] Boyd explains, "Since God determines whatever he wants to about world history, we should not find it surprising that the central defining event in world history—the crucifixion—included a number of predestined aspects. It seems that the incarnation and crucifixion were part of God's plan from 'before the foundation of the world.'"[28] Of course, holding this position has the advantage of avoiding the implication just noted, viz., of the uncertainty of the cross if God cannot know in advance what Christ will choose to do. But I am startled and incredulous that any open theist would want to solve this problem by asserting that the event of the crucifixion was divinely foreknown and predestined. After all, even if God may not know the roles that Pilate or Herod might play, if the event of the crucifixion is predestined, must God not know, at bare minimum, that his Son *will choose* to go to the cross? But just call to mind the strong and emotionally charged language open theists regularly offer in response to the notion that God can fore*know* what creatures *freely* do. If God knows what they will do, their actions cannot genuinely be free; rather, according to the openness view, they are robots, and there can be no true love, no true moral action, and no true relationship between the constrained agent and God. In fact, some open theists go so far as to call God's predetermination of future actions, carried out in a nonconsensual manner, as instances of divine rape![29] What can save Boyd's position from being charged with entailing, on openness grounds, that the

---

[27] Boyd, *God of the Possible*, 45.

[28] Ibid., 44-45. Boyd's full last paragraph of this discussion reads, "While Scripture portrays the crucifixion as a predestined event, it never suggests that the individuals who participated in this event were predestined to do so or foreknown as doing so. It was certain that Jesus would be crucified, but it was not certain from eternity that Pilot [*sic*], Herod, or Caiaphas would play the roles they played in the crucifixion. They participated in Christ's death *of their own free wills*" (ibid., 45, emphasis added). But, it seems impossible that when Boyd says, "it never suggests that the individuals who participated in this event were predestined to do so" he would include Christ's actual choice to go to the cross as left uncertain. If so, in what meaningful sense could we see "the crucifixion as a predestined event"?

[29] See, e.g., Sanders, *God Who Risks*, 240.

crucifixion of Christ, as predetermined by God, constituted the most egregious act of divine coercion perpetrated in the history of the universe? Furthermore, if the event of the crucifixion was predestined, does this not require that every act of Christ's earthly obedience was also constrained, since what was predestined was (obviously) an *efficacious* crucifixion, i.e., the crucifixion of a *truly sinless* atoning sacrifice? But if his life of obedience and crucifixion was constrained, are they not, then, morally vacuous, and is not the cross, then, worthless? And further yet, if the event of the crucifixion was predestined "before the foundation of the world," does this not entail God's foreknowledge of sin—i.e., how could God *predestine* a crucifixion to save from sin if sin is not certain? But what then of human freedom and moral responsibility in choosing originally to rebel against God? My own view is that consistent open theism will follow Sanders, not Boyd, on this point. In any event, I will proceed unfolding implications assuming Sanders's view.

7. Open theism's denial of exhaustive divine foreknowledge renders uncertain, by extension of the uncertainty of Christ's crucifixion, the resurrection of Jesus by which alone do believers in Christ have hope (1 Cor. 15:17).

Are the predictions of Jesus' future resurrection in Psalm 16 and by Jesus himself (e.g., Matt. 16:21) probabilistic or conditional in nature? Does Peter understand these predictions this way in Acts 2:24-32 as he quotes Psalm 16? Surely not. In Acts 2:31, Peter states, "[David] looked ahead and spoke of the resurrection of the Christ, that He was neither abandoned to Hades, nor did His flesh suffer decay" (NASB). But if the resurrection was not in question, then neither was the crucifixion merely probabilistic or conditional. Rather, both were set, fixed, certain, sure, and absolutely foreknown by God.

8. Open theism's denial of exhaustive divine foreknowledge jeopardizes the legitimacy of *God's justification of OT saints by faith* (e.g., Gen. 15:6).

Recall that in Romans 3:25-26 we are told that God passed over sins previously committed for the *demonstration of his righteousness at the present time.* So, what grounds the legitimacy of God's justification of OT believers is, not their sacrifices, not their faith per se, but the *future payment of Christ's death* on the cross, by which God demonstrates *now, in Christ,* that he is righteous in having forgiven those he did (as well as forgiving others yet future). But consider: For God to extend justification to OT saints, apart from *knowing* their sin *would be paid* by a subsequent death for sin, would be to extend what was in fact a groundless and unjustified justification.

9. Open theism's denial of exhaustive divine foreknowledge renders illusory the salvific value of OT atoning sacrifices for the forgiveness of sin.

The type/antitype reality in the OT sacrificial system requires the certainty of the future death of Christ, i.e., the *"Lamb of God* which *takes away* the sin of the world." But, of course, since God cannot have known whether his Son would freely offer himself as the once-for-all atonement for sin, God's institution of the sacrificial system was, strictly, a legal fiction. There was then no basis in the Old Testament period itself by which God could forgive sins through those sacrifices. Only if God *knows with certainty* that sin's debt *will be paid* in the future death of Christ can those OT sacrifices function as types by which God can genuinely forgive.

THE CHRISTIAN LIFE—ITS FAITH AND HOPE IN GOD

1. Open theism's denial of exhaustive divine foreknowledge undermines the Christian's confidence in the reliability and certainty of God's wise counsel and guidance for the Christian life.

Consider the Suzanne story in Boyd's *God of the Possible.* What assurances can she be given that God will do any better in his future leading than he has in the past? After all, Boyd accepts the notion that God truly did give his *best counsel and guidance* when he encouraged her marriage to the man that both he (God) and she learned over time was so deeply hurtful. Denying that God knows the future in this way undermines confidence and trust in accepting and following God's leading.

2. Open theism's denial of exhaustive divine foreknowledge undermines the Christian's hope that affliction, suffering, and trials in life are permitted by God for what he knows will turn out to be ultimately good purposes (e.g., Rom. 8:28; cf. Rom. 5:1-5; James 1:2-4).

Adding to the above point is the problem that any assurance we might have had that these hardships are part of a bigger wise and good plan is now taken away. God's plans change, and frankly many, many things happen that he wishes didn't. God simply cannot give assurances that things will work out for good because he doesn't know how the future will unfold. Face it, we may encounter gratuitous evil at any turn, unexpected and unwanted by God, and utterly pointless in its purpose for us. Don't expect God to know what you and I cannot know, viz., that there are good purposes ultimately for this suffering. Accept it; this is the nature of life lived with a God lacking such knowledge of the future.

3. Open theism's denial of exhaustive divine foreknowledge promotes presumptuous Christian prayers, in which we are encouraged to work together with God at devising what is best for the future.

Oh, the implicit arrogance embedded in the notion that God takes into consideration what I think before he and I decide together what is best to do, *as if* I, or we, could possibly contribute something that could be joined with God's understanding and wisdom resulting in an overall better plan. But hear how positively this is portrayed in the open view. Sanders writes:

> It is God's desire that we enter into a give-and-take relationship of love, and this is not accomplished by God's forcing his blueprint on us. Rather, God wants us to go through life together with him, making decisions together. Together we decide the actual course of my life. . . . To a large extent our future is open and we are to determine what it will be in dialogue with God.[30]

---

[30] Ibid., 276-277.

How strikingly contrasting this is with Jesus' approach to living life, in which he said repeatedly, "I have come to do the will of my Father who is in heaven." How presumptuous to think that we, together with God, could arrive at a better overall plan than the one God alone, in his infinite wisdom, can devise! The words of Isaiah 40:13-17 reveal how utterly foolish and deeply offensive this appeal in open theism is.

4. Open theism's denial of exhaustive divine foreknowledge calls into question the Church's ultimate eschatological hope that God will surely accomplish all his plans and purposes, exactly as he has told us in Scripture that he will, and openness assurances that he *will* succeed ring hollow, in that not even God knows (i.e., *can* know) what unexpected turns lie ahead and how severely these may thwart his purposes or cause him to change his plans.

Openness advocates want it both ways. They want high risk, and they also want high assurance of God's success. They cannot have it both ways. Clearly, what wins in the open view is risk; what loses is assurance of God's success. If even God cannot now know the outcome of his purposes with free creatures, we certainly cannot be sure whether those plans and purposes will prevail.

OPEN THEISM AND BOUNDARIES FOR EVANGELICALISM

So, we return to Dr. Pinnock's questions: "Why draw the line at foreknowledge? . . . . What church council has declared it to be impossible? Since when has this become the criterion of being orthodox or unorthodox, evangelical or not evangelical?"[31] Allow me two comments, and then my conclusion.

First, no church council took up this matter, because no serious proposal was ever set before the church that would deny what all Christians believed without question, viz., that God, as God, knew the future, as well as the past and present, exhaustively. Because church

---

[31] Pinnock, *Most Moved Mover*, 106, 110.

councils, creeds, and confessions are occasional in nature, and because no reason ever occasioned councils or synods to speak on this issue, therefore God's exhaustive foreknowledge was accepted without defense or formal creedal declaration. But does this history not also imply that when something as fundamental and basic to Christian commitment as, in this case, its confidence in God's exhaustive fore-knowledge is questioned, or rather denied, Christians ought to unite to declare now what we believe on this matter? In other words, as the church in past generations felt obligated to face these weighty doctrinal deviations and give voice to its most cherished and nonnegotiable commitments, so too in our day, thoughtful Christians, particularly Christian leaders, must speak out on the openness proposal to say what the glory of God, the truthfulness of Scripture, and our own consciences require.

Second, while the question of theological boundaries for evangelicalism is highly complicated, I agree with Derek Tidball in his *Who Are the Evangelicals?* who writes:

> The word 'evangelical' comes from the Greek word for 'good news' which takes us to the heart of the matter. Evangelicals are 'gospel' people. . . .[32] As gospel people, evangelicals stress that the heart of the gospel is the cross of Christ, usually insisting on that interpretation of the cross known as substitutionary atonement; that a personal response to Christ's work on the cross, usually called conversion, is necessary; that the fruits of the gospel should be subsequently seen in the believer's life and that the good news should be shared with all people through evangelism. . . .[33] Every definition [also] draws attention to the central place given by evangelicals to the Bible. They count it as their supreme authority and though they may differ over theories of inspiration and methods of interpretation they believe it to be the trustworthy record of God's revelation of himself to humankind, having superior authority to any other means of direction in the church (such as tradition, reason or contemporary scholarship), sufficient for all the church's needs and to be treated

---

[32] Derek J. Tidball, *Who Are the Evangelicals? Tracing the Roots of the Modern Movements* (London: Marshall Pickering, 1994), 11.

[33] Ibid., 12-13.

with the utmost seriousness as a guide both to what we are to believe and how we are to live.[34]

For evangelicals, what is central is gospel, cross, salvation, conversion, life of faith and good works, and the Bible, which reliably and sufficiently reveals the truths we believe and by which we live.

But given open theism's distinctive and essential tenet, viz., that God cannot know future free creaturely choices and actions, it is clear that certain central evangelical convictions are compromised to promote the open view. Consider where open theism leaves us in three areas discussed above that accord with these central evangelical commitments: We are left with a *Bible* somehow now devoid of specific and inviolable divine predictions involving future free human actions, an unintelligible canonical interconnectedness, a pervasive new interpretive proposal regarding hundreds of biblical passages, and the possibility of revealed predictions which are, frankly, wrong. We are left with a *gospel* unable to account for the eternal design of God's foreknowing and purposing to save those who God knew would sin against him, a gospel that jeopardizes the legitimacy of OT sacrifices and divine justification of sinners, a gospel where the substitutionary nature of Christ's death for sin and sinners arising after the crucifixion is, at best, impersonal and abstract, and a gospel where God's covenant promise to save and the very death and resurrection of Christ are rendered uncertain in God's salvific plans. And *Christian faith* is left possessing a heightened estimate of our own contribution to the unfolding future at the expense of God's diminished knowledge, wisdom, and certainty, a faith that cannot but be unsure of God's word, second-guessing God's direction, and ultimately lacking in confidence that God's purposes will prevail.

And yet another, perhaps the most, troubling area implicated by open theism is our understanding of God himself. Now, is it legitimate to ask whether changes in understanding God relate to the evangelical boundary question? The answer must be yes. Evangelicals have not

[34] Ibid., 12. For guidance on literature studying evangelicalism, see the helpful bibliographies provided in Edith L. Blumhofer and Joel A. Carpenter, *Twentieth-Century Evangelicalism: A Guide to the Sources* (New York: Garland, 1990); Norris A. Magnuson and William A. Travis, *American Evangelicalism: An Annotated Bibliography* (West Cornwall, Conn.: Locust Hill, 1990); idem, *American Evangelicalism II: First Bibliographical Supplement, 1990–1996* (West Cornwall, Conn.: Locust Hill, 1997); and Mark A. Noll, *American Evangelical Christianity: An Introduction* (Oxford: Blackwell, 2001), 289-308.

declared their distinctiveness or identity on the question of God, simply because this has been an area of substantial agreement with the broader orthodox and universal church. But now, within our own ranks, the openness proposal makes it incumbent for evangelicals to declare whether the open view of God is acceptable. Well, where does open theism leave us here? In short, it leaves us with a *God* who lacks massive knowledge of future human affairs, who possesses innumerable false beliefs about that future, whose wisdom is less than perfect, whose plans can prove faulty, whose actions might be regrettable, whose word may be mistaken, whose self-claim to deity is undermined, a God whose inability to declare future free human actions renders him strikingly similar to the pretender deities denounced by God himself.

My conclusion is this. The cost to doctrine and faith by open theism's denial of exhaustive divine foreknowledge is too great to be accepted within evangelicalism. It would be easier to say, let the discussion continue (which it will regardless, to be sure) and allow difference of opinion here as we do in other matters. After all, drawing the lines will no doubt be perceived by some as narrow, perhaps "fundamentalistic," and unloving, though these perceptions will be unfounded. Yet, to fail to challenge a proposal as massive in its harmful implications for theology and for the church as found in the openness proposal would be utterly irresponsible, and by its neglect, our failure would constitute complicity in the harmful effects these doctrinal innovations have for our evangelical theology and for the life of the church. So, with deep and abiding longings to honor God and his Word, to see the church strengthened, and to retain whatever integrity evangelicalism has through its core commitments, I would urge this conclusion: open theism, by its denial of exhaustive divine foreknowledge, has shown itself to be unacceptable as a viable, legitimate model within evangelicalism. May God grant mercy, wisdom, strength of character, fidelity, and love as we endeavor to follow him and his Word in days ahead.

General Index

Abraham, 52-53; open theism's view of the test of Abraham, 232-233
affliction. *See* suffering
anthropomorphism, 146n. 19
Aquinas, 38, 38n. 2
Argyle, A. W., 51
Arminianism, 63-64, 217; view of God, 108-109; view of the sovereignty of God, 64-66. *See also* freedom, libertarian; open theism
Arminius, Jacob, 92
Arnobius, 140n. 10
Assyria, as God's tool, 83-84, 88
Athanasius, 140n. 10
Athens, Paul's sermon at, 62, 77-78
Augustine, 38n. 2, 92, 101, 140n. 10, 144-145, 196

Barth, Karl, 40, 49, 55
Basinger, David, 63n. 2, 222
beatitudes, the, 206
Berkhof, Louis, 135-136
Boethius, 133
Boyd, Gregory A., 172, 221, 222, 230n. 21, 234, 234n. 28

Calvin, John, 92
Calvinism, 26-27

Christian life: fruitfulness in, 104; living *coram Deo* (before God), 181-183, 194 (*see also* prayer); living under God (*see* service); and the transformation of the Christian's character into the likeness of Christ, 94-95
classical theism, modern critique of, 37-39
compatibilist middle knowledge, 27-28, 76n. 13, 113-115, 115n. 10; and God's choice not to provide what he could have provided, 118-119; and God's relation to evil, 115-130; invoked by God as his basis for the final judgment, 118; not restricted to God's dealing with evil, 117-118
"Compatibility of Calvinism and Middle Knowledge, The" (Laing), 115n. 10
"Consider It Joy" (Kendrick), 178-179
conversion, 104
covenant, 52-53
Craig, William Lane, 25, 116n. 11
creation, 26, 51-52, 55-56, 59, 62-67, 71-72, 149, 165; *ex nihilo*,182; impossibility for it to affect God, 150

reasons it must be rejected, 112-113; Ware's response to, 92-95

freedom, of inclination, 25-26, 79-81, 87-88, 114-115; and necessary conditions, 114n. 9; and the sovereignty of God, 14-15, 81-84; and sufficient conditions, 114n. 9

Ganssle, Gregory E., 134n. 5
glory of God, 30, 58, 103-104, 159-160, 205-206
God: attributes of, 23, 28-29, 152-155; —contingent, 152-154; —eternal and necessary, 153-154; as both immanent and transcendent, 23, 35-37, 55-57; and change (*see* God, immutability of; God, mutability of); and contingency, 148-155; as Creator, 51-52, 62-63; emotions in, 144-147, 150-152, 154-155; —contingent, 148, 151; —eternal and necessary, 151-152; eternity of, 47-48, 134; grace of, 153; holiness of, 46-47; immanence of, 35-36, 51-55, 139-148; immutability of, 28, 139-148; —ethical immutability, 141; —ontological immutability, 140-141; love of, 56; mercy of, 153; misrepresentations of, 210-211; mutability of, 28; —relational mutability, 142-143; omnipotence of, 16n. 1; omnipresence of, 28, 133-139, 134; omnisapience of, 16n. 1; omniscience of, 16n. 1; omnitemporality of, 28, 133-139, 150; as only good,

165; "real relationality" with, 29-30, 57-58, 147-148, 155-159; as Redeemer, 52-54; relation to space and time (*see* God, omnipresence of; God, omnitemporality of); retributive justice of, 152; as revealed in Jesus Christ, 40-44; revelation of, 43-44, 59; roles in which he relates to us, 149; self-sufficiency of, 48-51, 57-58, 182-183, 185, 194, 196; transcendence of, 35-36, 46-51; tri-personal relationship of Father, Son, and Holy Spirit, 150. *See also* compatibilist middle knowledge; glory of God; God, asymmetrical relation to good and evil; God, generosity of to us; sovereignty of God; Trinity, the
God, asymmetrical relation to good and evil, 100-101, 102-109; God as good, not evil, 101-102; relation to evil, 105-109; relation to good, 102-105
God, generosity of to us: in calling us to live like Jesus, 201-202; in calling us to participate in a work that is his own, 203; in commanding us to obey him, 202-203; in giving us good, right, and holy commands, 201
God and Time (Ganssle, ed.), 134n. 5
God of the Possible (Boyd), 172, 222, 236
God's Lesser Glory (Ware), 24n. 4, 217n. 8, 225n. 15
Gregory of Nyssa, 140n. 10
Guthrie, Donald, 45-46n. 15

Scripture Index